Zaner-Bloser

SPELLING CONNECTIONS

J. Richard Gentry, Ph.D.

6

Series Author
J. Richard Gentry, Ph.D.

Editorial Development: Cottage Communications

Art and Production: PC&F

Photography: George C. Anderson: cover, pages 1, 4, 6, 7, 254, 255, 256, 257; The Stock Market: p. 12 © 88 Tom Martin, p. 30 © Ed Bohon 1983, p. 31 © Tom Bean 1988, p. 37 © 98 Douglas Whyte, p. 60 © 87 Richard Nicholas, p. 66 © Alan Schein, p. 67 © Peggy and Ronald Barnett 1998, p. 96 © 1992 Jon Feingersh, p. 108 © George Disario 1991, p. 139 © 85 David Frazier, p. 144 © 96 Ariel Skelley, p. 162 © Bob Abraham, p. 175 © 98 Don Mason, p. 192 © 97 Jeff Zaruba, p. 193 © 96 Bryan Peterson, p. 198 © 97 D. Stoecklein, p. 270 © 93 Kunio Owaki, p. 273 © 93 David Chalk, p. 286 © 97 Don Mason, p. 295 © 97 Arthur Beck, p. 297 © 95 Roy Morsch, p. 312 © 98 Ronnie Kaufman, p. 313 © 94 Mug Shots; Tony Stone Images: p. 13 © World Prospective, p. 24 © Lori Adamski Peek, p. 25 © Vince Streano, p. 36 © Kaluzny/Thatcher, p. 48 © Keren Su, p. 49 © A. Witte/C. Mahoney, p. 84 © Tom Ulrich, p. 97 © Stephen Johnson, p. 102 © Mark Lewis, p. 109 © Jane Gifford, p. 121 © Rich Frishman, p. 132 © Rex Ziak, p. 133 © Earth Imaging, p. 138 © Stuart McClymont, p. 157 © Peter Timmermans, p. 168 © Peter Pearson, p. 269 © Julian Calder, p. 271 © David Maisel, p. 272 © David Harry Stewart, p. 275 © John Millar, p. 279 © Brian Stablyk, p. 282 © Bruce Forster, p. 283 © Tom Bean, p. 285 © Laurence Dutton, p. 289 © Mark Wagner, p. 294 © Manoj Shah, p. 296 © Alejandro Balaguer, p. 309 © Vince Streano, p. 311 © Jon Gray; Corbis Bettmann ©: p. 18, p. 85, p. 126, p. 145 Richard Hamilton Smith, p. 277, p. 278, p. 284 Kelly-Mooney Photography, p. 287 Dimitri Iundt, TempSport, p. 290 Schenectady Museum, Hall of Electrical, p. 291 Kevin Fleming, p. 293 James Marshall, p. 300 Historical Picture Archive, p. 301 Kevin R. Morris, p. 305 Mike Zens, p. 306 Gianni Dagli Orti, p. 307 Richard Hamilton Smith, p. 308; FPG International: p. 19 © Telegraph Colour Library 1997, p. 54 © Mark Harmel 1993, p. 91 © Dennis Hallinan 1986, p. 169 © Ulf Sjostedt 1992, p. 174 © Spencer Jones 1997, p. 205 © Richard Harrington 1983, p. 210 © Gary Buss 1991, p. 211 © Steve Smith 1997; Artville ©: p. 55, p. 61, p. 72 © Burke-Triolo Productions, p. 90, p. 120, p. 216, p. 276, p. 292, p. 310; SUPER-STOCK ©: p. 156, p. 163, p. 180, p. 199, p. 204, p. 217.

Illustrations: Laurel Aiello: pages 106, 227, 248; Dave Blanchette: pages 15, 82, 130; Len Ebert: pages 10, 23, 33, 39, 40, 41, 42, 57, 75, 76, 78, 87, 95, 111, 112, 114, 148, 149, 150, 182, 183, 184, 219, 220, 221, 222; Tom Elliot: pages 73, 77, 103, 127, 147, 181; Ruth Flanigan: pages 11, 17, 29, 35, 47, 53, 59, 65, 71, 83, 89, 101, 107, 119, 125, 131, 137, 143, 197; Rusty Fletcher: pages 173, 209; Collin Fry: pages 155, 161; Bill Ogden: pages 16, 28, 34, 45, 52, 64, 88, 94, 100, 129, 142, 154, 160, 189.01, 190, 196; Remy Simard: pages 167, 171, 191, 203, 215; George Ulrich: pages 172, 179, 208

ISBN: 0-7367-0047-1

Zaner-Bloser, Inc., P.O. Box 16764, Columbus, Ohio 43216-6764 (1-800-421-3018)

Printed in the United States of America   00 01 02 03 QP 5 4 3

Contents

Spelling Study Strategy

Look ➡ **Say** ➡ **Cover** ➡ **See** ➡ **Write** ➡ **Check**

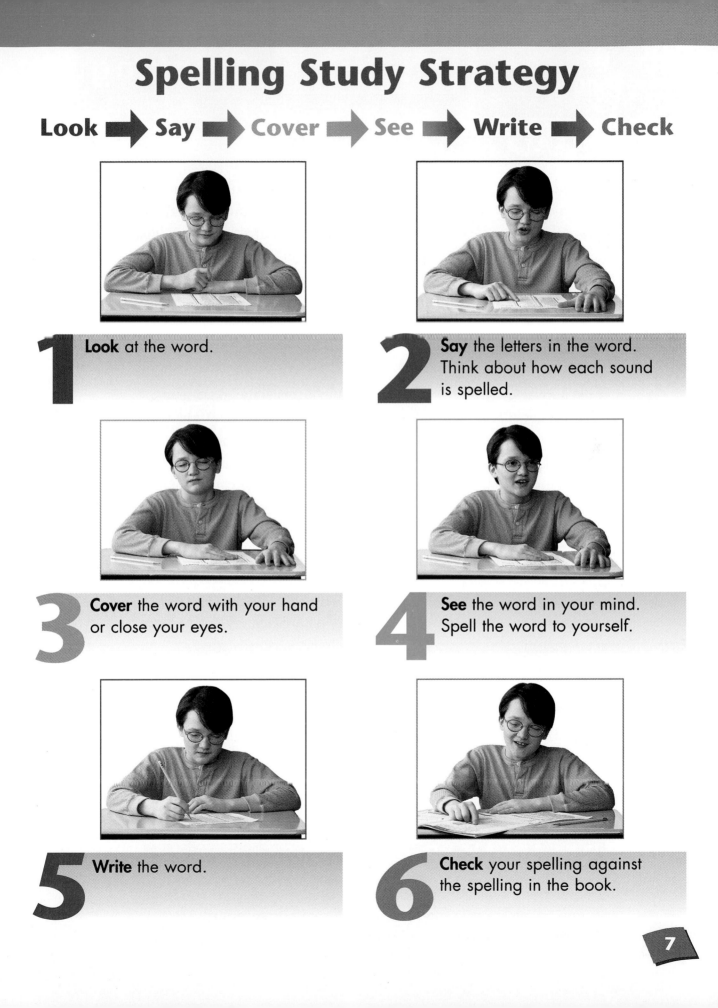

1 **Look** at the word.

2 **Say** the letters in the word. Think about how each sound is spelled.

3 **Cover** the word with your hand or close your eyes.

4 **See** the word in your mind. Spell the word to yourself.

5 **Write** the word.

6 **Check** your spelling against the spelling in the book.

Spelling and Thinking

READ THE SPELLING WORDS

1.	pattern	*pattern*	The leaves formed a colorful **pattern**.
2.	album	*album*	He arranged his pictures in an **album**.
3.	labor	*labor*	Scrubbing the floor was difficult **labor**.
4.	vacation	*vacation*	We delayed our summer **vacation**.
5.	exactly	*exactly*	The book cost **exactly** five dollars.
6.	chapter	*chapter*	I have read the first **chapter**.
7.	survey	*survey*	The engineer will **survey** the land.
8.	detain	*detain*	I must not **detain** you any longer.
9.	rapid	*rapid*	The rain caused a **rapid** river current.
10.	cancel	*cancel*	They might **cancel** the soccer game.
11.	obtain	*obtain*	You must **obtain** a permit to park here.
12.	admit	*admit*	This ticket will **admit** one person.
13.	trait	*trait*	His sense of humor is his best **trait**.
14.	accent	*accent*	She speaks with a British **accent**.
15.	complain	*complain*	They often **complain** about the service.
16.	advance	*advance*	The team will **advance** to the next level.
17.	natural	*natural*	He has **natural** artistic ability.
18.	daydream	*daydream*	You must try not to **daydream** in class.
19.	favorite	*favorite*	They played my **favorite** song.
20.	behave	*behave*	I am trying to teach my dog to **behave**.

SORT THE SPELLING WORDS

1.–10. Write the words with the **short a** sound.

11.–18. Write the words that spell **long a** as **a, ai,** or **ay.**

19.–20. Write the words that spell **long a** as **a-consonant-e** or **ey.**

Circle the letters that spell the **short a** sound or **long a** sound.

REMEMBER THE SPELLING STRATEGY

Remember that the **short a** sound in **rapid** is spelled **a.** The **long a** sound is spelled **a** in **labor, ai** in **trait, ay** in **daydream, a-consonant-e** in **behave,** and **ey** in **survey.**

Spelling and Vocabulary

Word Meanings

Write the spelling word that could best replace each underlined word or words.

1. The fabric has a floral <u>design</u>.
2. She speaks with a French <u>style of speech</u>.
3. I must not <u>delay</u> you with my questions.
4. I need to <u>call off</u> today's appointment.
5. This job requires hours of hard <u>work</u>.
6. You must <u>get</u> a permit to park here.
7. Never express <u>feelings of unhappiness</u> about life.

Word Analysis

Change the underlined part of each word to write a spelling word.

8. <u>day</u>light
9. sur<u>prise</u>
10. be<u>come</u>
11. <u>a</u>fter
12. sub<u>mit</u>
13. ad<u>vice</u>

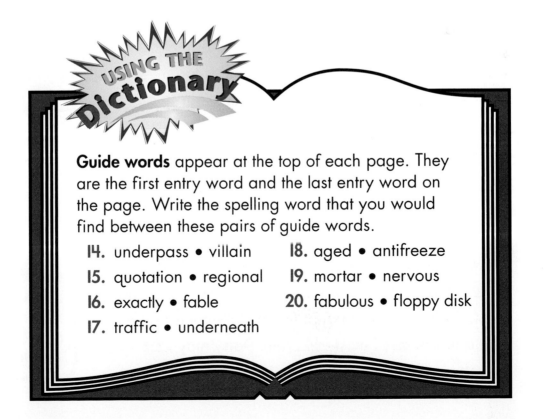

USING THE Dictionary

Guide words appear at the top of each page. They are the first entry word and the last entry word on the page. Write the spelling word that you would find between these pairs of guide words.

14. underpass • villain
15. quotation • regional
16. exactly • fable
17. traffic • underneath
18. aged • antifreeze
19. mortar • nervous
20. fabulous • floppy disk

Spelling and Reading

pattern	album	labor	vacation	exactly
chapter	survey	detain	rapid	cancel
obtain	admit	trait	accent	complain
advance	natural	daydream	favorite	behave

Complete the Sentences   Write the spelling word that completes each sentence.

1. Please _cancel_ my magazine subscription.
2. His vegetables grow in a neat _pattern_ of rows.
3. Sheila was lost in a long _____ about last summer.
4. Dan mixed the paints to _____ an unusual shade of red.
5. We should not _____ them any longer than we must.
6. You speak with a beautiful Spanish _____.
7. He tries to compliment people rather than _____ about them.
8. Jenny likes to do heavy physical _____.

Solve the Analogies   Write a spelling word to complete each analogy.

9. **Easy** is to **difficult** as **artificial** is to _____.
10. An **act** is to a **play** as a _____ is to a **book**.
11. **Recall** is to **remember** as **examine** is to _____.
12. A **recipe** is to a **cookbook** as a **photo** is to an _____.
13. **Finish** is to **complete** as **progress** is to _____.
14. **Work** is to a **job** as **relax** is to a _____.

Complete the Paragraph   Write the spelling words from the box to complete the paragraph.

Friendliness is the most desirable __15.__ a dog can have. Of all the dogs along my mail route, Daisy is my __16.__. Every day, she waits for me in __17.__ the same spot. The __18.__ wagging of her tail tells me how happy she is to see me. I must __19.__ that Daisy may __20.__ this way because of the treat I give her.

behave
exactly
rapid
trait
favorite
admit

Spelling ^{and} Writing

Proofread a Journal Entry

Six words are not spelled correctly in this journal entry. Write the words correctly.

Proofreading Marks

≡ Make a capital.

╱ Make a small letter.

∧ Add something.

℮ Take out something.

⊙ Add a period.

⌗ New paragraph

ⓈⓅ Spelling error

August 8, 1999

    I do not want to complane, but it has rained exactly five of the past six days of our vacashun. I must admitt, though, that I am still enjoying myself. I have taken lots of pictures of the beautiful nateral surroundings for my allbum. My favorate memory is watching a fawn follow its mother through a field.

Write a Journal Entry

Narrative Writing

A journal can be a valuable record of your experiences, thoughts, and memories. Write an entry for a personal journal.

- Describe something you did recently or something that is important to you.
- Follow the form used in the proofreading sample.

Use as many spelling words as you can.

Proofread Your Writing During ➤

Proofread your writing for spelling errors as part of the editing stage in the writing process. Be sure to check each word carefully. Use a dictionary to check spelling if you are not sure.

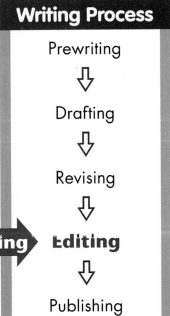

Writing Process

Prewriting

⇩

Drafting

⇩

Revising

⇩

Editing

⇩

Publishing

Vocabulary

Strategy
Words

Review Words: Short a, Long a

Write a word from the box to complete each sentence.

brand	claim	disobey	grayer	locate

1. Try this new _____ of cereal.
2. His hair is a little _____ than it was when I met him several years ago.
3. I am trying to _____ his town on this map.
4. Please _____ your prize by midnight tonight.
5. If you _____ the traffic laws of this town, you will get a ticket.

Preview Words: Short a, Long a

Write the word from the box that matches each clue.

anagram	caption	display
entertain	mistake	

6. This is a short explanation for a picture in a book, magazine, or newspaper.
7. A comedian might stand on a stage to do this for an audience.
8. You might apologize for this.
9. An athlete might do this with her trophies.
10. **Tap** and **pat** are examples of this word puzzle.

Connections

Content Words

Fine Arts: Sculpture

Write the word from the box that fits each definition.

chisel	sculptor	engraving	woodcut	marble

1. a person who carves figures
2. an engraved block of wood to print from
3. the art of cutting designs into a surface
4. a hard rock made from limestone
5. a metal tool with a sharp edge

Science: Astronomy

Write the words from the box to complete the paragraph.

crater	module	lunar	terrain	meteorite

On July 20, 1969, the first astronauts were about to set foot on the moon. Neil Armstrong and Buzz Aldrin climbed into the landing __6.__. They guided their vehicle toward the __7.__ surface, narrowly missing a deep __8.__. The two men explored the moon's rugged and dusty __9.__. Unless a __10.__ hits that area of the moon, their footprints will probably last for millions of years.

Apply the Spelling Strategy

Circle the letters that spell the **long a** sound in three of the content words you wrote.

Spelling and Thinking

READ THE SPELLING WORDS

1.	text	*text*	We revised the speechwriter's **text**.
2.	feeble	*feeble*	Grandpa is **feeble** but has a sharp mind.
3.	gravity	*gravity*	The pull of **gravity** gives us weight.
4.	dealt	*dealt*	He **dealt** with his problem with courage.
5.	theme	*theme*	The **theme** of my report is earthquakes.
6.	sleet	*sleet*	The cold air changed the rain to **sleet**.
7.	excellent	*excellent*	She has an **excellent** attendance record.
8.	cleanse	*cleanse*	Be sure to **cleanse** the wound carefully.
9.	melody	*melody*	He was humming a familiar **melody**.
10.	employee	*employee*	The new **employee** arrived at work early.
11.	method	*method*	We are trying a new cooking **method**.
12.	indeed	*indeed*	She is **indeed** a very bright woman.
13.	develop	*develop*	A storm might **develop** overnight.
14.	regular	*regular*	The **regular** price has been reduced.
15.	scheme	*scheme*	She has a **scheme** for making money.
16.	crease	*crease*	He ironed the **crease** in his pants.
17.	leather	*leather*	The shoes are made of genuine **leather**.
18.	attend	*attend*	Hundreds will **attend** tonight's lecture.
19.	release	*release*	I will **release** the name of the winner.
20.	meadow	*meadow*	Plant life abounds in the **meadow**.

SORT THE SPELLING WORDS

1.–2. Write the words with both the **short e** and the **long e** sounds.

3.–12. Write the other words with the **short e** vowel sound.

13.–20. Write the other words with the **long e** vowel sound.

Circle the letters that spell the **short e** sound or the **long e** sound.

REMEMBER THE SPELLING STRATEGY

Remember that the **short e** sound is spelled **e** in **text** and **ea** in **dealt**. The **long e** sound is spelled **ee** in **sleet**, **ea** in **crease**, **e-consonant-e** in **theme**, and **y** in **gravity**.

Spelling and Vocabulary

Word Meanings

Write the spelling word for each clue.

1. to grow
2. system
3. better than good
4. musical tones
5. past tense of **deal**
6. topic

Beginning and Ending Sounds

7.–10. Write the spelling words that begin with a two-letter consonant cluster.

11. Write the spelling word that begins with the /**sk**/ sound spelled **sch**.

12.–13. Write the spelling words that begin and end with the same consonant sound.

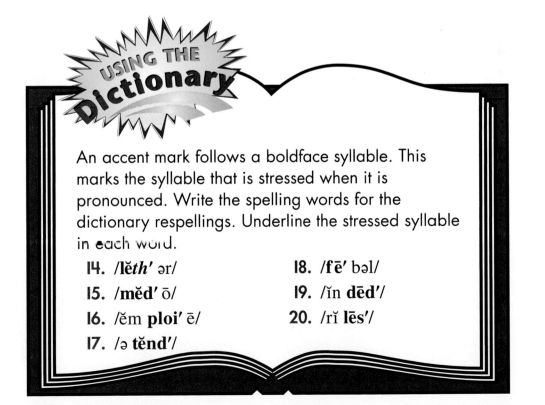

USING THE Dictionary

An accent mark follows a boldface syllable. This marks the syllable that is stressed when it is pronounced. Write the spelling words for the dictionary respellings. Underline the stressed syllable in each word.

14. /lĕ*th*′ ər/
15. /mĕd′ ō/
16. /ĕm ploi′ ē/
17. /ə tĕnd′/
18. /fē′ bəl/
19. /ĭn dēd′/
20. /rĭ lēs′/

Spelling and Reading

text	feeble	gravity	dealt	theme
sleet	excellent	cleanse	melody	employee
method	indeed	develop	regular	scheme
crease	leather	attend	release	meadow

Complete the Sequences   Write a spelling word to complete each sequence.

1. field, pasture, grassland, _____
2. hail, rain, snow, _____
3. normal, usual, ordinary, _____
4. worker, laborer, attendant, _____
5. weak, frail, shaky, _____

Solve the Analogies   Write a spelling word to complete each analogy.

6. **Sweater** is to **wool** as **belt** is to _____.
7. **Painting** is to **color** as **music** is to _____.
8. **Argue** is to **agree** as **restrain** is to _____.
9. **Dirt** is to **smudge** as **soap** is to _____.
10. **Foolish** is to **wise** as **poor** is to _____.
11. **Devise** is to **plan** as **concoct** is to _____.
12. **Meet** is to **met** as **deal** is to _____.

Complete the Sentences   Write the spelling word that completes each sentence.

13. The force of _____ made rocks roll down the hill.
14. We would like you to _____ tonight's meeting.
15. Electronic mail is a fairly new _____ of communication.
16. This tiny bud will _____ into an enormous flower.
17. Fold the paper and cut the design along the _____.
18. Modern art is the _____ of the lecture series.
19. I found the answer on page five of the _____.
20. The play was _____ enjoyable.

Spelling and Writing

Proofread a Play Description

Six words are not spelled correctly in this play description. Write the words correctly.

Proofreading Marks

≡ Make a capital.

/ Make a small letter.

∧ Add something.

ℓ Take out something.

⊙ Add a period

¶ New paragraph

(SP) Spelling error

The Mystery of the Missing Worker

Type of play: comedy

Setting: an office in a leather goods company

The play opens with a group of workers discussing the gravitey of a situation in which one of their co-workers has disappeared. They agree that they indede need to devellop a skeme to find the missing employee. After their feebel attempts fail, the worker reappears just as suddenly as he had vanished.

Write a Play Description

Expository Writing

The action of a play is divided into acts and scenes, just as a book is divided into chapters and paragraphs. Each act tells a part of the story. Write a description for a play.

- Describe the type of play and the setting, or where the play takes place. Also describe the cast of characters.
- Follow the form used in the proofreading sample.

Use as many spelling words as you can.

Proofread Your Writing During ➤

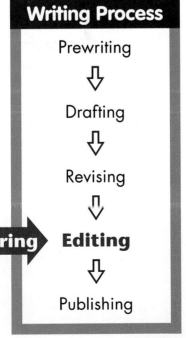

Writing Process

Prewriting

⇩

Drafting

⇩

Revising

⇩

Editing

⇩

Publishing

Proofread your writing for spelling errors as part of the editing stage in the writing process. Be sure to check each word carefully. Use a dictionary to check spelling if you are not sure.

Vocabulary

Strategy Words

Review Words: Short e, Long e

Write the words from the box to complete the paragraph.

beneath	expect	homestead	memory	needle

With a __1.__ and thread, Abigail had captured the __2.__ of the old family __3.__ in Kansas. Her quilt now hangs on the wall in the historical society. A description of the quilt is __4.__ it. I __5.__ that everyone who sees the quilt admires it.

Preview Words: Short e, Long e

Write the word from the box that matches each clue.

activities	extreme	headline	league	newsreel

6. This appears on the front page of a newspaper.

7. Sports teams might come together to form this.

8. Plan a lot of these to keep a group of two-year-olds busy all day.

9. This would show motion pictures of news events.

10. This could describe the heat of the desert.

Connections

Language Arts: Genres

Write the word from the box that fits each definition.

autobiography	journal	serial	novel	trilogy

1. a record of the events in your day
2. the story of your life
3. a series of three related plays, operas, or novels
4. a story that is published one part at a time
5. a long work of fiction

Health: First Aid

Write the words from the box to complete the paragraph.

artery	pressure	bleed	tourniquet	emergency

After the accident, the __6.__ team immediately set to work. First they checked the victim's blood __7.__. They tied a __8.__ around his arm so that the wound would not continue to __9.__. Fortunately, the broken glass had missed an __10.__ in his arm. He will be released from the hospital today.

Apply the Spelling Strategy

Circle the words that spell the **long e** sound **ee** or **y** in five of the content words you wrote.

Spelling and Thinking

READ THE SPELLING WORDS

1. attic	*attic*	I found the old clothes in the **attic**.
2. ideal	*ideal*	The weather is **ideal** for sailing.
3. limit	*limit*	The speed **limit** is forty miles an hour.
4. confide	*confide*	I **confide** my worries to my friend.
5. district	*district*	The school **district** covers five miles.
6. disguise	*disguise*	He tried to **disguise** his handwriting.
7. exhibit	*exhibit*	The art will be on **exhibit** for a month.
8. classify	*classify*	Librarians **classify** novels as literature.
9. require	*require*	Laws will **require** the use of seat belts.
10. permit	*permit*	We will **permit** you to leave at noon.
11. consider	*consider*	I **consider** him to be an expert on cars.
12. item	*item*	She had one **item** in her grocery cart.
13. empire	*empire*	The **empire** fell in the fifth century.
14. satisfy	*satisfy*	We try to **satisfy** all of our customers.
15. system	*system*	The bank installed a new alarm **system**.
16. strike	*strike*	The workers voted to begin the **strike**.
17. assign	*assign*	Your teacher will **assign** your seats.
18. apply	*apply*	I decided to **apply** for the job.
19. inherit	*inherit*	The baby might **inherit** your blue eyes.
20. examine	*examine*	The detective will **examine** the evidence.

SORT THE SPELLING WORDS

1.–2. Write the words with both the **short i** and **long i** sounds.

3.–11. Write the other words that have the **short i** vowel sound.

12.–20. Write the other words that have the **long i** vowel sound.

Circle the letters that spell the **short i** sound or **long i** sound.

REMEMBER THE SPELLING STRATEGY

Remember that the **short i** sound is spelled **i** in **permit** and **y** in **system**. The **long i** sound is spelled **i** in **item**, **i-consonant-e** in **strike**, and **y** in **satisfy**.

20

Spelling ^{and} Vocabulary

Word Structure

Change each of these nouns into verbs to write a spelling word.

1. consideration
2. classification
3. examination
4. requirement
5. limitation

Word Meanings

Write the spelling word that could best replace each underlined word or words.

6. He tried to <u>conceal</u> his voice on the phone.
7. You forgot to buy one <u>article</u> on the list.
8. The artist's works are on <u>public display</u> at the museum.
9. Be sure to <u>put on</u> the paint with a thick brush.
10. He ate, and ate, but he could not <u>put an end to</u> his hunger.
11. The coach is using a new <u>way of doing something</u>.
12. She will <u>receive</u> a clock from her grandfather.
13. The weather was <u>perfect</u> for the race.
14. There was a lightning <u>hit</u> in our neighborhood.

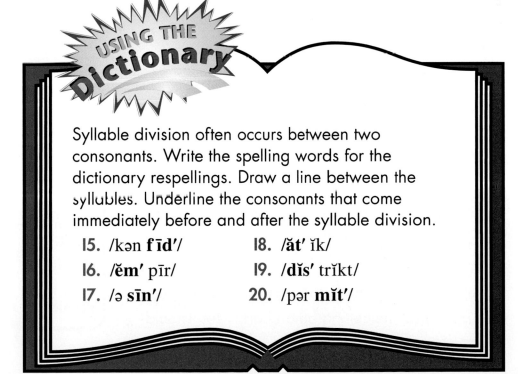

USING THE Dictionary

Syllable division often occurs between two consonants. Write the spelling words for the dictionary respellings. Draw a line between the syllables. Underline the consonants that come immediately before and after the syllable division.

15. /kən **fīd'**/
16. /**ĕm'** pīr/
17. /ə **sīn'**/
18. /**ăt'** ĭk/
19. /**dĭs'** trĭkt/
20. /pər **mĭt'**/

Spelling ᴬⁿ𝐝 Reading

attic	ideal	limit	confide	district
disguise	exhibit	classify	require	permit
consider	item	empire	satisfy	system
strike	assign	apply	inherit	examine

Solve the Analogies Write a spelling word to complete each analogy.

1. **Help** is to **aid** as **display** is to _____.
2. **Down** is to **up** as **basement** is to _____.
3. **Argue** is to **agree** as **disappoint** is to _____.
4. **President** is to **nation** as **emperor** is to _____.
5. **Idea** is to **suggest** as **secret** is to _____.

Complete the Sentences Write spelling words to complete the sentences.

6. Children _____ traits from their parents.
7. I will _____ your homework for tomorrow.
8. Always _____ the evidence before drawing a conclusion.
9. The voters in this _____ approved the new school.
10. I read an interesting _____ in the newspaper.
11. The heart is part of the circulatory _____.
12. The clock should _____ midnight soon.
13. You can _____ your math knowledge to the science project.
14. No one recognized the man with the _____.

Complete the Paragraph Write spelling words from the box to complete the paragraph.

The __15.__ science fiction story includes scientific facts. Even so, librarians __16.__ science fiction as fiction, not as science. If you write science fiction, __17.__ your imagination to soar. Do not feel that you should __18.__ the time to the present. These stories do not __19.__ that the setting be on Earth. You should __20.__ all possibilities for your story.

limit
require
ideal
classify
permit
consider

Spelling and Writing

Proofread a Science Fiction Story

Six words are not spelled correctly in this science fiction story. Write the words correctly.

Julia could not believe her eyes. Her computer sistem had shut down without warning. When it restarted, a voice announced, "Please permmit me to introduce myself. I am Commander X from Galaxy Gorp. I am here to assigne you the role of ambassador. There is no limit to your powers. The usual rules do not applie to you. I only rekwire that you considor this project a deeply held secret."

Proofreading Marks

≡	Make a capital.
/	Make a small letter.
∧	Add something.
ℓ	Take out something.
⊙	Add a period.
⌗	New paragraph
SP	Spelling error

Write a Science Fiction Story

Narrative Writing

A work of science fiction changes life as we know it in some dramatic way. Write a science fiction story.

- Describe something that might happen in a futuristic world, or describe a condition in today's world that suddenly changes.
- Follow the form used in the proofreading sample.

Use as many spelling words as you can.

Proofread Your Writing During

Proofread your writing for spelling errors as part of the editing stage in the writing process. Be sure to check each word carefully. Use a dictionary to check spelling if you are not sure.

Writing Process

Prewriting
⇩
Drafting
⇩
Revising
⇩
Editing
⇩
Publishing

23

Vocabulary

Strategy Words

Review Words: Short i, Long i

Write words from the box to complete the paragraph.

arrive	bicycle	digit	signs	simplify

This year we are trying to __1.__ the rules of the __2.__ race. The route of the race through town will be clearly marked. Along the route, volunteers will hold __3.__ with two- __4.__ numbers on them. These signs will indicate the number of kilometers left in the race. When you __5.__ at the finish line, someone will hand you a card with your time.

Preview Words: Short i, Long i

Write the word from the box that matches each clue.

admire	alliance	byline	hinder	resign

6. Marriage is an example of this.

7. Heavy snow could do this to road travel.

8. This tells you the author of a newspaper article.

9. You might do this if you were unhappy with your job.

10. After you finish a painting, you might stand back and do this.

Connections

Language Arts: Genres

Write the word from the box to complete each sentence.

| legend | fable | myth | ballad | short story |

1. A narrative poem set to music is a _____.
2. The _____ told how Zeus's anger caused lightning.
3. The story of King Arthur and his knights is an English _____.
4. A _____ is a brief story in which animals are the main characters.
5. A short piece of fiction is called a _____.

Social Studies: Petroleum

Write the words from the box to complete the paragraph.

| derrick | platform | petroleum | tanker | pipeline |

Oil, or __6.__, is often found under the ocean. A steel or concrete __7.__ provides a stable structure, and the drilling and pumping equipment is attached to the __8.__. The oil is brought ashore by an underwater __9.__ or an oil __10.__.

Apply the Spelling Strategy

Circle the letters that spell the **short i** or the **long i** sound in three of the content words you wrote.

Spelling and Thinking

READ THE SPELLING WORDS

1.	profit	*profit*	The store made a **profit** from the sale.
2.	oppose	*oppose*	The mayor will **oppose** the new highway.
3.	bronze	*bronze*	The lamp base is made of solid **bronze**.
4.	video	*video*	I watched a **video** about dog training.
5.	constant	*constant*	His **constant** humming was annoying.
6.	approach	*approach*	Slow down as you **approach** the light.
7.	pose	*pose*	The photographer asked us to **pose**.
8.	associate	*associate*	She consulted her business **associate**.
9.	contact	*contact*	I use the Internet to **contact** friends.
10.	opportunity	*opportunity*	I cannot pass up this **opportunity**.
11.	positive	*positive*	She is **positive** that she saw them.
12.	donate	*donate*	He will **donate** the proceeds to charity.
13.	stereo	*stereo*	The **stereo** speakers are ten feet apart.
14.	beyond	*beyond*	We drove **beyond** our destination.
15.	charcoal	*charcoal*	He sketched the portrait in **charcoal**.
16.	notice	*notice*	She did not **notice** the missing cookies.
17.	opposite	*opposite*	We stood on **opposite** sides of the room.
18.	emotion	*emotion*	He did not cry or show any **emotion**.
19.	project	*project*	The class **project** is nearly done.
20.	respond	*respond*	They did not **respond** to my phone call.

SORT THE SPELLING WORDS

1.–10. Write the words that spell **short o** as **o**.

11.–16. Write the words that spell **long o** as **o**.

17.–18. Write the words that spell **long o** as **o-consonant-e**.

19.–20. Write the words that spell **long o** as **oa**.

REMEMBER THE SPELLING STRATEGY

Remember that the **short o** sound in **bronze** is spelled **o**. The **long o** sound is spelled **o** in **notice, o-consonant-e** in **pose,** and **oa** in **approach**.

Spelling and Vocabulary

Word Groups

Write a spelling word to complete each sequence.

1. connect, communicate, _____
2. reaction, feeling, _____
3. answer, reply, _____
4. steady, continual, _____
5. chance, occasion, _____
6. connect, correlate, _____
7. give, provide, _____
8. past, farther, _____
9. announcement, report, _____

Sound and Letter Patterns

10.–13. Write the spelling words that begin with a two-letter consonant cluster.

14.–15. Write the spelling words that begin or end with **ch**.

16. Write the spelling word that begins like **voice** and ends in two long vowel sounds.

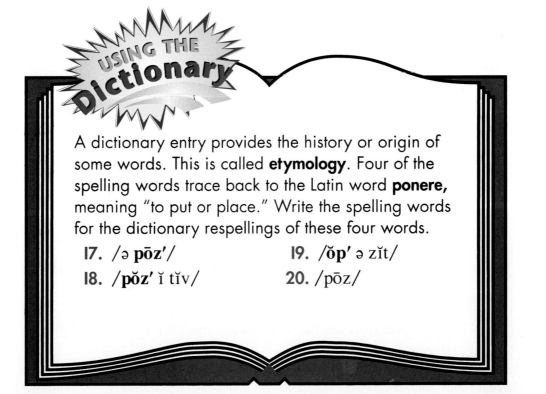

USING THE Dictionary

A dictionary entry provides the history or origin of some words. This is called **etymology**. Four of the spelling words trace back to the Latin word **ponere,** meaning "to put or place." Write the spelling words for the dictionary respellings of these four words.

17. /ə pōz′/   19. /ŏp′ ə zĭt/
18. /pŏz′ ĭ tĭv/   20. /pōz/

Spelling and Reading

profit	oppose	bronze	video	constant
approach	pose	associate	contact	opportunity
positive	donate	stereo	beyond	charcoal
notice	opposite	emotion	project	respond

Solve the Analogies Write a spelling word to complete each analogy.

1. **Fame** is to **stardom** as **chance** is to _____.
2. **Defeat** is to **victory** as **loss** is to _____.
3. **Regret** is to **mistake** as **feel** is to _____.
4. **White** is to **snow** as **black** is to _____.
5. **Opponent** is to **rival** as **co-worker** is to _____.

Complete the Sentences Write a spelling word to complete each sentence.

6. The live concert was reproduced in _____.
7. The school needs to know whom to _____ in an emergency.
8. We walked two blocks _____ the park.
9. My reaction to the book was the _____ of his.
10. You will recognize the building as you _____ it.
11. Please _____ to the invitation by Friday.
12. We heard the _____ roar of the waterfall.

Complete the Paragraph Write the spelling words that could replace the boldfaced words in the paragraph.

     Spectators at the race asked the chairman to **direct** his voice ^{13.}
when he announced the winner of the **metal** trophy. The winner ^{14.}
said she was **certain** that she would **give** the prize money to the ^{15.} ^{16.}
animal shelter. The chairman did not **resist** her request. He asked ^{17.}
the racers to **pay attention to** the woman with the camera and ^{18.}
hold their expression for her. He also invited them to watch the ^{19.}
taped recording of the race. ^{20.}

28

Spelling and Writing

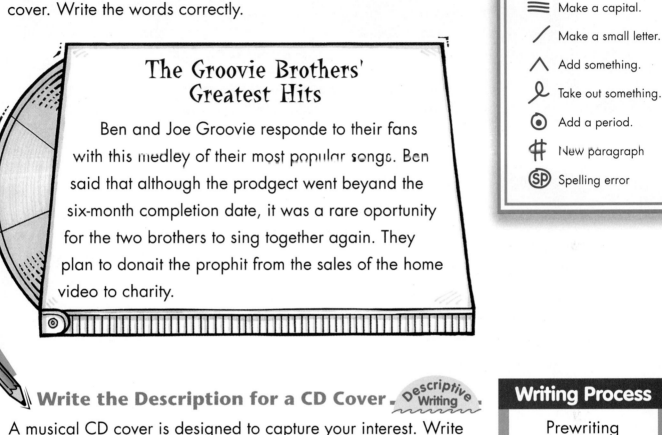

Proofread a Description for a CD Cover

Six words are not spelled correctly in this description for a CD cover. Write the words correctly.

The Groovie Brothers' Greatest Hits

Ben and Joe Groovie responde to their fans with this medley of their most popular songs. Ben said that although the prodgect went beyand the six-month completion date, it was a rare oportunity for the two brothers to sing together again. They plan to donait the prophit from the sales of the home video to charity.

Proofreading Marks

≡ Make a capital.

/ Make a small letter.

∧ Add something.

℘ Take out something.

⊙ Add a period.

⌗ New paragraph

⑤Ⓟ Spelling error

Write the Description for a CD Cover _Descriptive Writing_

A musical CD cover is designed to capture your interest. Write the description for a CD.

- Describe the musicians and their music.
- What is special about the music?
- Follow the form used in the proofreading sample.

Use as many spelling words as you can.

Proofread Your Writing During

Proofread your writing for spelling errors as part of the editing stage in the writing process. Be sure to check each word carefully. Use a dictionary to check spelling if you are not sure.

Writing Process

Prewriting

⇩

Drafting

⇩

Revising

⇩

Editing

⇩

Publishing

Vocabulary

Strategy Words

Review Words: Short o, Long o

Write words from the box to complete the paragraph.

colonist	loaves	Ohio	promise	slope

It was May of 1787. The __1.__ and his family were settling in a part of the country that would later become the state of __2.__. Just a few __3.__ of bread remained at the end of the long trip. They built a log cabin on a __4.__ overlooking their newly cleared farmland. Their future held much __5.__.

Preview Words: Short o, Long o

Write the word from the box that matches each clue.

oval	monotone	pronto	trophy	toxic

6. It is an informal way of saying **immediately**.
7. It begins with **mono,** which means "one" or "single."
8. This goes to the winner of the race.
9. It is a synonym for **poisonous**.
10. An egg has this shape.

Connections

Language Arts: Periodicals

Write the word from the box that fits each clue.

| brochure | periodical | pamphlet | catalog | publication |

1. It begins with a /**k**/ sound spelled **c**.
2. It has a **long e** sound spelled **i**.
3. It has an /**f**/ sound spelled **ph**.
4. It has an /**sh**/ sound spelled **ch**.
5. It ends like **vacation**.

Science: The Environment

Write the words from the box to complete the paragraph.

| conservation | depletion | erosion | fertilizer | topsoil |

Imagine if you woke up one morning and found that all of the surface layer of earth, or __6.__, had washed away overnight. Heavy rain can cause __7.__ of unprotected land. A loss of vegetation will result in a __8.__ of the soil's basic components. Using __9.__ can help restore the loss, but it can be harmful to our water supply. We must create __10.__ laws that will protect all of our valuable resources.

Apply the Spelling Strategy

Circle the letters that spell the **short o** or the **long o** sound in five of the content words you wrote.

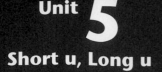
Spelling and Thinking

READ THE SPELLING WORDS

1.	stubborn	*stubborn*	The **stubborn** man will not move.
2.	computer	*computer*	Our files are on the **computer**.
3.	customer	*customer*	The **customer** waited in line.
4.	contribute	*contribute*	I will **contribute** to the charity.
5.	budge	*budge*	We could not **budge** the heavy rock.
6.	barbecue	*barbecue*	I will serve chicken at the **barbecue**.
7.	union	*union*	The first colonies formed a **union**.
8.	dispute	*dispute*	The company settled the **dispute**.
9.	community	*community*	We planned a **community** picnic.
10.	uniform	*uniform*	All officers will wear a **uniform**.
11.	smudge	*smudge*	The paint will **smudge** if it is wet.
12.	custody	*custody*	The thief is in police **custody**.
13.	bugle	*bugle*	You will hear the **bugle** at dawn.
14.	confuse	*confuse*	Too many details will **confuse** us.
15.	acute	*acute*	A bad sprain causes **acute** pain.
16.	insult	*insult*	His thoughtless comments **insult** her.
17.	suffer	*suffer*	Some people **suffer** from back pain.
18.	punish	*punish*	We had to **punish** our puppy once.
19.	accuse	*accuse*	Do not **accuse** me of laziness.
20.	result	*result*	The game **result** was announced.

SORT THE SPELLING WORDS

1.–9. Write the spelling words with the **short u** sound.

10.–14. Write the words with the **long u** sound spelled **u**.

15.–20. Write the words with the **long u** sound spelled
u-consonant-e or **ue**.

REMEMBER THE SPELLING STRATEGY

Remember the **short u** sound in **result** is spelled **u**. The **long u**
sound is spelled **u** in **union**, **u-consonant-e** in **acute**, and **ue** in
barbecue.

Spelling and Vocabulary

Word Groups

Write a spelling word to complete each group.

1. trumpet, horn, _____
2. safekeeping, care, _____
3. picnic, cookout, _____
4. difficult, inflexible, _____
5. discipline, reprimand, _____
6. mark, smear, _____
7. blame, criticize, _____
8. outcome, effect, _____
9. argue, debate, _____
10. baffle, puzzle, _____
11. keyboard, monitor, _____
12. move, advance, _____

Letters and Syllables

Add the missing syllable and write a spelling word.

13. con__ __ __ __ute   15. suf__ __ __   17. __ __sult
14. __ __ __tomer   16. a__ __ __ __

USING THE Dictionary

A dictionary often provides the history or origin of a word. Write the spelling words that have these similar origins.

18. From Latin **unus,** and **forma,** meaning "shape."
19. From Latin **unus** meaning "one."
20. From Latin **communis,** meaning "common."

Spelling and Reading

stubborn	computer	customer	contribute	budge
barbecue	union	dispute	community	uniform
smudge	custody	bugle	confuse	acute
insult	suffer	punish	accuse	result

Complete the Sentences   Write spelling words to complete the sentences.

1. The ink left a _____ on the paper.
2. I did not mean to _____ you with my critical remark.
3. The parents have joint _____ of the children.
4. He was too _____ to listen to my explanation.
5. I hope they will not _____ me for being late.
6. We will hold the _____ in spite of the rain.

Solve the Analogies   Write a spelling word to complete each analogy.

7. **Country** is to **nation** as **neighborhood** is to _____.
8. **Actor** is to **costume** as **officer** is to _____.
9. **Painting** is to **brush** as **music** is to _____.
10. **Hospital** is to **patient** as **store** is to _____.
11. **Photographer** is to **camera** as **programmer** is to _____.
12. **Safe** is to **dangerous** as **mild** is to _____.
13. **Depart** is to **arrive** as **clarify** is to _____.

Complete the Paragraph   Write the spelling words from the box that complete the paragraph.

Members of the postal __14.__ were willing to __15.__ the consequences of a strike. The workers said they would __16.__ some of their pay, but the employers refused to __17.__ . Each side was eager to __18.__ the other of unfair practices. The __19.__ of this __20.__ is that we are still waiting to receive our mail.

accuse
dispute
budge
contribute
union
suffer
result

Spelling and Writing

Proofread a List of Rules

Six words are not spelled correctly in this list of employee rules. Write the words correctly.

Rules for Restaurant Employees

1. Do not argue with a stuborn custimer. Arguing will only result in a loss of business to us.
2. Any despute should be resolved by consulting with the manager.
3. Wear a clean unaform at all times.
4. Check the computor for your schedule.
5. Waiters will contributte a portion of their tips to the dishwashers.

Proofreading Marks

≡ Make a capital.

/ Make a small letter.

∧ Add something.

ℓ Take out something.

⊙ Add a period

New paragraph

SP Spelling error

Write a List of Rules

Expository Writing

Rules help people get along in a group. Write some rules that would help things run smoothly in your classroom.

- Be sure the rules you write are fair to everyone.
- Follow the form used in the proofreading sample.

Use as many spelling words as you can.

Writing Process

Prewriting

⇩

Drafting

⇩

Revising

⇩

Editing

⇩

Publishing

Proofread Your Writing During

Proofread your writing for spelling errors as part of the editing stage in the writing process. Be sure to check each word carefully. Use a dictionary to check spelling if you are not sure.

Vocabulary

Strategy Words

Review Words: Short u, Long u

Write words from the box to complete the letter.

amuse	discuss	publish	unit	value

Dear Editor,

I would like to __1.__ a recent article. I wonder why you __2.__ material like this, since it appears to have no __3.__. Perhaps your intent is to __4.__ the reader. Well, you can decrease the number of copies to print by a __5.__ of one, because I have canceled my subscription.

        Sincerely,

        I. M. Annoyed

Preview Words: Short u, Long u

Write the word from the box that matches each clue.

commute	culprit	mutual	tuxedo	unison

6. My friend and I have many _____ interests.

7. He rented a _____ to wear to the wedding.

8. The musical group sang in _____.

9. She has a one-hour _____ to work.

10. The fingerprints led us to the _____.

Connections

Fine Arts: Canvas, Pen, and Thread

Write a word from the box to complete each sentence.

pigment	mural	tapestry	hue	etching

1. We hung the woven _____ on the wall.
2. **Color** is a synonym for _____.
3. The wall is decorated with a painted _____.
4. The artist added green _____ to the paint.
5. An _____ is a design made from a metal plate.

Science: Measurement

Write a word from the box that matches each clue.

capacity	volume	dimensions	velocity	mass

6. This is the amount of space an object occupies.
7. The weight of an object can change, but this will always stay the same.
8. These are the measurements of length, width, and height.
9. This is the rate at which an object moves in a specific direction.
10. This is the amount that something can hold.

Apply the Spelling Strategy

Circle the letters that spell the **long u** sound **ue** or **u-consonant-e** in two of the content words you wrote.

Assessment and Review

Assessment — Units 1–5

Each Assessment Word in the box fits one of the spelling strategies you have studied over the past five weeks. Read the spelling strategies. Then write each Assessment Word under the unit number it fits.

Unit 1

1.–4. The **short a** sound in **rapid** is spelled **a**. The **long a** sound is spelled **a** in **labor**, **ai** in **trait**, **ay** in **daydream**, **a-consonant-e** in **behave**, and **ey** in **survey**.

Unit 2

5.–9. The **short e** sound is spelled **e** in **text** and **ea** in **dealt**. The **long e** sound is spelled **ee** in **sleet**, **ea** in **crease**, **e-consonant-e** in **theme**, and **y** in **gravity**.

Unit 3

10.–12. The **short i** sound is spelled **i** in **permit** and **y** in **system**. The **long i** sound is spelled **i** in **item**, **i-consonant-e** in **strike**, and **y** in **satisfy**.

Unit 4

13.–16. The **short o** sound in **bronze** is spelled **o**. The **long o** sound is spelled **o** in **notice**, **o-consonant-e** in **pose**, and **oa** in **approach**.

Unit 5

17.–20. The **short u** sound in **result** is spelled **u**. The **long u** sound is spelled **u** in **union**, **u-consonant-e** in **acute**, and **ue** in **barbecue**.

estate
treasury
critic
oatmeal
secure
cue
patrol
specify
plenty
praise
granite
retreat
besides
popular
deduct
bundle
polish
wheeze
cactus
despise

Unit 1: Short a, Long a

favorite	vacation	natural	exactly	rapid
pattern	admit	behave	daydream	complain

Write the spelling word that matches each clue.

1. whine about
2. act a certain way
3. regular design
4. fantasize or wish
5. fast

6. let in
7. best, in one's opinion
8. precisely
9. time away from school
10. actual or real

Review Unit 2: Short e, Long e

develop	method	scheme	melody	regular
attend	meadow	leather	indeed	release

Write a spelling word for each clue.

11. It has the **short e** sound in the <u>middle</u> of three syllables.
12. It begins with the same two letters as **melody** and **meadow**.
13. It means "tune."
14. It means "ordinary" or "common."
15. The **long e** sound is spelled **ea**.
16.–17. In these two words, **short e** is spelled **ea**.
18. The **long e** sound is spelled **e-consonant-e**.
19. It ends with **end**.
20. The **long e** sound is spelled **ee**.

| exhibit | examine | disguise | assign | limit |
| attic | system | consider | item | strike |

Write the spelling word that completes each sentence.

1. Let the doctor _____ the cut on your arm.
2. That was a wonderful art _____!
3. Did the director _____ the play parts yet?
4. No one will know you with that funny _____.
5. The umpire has called one ball and one _____.
6. Put a check beside the first _____ on the list.
7. Our new public address _____ has been installed.
8. I hope you will _____ voting for me.
9. There is a _____ of two on the number you can buy.
10. The old photos are kept in a box up in the _____.

Review Unit 4: Short o, Long o

| opportunity | positive | approach | video | constant |
| project | beyond | opposite | notice | respond |

Change the underlined part of these words to write spelling words.

11. pos<u>sible</u>
12. <u>re</u>proach
13. vi<u>sion</u>
14. pro<u>duce</u>
15. be<u>side</u>
16. com<u>posite</u>
17. resp<u>ect</u>
18. not<u>ion</u>
19. <u>instant</u>
20. <u>community</u>

40

stubborn	customer	barbecue	contribute	suffer
result	confuse	punish	computer	community

Write spelling words to complete the paragraph.

   This year we had a street fair in our __1.__. The businesses agreed to __2.__ something. The John's Ribs store made their delicious __3.__ to sell. Each paying __4.__ bought tokens to use. The tokens were different sizes so that we wouldn't __5.__ them. Mr. Hempstead kept track of all the sales on his __6.__. We were pleased with the __7.__ of the fair. We decided not to __8.__ ourselves in the future by trying our old fund-raising methods. We wouldn't __9.__ any more by going door to door asking for money. Even the most __10.__ residents agreed that the fair was a great idea.

GAME Spelling Study Strategy

Spelling Capture

Swap spelling lists with a partner. On a sheet of paper, make five rows of dots with five dots in each row. Decide who is Player 1 and who is Player 2.

Player 2 says the first word on Player 1's list, and Player 1 spells the word. If it's correct, Player 1 uses a pencil to connect any two dots that are side by side. If Player 1 misspells the word, no dots are connected. Player 2 spells the misspelled word aloud correctly. Then it's Player 2's turn to spell the first word on his or her list.

Continue to take turns, spelling the next word on each list. Each time a player connects two dots to make a square, that player writes initials in the square. That square is "captured." The player who has the most initialed squares at the end of the game wins.

Grammar, Usage, and Mechanics

Sentences and Their Parts

There are four kinds of sentences: declarative (ones that tell), interrogative (ones that ask), imperative (ones that command), and exclamatory (ones that show strong feeling).

Every sentence has a subject and a predicate. The simple subject tells whom or what the sentence is about. The simple predicate tells what the subject is, has, or does. In a command, the subject is often not named. It is understood to be **you,** the person being spoken to.

Practice Activity

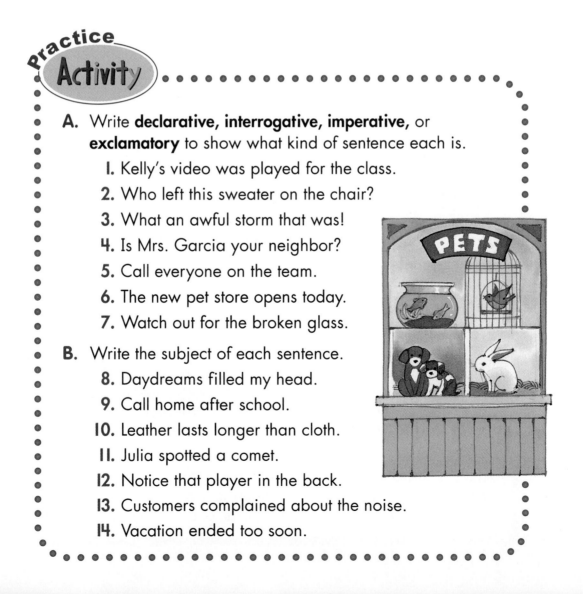

A. Write **declarative, interrogative, imperative,** or **exclamatory** to show what kind of sentence each is.

1. Kelly's video was played for the class.
2. Who left this sweater on the chair?
3. What an awful storm that was!
4. Is Mrs. Garcia your neighbor?
5. Call everyone on the team.
6. The new pet store opens today.
7. Watch out for the broken glass.

B. Write the subject of each sentence.

8. Daydreams filled my head.
9. Call home after school.
10. Leather lasts longer than cloth.
11. Julia spotted a comet.
12. Notice that player in the back.
13. Customers complained about the noise.
14. Vacation ended too soon.

WORKSHOP

Proofreading Strategy

One at a Time!

Good writers always proofread their writing for spelling mistakes. Here's a strategy you can use to proofread your papers.

Look for one kind of mistake at a time. First, skim your paper and look at any word endings. Then, look for words that contain **ie** or **ei**. Go through again and check contractions.

This may sound like a lot of work, but it's not. You do not read many words each time. Instead, you focus on a small group each time. You look for particular problems. Try it!

Electronic Spelling

Search Engines

Search engines are wonderful tools. They help you find information on the Internet, in encyclopedias, and in many programs. To use them, you simply type a word or phrase. However, you have to be sure you type this word or phrase correctly. A search engine can't guess what you are looking for; it can only look.

Some words are often misspelled by many people. Some have silent letters or double consonants. Others may just be hard to remember. If you are unsure of a word's spelling, look it up.

Look at these frequently misspelled words, which are often used in searches. Which are misspelled here? Write them correctly. Write **OK** if a name is correct.

1. sistem
2. community
3. exibit
4. examin
5. project
6. vidio

Spelling and Thinking

READ THE SPELLING WORDS

1.	aptitude	*aptitude*	He has an **aptitude** for languages.
2.	understood	*understood*	I **understood** the reason for the rule.
3.	intrude	*intrude*	We should not **intrude** on a meeting.
4.	routine	*routine*	The car is here for a **routine** checkup.
5.	proof	*proof*	We have **proof** that Pluto exists.
6.	neighborhood	*neighborhood*	I just moved to this **neighborhood**.
7.	would've	*would've*	I **would've** helped you make dinner.
8.	cushion	*cushion*	The **cushion** is comfortable.
9.	fluid	*fluid*	Your car is low on engine **fluid**.
10.	tablespoon	*tablespoon*	Add a **tablespoon** of flour.
11.	could've	*could've*	I **could've** helped you clean up.
12.	should've	*should've*	You **should've** attended the meeting.
13.	through	*through*	Walk **through** the door on the left.
14.	goodness	*goodness*	His **goodness** is known to everyone.
15.	approve	*approve*	Do you **approve** of the new rules?
16.	bulletin	*bulletin*	A **bulletin** warned us to stay inside.
17.	conclude	*conclude*	I will **conclude** my speech with a joke.
18.	introduce	*introduce*	I want to **introduce** you to my family.
19.	teaspoon	*teaspoon*	Add a **teaspoon** of salt to the mix.
20.	assume	*assume*	I **assume** you brought your umbrella.

SORT THE SPELLING WORDS

1.–12. Write the words with the /oo/ vowel sound spelled **oo**, **ou**, **u**, or **vowel-consonant-e**. Circle the letters that spell this vowel sound.

13.–20. Write the words with the /ŏŏ/ vowel sound spelled **oo**, **ou**, or **u**. Circle the letters that spell this vowel sound.

REMEMBER THE SPELLING STRATEGY

Remember that the /oo/ sound is spelled **oo** in **proof**, **ou** in **routine**, **u** in **fluid**, and **vowel-consonant-e** in **assume**. The /ŏŏ/ sound is spelled **oo** in **goodness**, **ou** in **could've**, and **u** in **bulletin**.

44

Spelling and Vocabulary

Word Groups

Write a spelling word to complete each group.

1. schedule, system, _____
2. pillow, buffer, _____
3. kindness, decency, _____
4. news report, notice, _____
5. water, liquid, _____
6. guarantee, evidence, _____
7. accept, suppose, _____

Word Structure

8.–10. Write the spelling words that are contractions.

11. Write the spelling word that ends in the suffix **-hood**.

12.–13. Write the spelling words that are compound words and that name units of measure.

14. Write the spelling word that ends in silent **gh**.

15. Write the spelling word that is the verb form of the noun **introduction**.

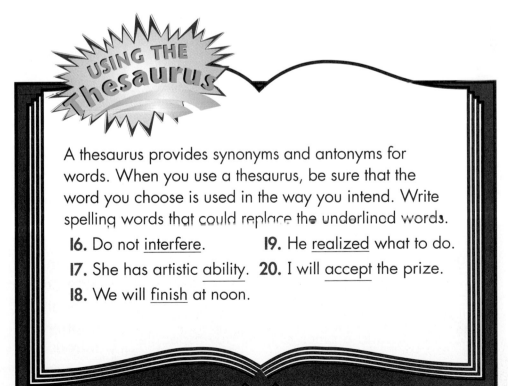

USING THE Thesaurus

A thesaurus provides synonyms and antonyms for words. When you use a thesaurus, be sure that the word you choose is used in the way you intend. Write spelling words that could replace the underlined words.

16. Do not <u>interfere</u>.
17. She has artistic <u>ability</u>.
18. We will <u>finish</u> at noon.
19. He <u>realized</u> what to do.
20. I will <u>accept</u> the prize.

Spelling and Reading

aptitude	understood	intrude	routine
proof	neighborhood	would've	cushion
fluid	tablespoon	could've	should've
through	goodness	approve	bulletin
conclude	introduce	teaspoon	assume

Solve the Analogies Write a spelling word to complete each analogy.

1. **Progress** is to **growth** as **talent** is to _____.
2. **Bed** is to **pillow** as **chair** is to _____.
3. **Rock** is to **solid** as **water** is to _____.
4. **Inhale** is to **exhale** as **start** is to _____.
5. **Break** is to **broke** as **understand** is to _____.
6. **Weak** is to **weakness** as **good** is to _____.
7. **They will** is to **they'll** as **could have** is to _____.

Complete the Sentences Write spelling words to complete the sentences.

8. You _____ seen the surprised look on his face.
9. A _____ is equal to three teaspoons.
10. His morning _____ begins with a long walk.
11. I know you _____ enjoyed the play last night.
12. She did not want to _____ on our conversation.
13. I am not certain, but I _____ he will be here.

Complete the Paragraph Write spelling words from the box to complete the paragraph.

Chef Fidelia shares her recipes __14.__ a weekly __15.__. Her crowded __16.__ restaurant is __17.__ of her good cooking. Chef Fidelia tries to __18.__ one new dish a week to her menu. When asked about her trade secrets, Chef Fidelia says, "I simply add a __19.__ of this and a pinch of that." Townspeople enthusiastically __20.__ of this new restaurant.

neighborhood
proof
bulletin
teaspoon
through
approve
introduce

Spelling <small>and</small> ▶ Writing

🔍 Proofread a Friendly Letter

Six words are not spelled correctly in this letter. Write the words correctly.

October 2, 2004

Dear Sophia,

Our soccer team has not been the same since you moved. We couldv'e used you this season. Our 3–6 record is proofe that we miss your goal-scoring skills. I heard throogh your aunt that you are on a team in your new nieghborhood. I asume you are one of the stars already! I will conclud this letter with a request. Please visit me soon. I will introduce you to my new kitten!

Sincerely,

Carolina

✏️ Write a Friendly Letter

Narrative Writing

Write a letter to a friend to whom you have not spoken in a long time.

- Share a story or describe a memorable day. Include facts and details to make your letter interesting to read.
- Follow the form used in the proofreading sample.

Use as many spelling words as you can.

Proofread Your Writing During

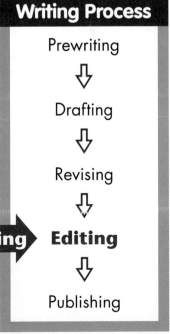

Writing Process

Prewriting

⬇

Drafting

⬇

Revising

⬇

Editing

⬇

Publishing

Proofread your writing for spelling errors as part of the editing stage in the writing process. Be sure to check each word carefully. Use a dictionary to check spelling if you are not sure.

Vocabulary

Strategy
Words

Review Words: Vowels /o͞o/, /o͝o/

Write a word from the box to complete each sentence.

| foolish | good-bye | goulash | solution | woodwind |

1. He ordered the homemade beef _____.
2. It would be _____ to go out in the cold without your coat.
3. I think I have the _____ to your problem.
4. He plays the bassoon in the _____ section of the city's orchestra.
5. She abruptly said _____ and left.

Preview Words: Vowels /o͞o/, /o͝o/

Write the word from the box that matches each clue.

| bamboo | boutique | footage | pollutant | pursuit |

6. This is the panda bear's favorite food.
7. Exhaust from cars is an example of this.
8. This is a hobby, an interest, or a high-speed chase.
9. This is a small and fashionable shop.
10. This is the length or amount of motion picture film.

Connections

Social Studies: The Caribbean

Write the word from the box that matches each clue.

Caribbean	sunset	coral	tropics	lagoon

1. the region of the earth near the equator
2. a shallow body of water
3. an arm of the Atlantic Ocean between Central and South America
4. the time when the sun disappears below the western horizon
5. a hard substance formed by skeletons of tiny sea animals

Social Studies: International Relations

Write the words from the box to complete the paragraph.

diplomat	rumor	protect	enlist	quota

A __6.__ was spreading among the immigrants that the president was going to restrict their __7.__ of persons entering the country. The president decided to __8.__ help. He appointed a __9.__ to assure the immigrants that every effort would be made to __10.__ their rights.

Apply the Spelling Strategy

Circle the letters that spell the /$\overline{oo}$/ or /$\breve{oo}$/ sound in two of the content words you wrote.

49

Spelling and Thinking

READ THE SPELLING WORDS

1.	mischief	*mischief*	A puppy often gets into **mischief**.
2.	ceiling	*ceiling*	Paint was peeling from the **ceiling**.
3.	siege	*siege*	The town was under **siege** for two months.
4.	relief	*relief*	It was a **relief** to have the test over.
5.	reign	*reign*	The queen's **reign** lasted for fifty years.
6.	niece	*niece*	His **niece** is in sixth grade.
7.	leisure	*leisure*	He spends his **leisure** time fishing.
8.	achieve	*achieve*	She will try to **achieve** good grades.
9.	yield	*yield*	The driver slowed down at the **yield** sign.
10.	weird	*weird*	I thought the movie had a **weird** ending.
11.	conceit	*conceit*	His **conceit** caused him to lose friends.
12.	grief	*grief*	Her sad expression revealed her **grief**.
13.	shriek	*shriek*	We heard her **shriek** with laughter.
14.	fierce	*fierce*	The **fierce** wind blew the door open.
15.	seize	*seize*	At the signal, **seize** the ball and run.
16.	thief	*thief*	The police caught the **thief** in the act.
17.	receive	*receive*	You will **receive** the letter in the mail.
18.	sleigh	*sleigh*	The horse pulled the **sleigh** down the path.
19.	receipt	*receipt*	The sales clerk handed her the **receipt**.
20.	shield	*shield*	The hat will **shield** you from the rain.

SORT THE SPELLING WORDS

1.–11. Write the words that have the **ie** spelling pattern. Circle this vowel combination in the words you write.

12.–20. Write the words that have the **ei** spelling pattern. Circle this vowel combination in the words you write.

REMEMBER THE SPELLING STRATEGY

Remember this rhyme can often help you decide when to use **ie** and when to use **ei**: Use **i** before **e**, except after **c**, or when sounded as **a**, as in **neighbor** and **weigh**.

Spelling ^a_{nd} Vocabulary

Word Groups

Write a spelling word to complete each sequence.

1. sorrow, sadness, _____
2. trouble, misconduct, _____
3. free time, rest, _____
4. submit, give up, _____
5. grasp, grab, _____

6. realize, reach, _____
7. strange, unusual, _____
8. robber, burglar, _____
9. wild, violent, _____
10. rule, govern, _____

Ending Sounds

Write a spelling word that fits each sentence. The spelling word will rhyme with the underlined word.

11. Dropping at her <u>feet</u> was the grocery store _____.
12. Causing the candidate's <u>defeat</u> was his annoying _____.
13. The boards will <u>creak</u>, and the children will _____.
14. He cut a <u>piece</u> of cake and gave it to his _____.
15. They piled the <u>hay</u> into the wooden _____.
16. The knight in the <u>field</u> was protected by his _____.

USING THE Dictionary

Dictionary **guide words** help you find a word easily. The guide words appear at the top of the page and are the first entry word and the last entry word on a page. Write the spelling word that you would find between each of these pairs of guide words.

17. quotation • regional
18. regular • rival
19. candidate • CEO
20. secondary • skyscraper

Spelling and Reading

mischief	ceiling	siege	relief	reign
niece	leisure	achieve	yield	weird
conceit	grief	shriek	fierce	seize
thief	receive	sleigh	receipt	shield

Solve the Analogies   Write a spelling word to complete each analogy.

1. **President** is to **term** as **king** is to _____.
2. **Wheel** is to **car** as **runner** is to _____.
3. **Brother** is to **sister** as **nephew** is to _____.
4. **Delight** is to **joy** as **sorrow** is to _____.
5. **House** is to **roof** as **room** is to _____.
6. **Construct** is to **destroy** as **give** is to _____.

Complete the Sentences   Write a spelling word to complete each sentence.

7. I cannot return the shirt without the _____.
8. You should _____ the opportunity to see the movie.
9. She enjoys painting in her _____ time.
10. It is good to have confidence but not _____.
11. The package arrived safely, to my great _____.
12. I know she will _____ with delight at the news.
13. The shadows made _____ figures on the wall.
14. Police apprehended the _____ outside the bank.

Complete the Paragraph   Write spelling words from the box to complete the paragraph.

There are many legends about noble knights of medieval times who traveled the land defending the helpless against __15.__ intruders. With only their sword and __16.__, they were able to __17.__ noble deeds, preventing the __18.__ of a castle. Other stories tell of daring knights who forced robbers to __19.__ their weapons, keeping them from causing further harm and __20.__.

siege
achieve
yield
fierce
shield
mischief

Spelling and Writing

Proofread a Story

Six words are not spelled correctly in this story about medieval times. Write the words correctly.

> The queen's riegn ran smoothly until the winter of 1524, when barbarians attempted to sieze the cusile. The selge lasted for months and caused the queen much grief. One morning her golden crown was missing. The queen commanded, "Bring me the villain! Whoever rescues my crown will receive a jewel-studded sheild." Each knight strutted to his horse with an air of conciet as he imagined himself capturing the theif.

Proofreading Marks

≡ Make a capital.

/ Make a small letter.

∧ Add something.

℮ Take out something.

⊙ Add a period.

⌗ New paragraph

⑤⑭ Spelling error

Write a Story

Narrative Writing

Knights of medieval times swore an oath to serve their king and queen and to bring honor to their land. Finish the story above.

- Describe the knight who captured the robber and how he captured him. Describe the knight's triumphant return to the queen's castle to receive his reward.
- Follow the form used in the proofreading sample.

Use as many spelling words as you can.

Proofread Your Writing During ▶

Proofread your writing for spelling errors as part of the editing stage in the writing process. Be sure to check each word carefully. Use a dictionary to check spelling if you are not sure.

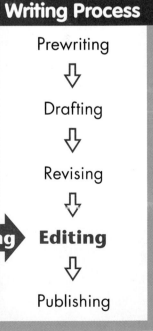

Writing Process

Prewriting

⇩

Drafting

⇩

Revising

⇩

Editing

⇩

Publishing

Vocabulary

Strategy Words

Review Words: ie, ei

Write a word from the box that matches each clue.

chiefs	midfield	pierce	protein	weight

1. This is what a nail might do to a tire.
2. Meat, milk, eggs, and some beans have this.
3. This is the middle of the field.
4. This would decrease if you were on the moon.
5. This is what you would call two fire department leaders.

Preview Words: ie, ei

Write words from the box to complete the movie review.

achieving	believable	fierceness	mischievous	briefly

In this his first attempt at directing a movie, David Parker seems to be __6.__ near perfection. In his playful and __7.__ way, Parker weaves reality with fiction, combining the __8.__ of battle scenes with touching moments. The result is a __9.__ story that even I found convincing. Pausing only __10.__ to enjoy his success, Parker is already planning his next movie.

Connections

Science: Radios

Write a word from the box that matches each clue.

amplitude   receiver   decibel   reverberate   loudness

1. part of a radio that picks up signals
2. a unit used for measuring the intensity of sounds
3. to sound again
4. the distance between the highest and lowest point of a sound wave
5. the volume of a sound

Health: Skin

Write the words from the box that complete the paragraph.

dermis   hygiene   epidermis   dermatologist   complexion

Dr. Wong is a __6.__. She told me that proper __7.__ is the key to keeping my __8.__ healthy. She says the skin has layers. The __9.__, or outer layer, suffers the most wear and tear. The __10.__, the layer just below the outer layer, contains the structures that allow the skin to sweat.

Apply the Spelling Strategy

Circle the **ie** or **ei** spelling pattern in two of the content words you wrote.

Spelling and Thinking

READ THE SPELLING WORDS

1.	carpenter	*carpenter*	The **carpenter** repaired the door frame.
2.	adore	*adore*	I know that they **adore** seafood.
3.	therefore	*therefore*	It is raining; **therefore,** the game is off.
4.	dirty	*dirty*	Please leave your **dirty** shoes at the door.
5.	purchase	*purchase*	She made a ten-dollar **purchase**.
6.	carbon	*carbon*	Charcoal has **carbon** in it.
7.	authority	*authority*	He is an **authority** on birds.
8.	confirm	*confirm*	Call the airline to **confirm** your flight.
9.	territory	*territory*	This **territory** is used for agriculture.
10.	curfew	*curfew*	The teenagers have a ten o'clock **curfew**.
11.	carton	*carton*	The **carton** broke, and the books fell out.
12.	ignore	*ignore*	You should **ignore** his rude remark.
13.	furnace	*furnace*	Check the **furnace** before winter arrives.
14.	concern	*concern*	My main **concern** is for your safety.
15.	foreman	*foreman*	The **foreman** asked us to work overtime.
16.	partner	*partner*	He is my **partner** in science class.
17.	mortar	*mortar*	A mason puts **mortar** between bricks.
18.	curtain	*curtain*	She chose a heavy fabric for the **curtain**.
19.	insert	*insert*	First **insert** the ticket in the slot.
20.	circular	*circular*	The house has a wide **circular** staircase.

SORT THE SPELLING WORDS

1.–9. Write the words that spell the /ûr/ sound **er, ir,** or **ur.**

10.–13. Write the words that spell the /är/ sound **ar.**

14. Write the word that spells the /âr/ sound **er** and the /ôr/ sound **ore.**

15.–20. Write the other words that spell the /ôr/ sound **or** or **ore.**

REMEMBER THE SPELLING STRATEGY

Remember that **r**-controlled vowel sounds can be spelled in different ways, including /ûr/ spelled **er, ir,** and **ur;** /är/ spelled **ar;** /âr/ spelled **er;** and /ôr/ spelled **or** and **ore.**

Spelling and Vocabulary

Related Words

Write a spelling word to complete each group.

1. box, package, crate, _____
2. worry, distress, anxiety, _____
3. area, region, zone, _____
4. filthy, unclean, soiled, _____
5. builder, woodworker, cabinetmaker, _____
6. tin, lead, silicon, _____
7. heater, radiator, boiler, _____
8. glue, sealant, filler, _____
9. shade, blinds, drapes, _____
10. supervisor, boss, manager, _____
11. deadline, time limit, _____
12. avoid, disregard, _____

Word Analysis

Change the underlined part of each word to write a spelling word.

13. thereafter
14. community

15. purpose
16. particular

USING THE Dictionary

Write the spelling word that is the base word of each word below. Write the part of speech after each word you write.

17. adorable, adj.
18. confirmation, n.

19. partnership, n.
20. insertion, n.

◆ ◆ ◆

Dictionary Check Be sure to check your answers in your **Spelling Dictionary**.

Spelling and Reading

carpenter	adore	therefore	dirty	purchase
carbon	authority	confirm	territory	curfew
carton	ignore	furnace	concern	foreman
partner	mortar	curtain	insert	circular

Answer the Questions   Write the spelling word that answers each question.

1. What pattern of motion does a windmill have?
2. What do you call a cardboard milk container?
3. What kind of paper was once used to make copies?
4. What requires someone to be home before dark?
5. What mixture is made with cement, sand, and water?
6. What does a customer do in a store?
7. Who works side by side with someone else?

Complete the Meaning   Write a spelling word to complete each sentence.

8. To open the box, _____ the key and turn.
9. He dumped the _____ laundry into the washer.
10. We are late; _____, we should walk fast.
11. An ornithologist is an _____ on birds.
12. I will ask him to play a song that I _____.
13. The director signaled me to open the _____ on the stage.
14. Much of the _____ in northern Africa is desert.

Complete the Paragraph   Write spelling words from the box to complete the paragraph.

The __15.__ of the construction project gathered his crew to express his __16.__. He wanted to __17.__ that the house would be completed on time. The __18.__ had finished the framing. The __19.__ had been installed. The crew was prepared to __20.__ the rainy weather and work until the job was done.

furnace
concern
foreman
confirm
carpenter
ignore

58

Spelling **and** Writing

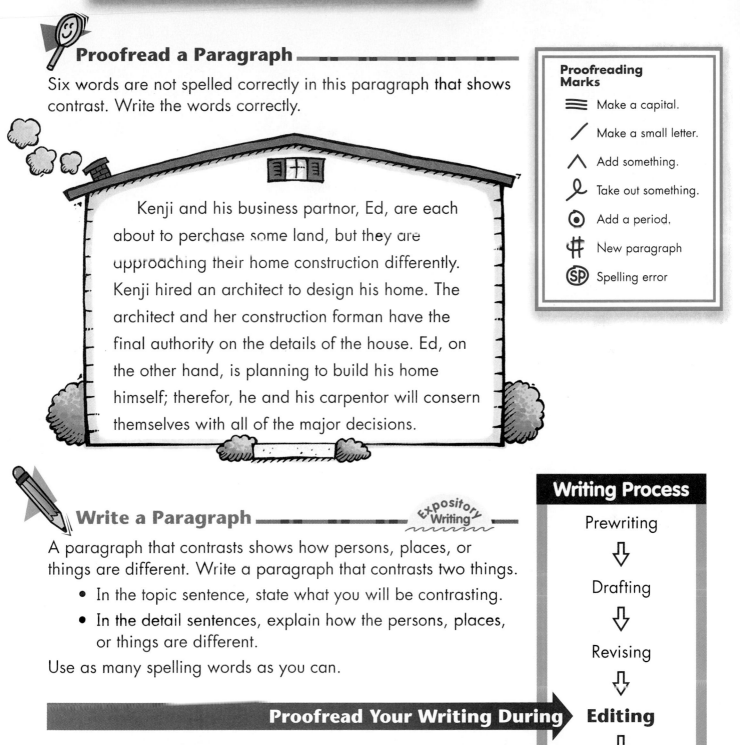

Proofread a Paragraph

Six words are not spelled correctly in this paragraph that shows contrast. Write the words correctly.

Kenji and his business partnor, Ed, are each about to perchase some land, but they are upproaching their home construction differently. Kenji hired an architect to design his home. The architect and her construction forman have the final authority on the details of the house. Ed, on the other hand, is planning to build his home himself; therefor, he and his carpentor will consern themselves with all of the major decisions.

Proofreading Marks

≡ Make a capital.

／ Make a small letter.

∧ Add something.

℘ Take out something.

⊙ Add a period.

＃ New paragraph

(SP) Spelling error

Write a Paragraph

Expository Writing

A paragraph that contrasts shows how persons, places, or things are different. Write a paragraph that contrasts two things.

- In the topic sentence, state what you will be contrasting.
- In the detail sentences, explain how the persons, places, or things are different.

Use as many spelling words as you can.

Writing Process

Prewriting

⇩

Drafting

⇩

Revising

⇩

Editing

⇩

Publishing

Proofread Your Writing During ➤ Editing

Proofread your writing for spelling errors as part of the editing stage in the writing process. Be sure to check each word carefully. Use a dictionary to check spelling if you are not sure.

59

Vocabulary

Strategy Words

Review Words: r-Controlled Vowels

Write a word from the box to match each definition.

birthmark	carpet	fortune	murmur	service

1. a mark on the body since birth
2. say something in a low voice
3. the act of helping others
4. the good or bad luck that comes to someone
5. a heavy covering for a floor

Preview Words: r-Controlled Vowels

Write words from the box that complete this letter to an editor.

awareness	affirm	endorse	furthermore	refer

Dear Editor:

    Regarding tomorrow's election, I would like to __6.__ Julio Flores for governor. For proof of his skill, you need only __7.__ to his excellent performance as attorney general. And __8.__, his __9.__ of the needs of the people of our state serves to __10.__ his ability to lead.

Mun Sook Kim
Middletown

Connections

Content Words

Fine Arts: Music

Write the word from the box that matches each clue.

castanets	percussion	chimes	timpani	marimba

1. instrument that makes bell-like sounds
2. a large xylophone
3. instruments that are struck to produce sounds
4. Spanish dancer's instrument
5. kettledrums

Science: Respiratory System

Write the word from the box that completes each sentence.

cartilage	respiratory	exhale	trachea	inhale

6. The _____ system controls breathing.
7. Your joints have _____ to protect the bones from wear and tear.
8. When you _____, your lungs expand.
9. The windpipe is another name for the _____.
10. When you breathe out, you _____ carbon dioxide.

Apply the Spelling Strategy

Not all vowels followed by **r** are **r**-controlled. The vowel must be in the same syllable as the **r** and affected by the **r** in pronunciation. Circle the letters that spell the **r**-controlled vowel sound in two of the content words you wrote.

Spelling and Thinking

READ THE SPELLING WORDS

1. unpleasant	*unpleasant*	Washing a pan is an **unpleasant** task.
2. absent	*absent*	She was **absent** from school today.
3. practical	*practical*	His **practical** answer surprised us.
4. neutral	*neutral*	You can take sides, but I am **neutral**.
5. turbulent	*turbulent*	The ocean was **turbulent** from a storm.
6. rival	*rival*	We will play our **rival** in today's game.
7. rational	*rational*	He gave us a **rational** explanation.
8. instant	*instant*	I saw the rainbow for only an **instant**.
9. talent	*talent*	She is known for her musical **talent**.
10. partial	*partial*	He gave only a **partial** answer.
11. label	*label*	The **label** says the tie is made of silk.
12. legal	*legal*	He asked a lawyer for **legal** advice.
13. cruel	*cruel*	It is **cruel** to leave the dog alone.
14. distant	*distant*	She seemed shy and **distant** at first.
15. tunnel	*tunnel*	The truck stalled in the **tunnel**.
16. typical	*typical*	Her **typical** day begins with a jog.
17. channel	*channel*	The boat sailed through the **channel**.
18. ignorant	*ignorant*	He was **ignorant** of the game rules.
19. central	*central*	I live in the **central** part of the state.
20. material	*material*	The new **material** was delivered today.

SORT THE SPELLING WORDS

1.–9. Write the words that have the /əl/ sound spelled **al**.

10.–13. Write the words that have the /əl/ sound spelled **el**.

14.–16. Write the words that have the /ənt/ sound spelled **ent**.

17.–20. Write the words that have the /ənt/ sound spelled **ant**.

REMEMBER THE SPELLING STRATEGY

Remember that the **schwa** sound (/ə/) often occurs in unstressed final syllables. Think about how /ə/ is spelled in the final syllable in **legal, label, talent,** and **distant**.

Spelling ^{and} Vocabulary

Synonyms

Write a spelling word that is a synonym for each word.

1. lawful
2. opponent
3. useful
4. normal
5. substance
6. middle
7. tag

Word Structure

8. Write the spelling word that has the /o͞o/ sound spelled **eu**.

9. Write the spelling word that has the /o͞o/ sound spelled **u**.

10. Write the spelling word that begins with the consonant digraph **ch**.

11.–12. Change the first letter in **national** and in **funnel**. Write the spelling words.

Antonyms

Write the spelling words that complete the meaning.

13. **Tie** is to **untie** as **pleasant** is to _____.

14. **Whole** is to **piece** as **complete** is to _____.

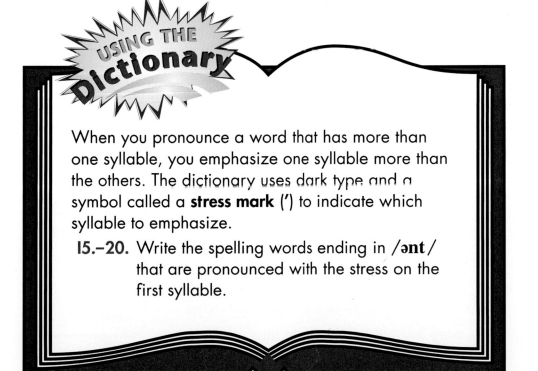

USING THE Dictionary

When you pronounce a word that has more than one syllable, you emphasize one syllable more than the others. The dictionary uses dark type and a symbol called a **stress mark** (') to indicate which syllable to emphasize.

15.–20. Write the spelling words ending in /ənt/ that are pronounced with the stress on the first syllable.

Spelling and Reading

unpleasant	absent	practical	neutral	turbulent
rival	rational	instant	talent	partial
label	legal	cruel	distant	tunnel
typical	channel	ignorant	central	material

Solve the Analogies Write a spelling word to complete each analogy.

1. **Angry** is to **pleased** as **present** is to _____.
2. **Famous** is to **unknown** as **educated** is to _____.
3. **Arrive** is to **depart** as **near** is to _____.
4. **Low** is to **high** as **slow** is to _____.
5. **Wind** is to **fierce** as **water** is to _____.
6. **Quiet** is to **calm** as **useful** is to _____.

Complete the Sentences Write a spelling word to complete each sentence.

7. This painting demonstrates his remarkable _____.
8. Switzerland remained _____ during two world wars.
9. The _____ joke hurt his feelings.
10. He was so angry that he was not behaving in a _____ way.
11. It is not _____ to park here so you will get a ticket.
12. Read the _____ before you buy the product.
13. I watch the morning news on another _____.

Complete the Paragraph Write spelling words from the box to complete the paragraph.

Building a __14.__ in the 1920s was a difficult and __15.__ task. Every day, __16.__ progress was made toward the goal. A __17.__ problem was preventing soft __18.__ from sliding into the hole as workers dug. Often two __19.__ digging crews worked from opposite sides. They met in the __20.__ area known as the "hole through."

typical
rival
unpleasant
tunnel
partial
material
central

64

Spelling and Writing

Proofread a Paragraph

Six words are not spelled correctly in this paragraph. Write the words correctly.

Levi Strauss had a special talent for business. During the gold rush of the 1850s, Strauss sold canvas for tents. Knowing that the tipical miner needed heavy-duty pants, Strauss had a practicle solution. He used some of his canvas to stitch overalls. Later, Strauss replaced the canvas with a new materiel called denim. He changed the nuetral color of the denim by dyeing it a dark blue. Customers were parcial to this softer, darker fabric. Strauss's pants, or Levi's, were an instent hit.

Proofreading Marks

≡ Make a capital.
/ Make a small letter.
∧ Add something.
℘ Take out something.
⊙ Add a period
New paragraph
(SP) Spelling error

Write a Paragraph

Descriptive Writing

Every paragraph has a main idea, which is stated in the topic sentence. The other sentences in the paragraph support or develop that central idea. Write a paragraph that describes something.

- Write about something that you have done or someone else has done.
- Follow the form used in the proofreading sample.

Use as many spelling words as you can.

Proofread Your Writing During

Writing Process

Prewriting
⇩
Drafting
⇩
Revising
⇩
Editing
⇩
Publishing

Proofread your writing for spelling errors as part of the editing stage in the writing process. Be sure to check each word carefully. Use a dictionary to check spelling if you are not sure.

Unit 10 enrichment

Vocabulary

Strategy Words

Review Words: /ə/ in Final Syllables

Write words from the box to complete this thank-you note.

angel	final	incident	loyal	pleasant

Dear Lucy,

   You were an __1.__ to come to my rescue last night when I had a flat tire. You even helped me through the __2.__ of the empty gas tank. You are a __3.__ friend indeed. I promise you that that was the __4.__ episode in my adventures. Our next occasion together will be more __5.__.

                              Your grateful friend,
                              Dave

Preview Words: /ə/ in Final Syllables

Write the word from the box that completes each sentence.

apparent	diesel	equidistant	confidential	ordinal

6. Most trucks have a _____ engine.
7. Something that is private is _____.
8. Something that is easily understood is _____.
9. If the store is a mile from each of our homes, it is _____ from our homes.
10. **First, second,** and **third** are examples of _____ numbers.

66

Connections

Content Words

Math: Proportions

Write the word from the box that completes each sentence.

| equivalent | ratio | invert | reciprocal | proportion |

1. Twelve inches are _eq_ to one foot.
2. The _rat_ of ⁴/₃ is ³/₄.
3. If you _inv_ ¹/₄, the result is ⁴/₁.
4. The size of things in comparison to each other refers to _pro_.
5. The _rec_ of 2 to 3 is ²/₃.

Social Studies: Debate

Write the words from the box that complete the paragraph.

| debate | opinion | disagreement | panelist | logical |

Jurors __6.__ the issues that have been discussed during a trial. A jury __7.__ must form his or her own __8.__ and make __9.__ decisions based on what the jury learned during the trial. Any major __10.__ must be solved among the jurors before their verdict is delivered.

Apply the Spelling Strategy

Circle the letters that spell the /əl/ or the /ənt/ sound in the final syllable of four of the content words you wrote.

67

Spelling and Thinking

READ THE SPELLING WORDS

1. completely	*completely*	The food is **completely** gone.
2. additionally	*additionally*	He is, **additionally,** a skilled artist.
3. downward	*downward*	This **downward** path leads to a pond.
4. homeward	*homeward*	Seeing the storm, we headed **homeward**.
5. especially	*especially*	He is **especially** fond of spaghetti.
6. certainly	*certainly*	I am **certainly** happy that you are home.
7. eastward	*eastward*	The storm is moving **eastward**.
8. carefully	*carefully*	Please open the package **carefully**.
9. skyward	*skyward*	We looked **skyward** to see the plane.
10. outward	*outward*	Fire laws say doors must open **outward**.
11. scarcely	*scarcely*	I have **scarcely** finished my breakfast.
12. inward	*inward*	These windows open **inward**.
13. ideally	*ideally*	This is **ideally** the best place to meet.
14. upward	*upward*	The wind carried the balloons **upward**.
15. possibly	*possibly*	She is **possibly** the best soccer player.
16. finally	*finally*	They **finally** arrived at midnight.
17. barely	*barely*	I have **barely** started my homework.
18. loosely	*loosely*	Place the flowers **loosely** in the vase.
19. afterward	*afterward*	I will answer your question **afterward**.
20. directly	*directly*	You should go **directly** to the bus.

SORT THE SPELLING WORDS

1.–8. Write the spelling words that end in **-ward**.

9. Write the spelling word in which the spelling of the base word changed when the suffix **-ly** was added.

10.–20. Write the spelling words that end in **-ly** with no changes to the spelling of the base word.

REMEMBER THE SPELLING STRATEGY

Remember that the suffix **-ward** means "direction" or "tendency." The suffix **-ly** means "in a specific manner." These suffixes are added to base words to form adverbs.

Spelling ᴬⁿᵈ Vocabulary

Word Replacement

Write the spelling word that could replace the underlined word or words in each sentence.

1. I <u>in particular</u> enjoyed the ice skating.
2. We promised that we would come home <u>immediately</u> after school.
3. You, <u>moreover</u>, have earned a second award.
4. She <u>cautiously</u> drove down the narrow street.
5. And, <u>lastly</u>, I would like to thank my good friends.
6. We thought that you could <u>perhaps</u> help us.
7. The car at the top of the hill rolled <u>toward a lower place</u>.
8. The stock market is headed <u>toward a higher position</u>.

Antonyms

Write a spelling word that is an antonym for each word.

9. westward
10. tightly
11. doubtfully
12. partially
13. beforehand

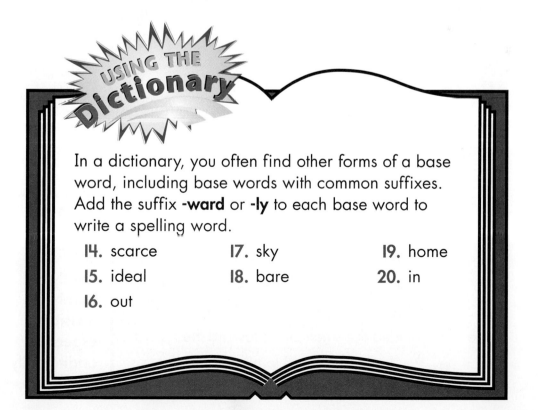

USING THE Dictionary

In a dictionary, you often find other forms of a base word, including base words with common suffixes. Add the suffix **-ward** or **-ly** to each base word to write a spelling word.

14. scarce
15. ideal
16. out
17. sky
18. bare
19. home
20. in

Spelling and Reading

completely	additionally	downward	homeward
especially	certainly	eastward	carefully
skyward	outward	scarcely	inward
ideally	upward	possibly	finally
barely	loosely	afterward	directly

Solve the Analogies   Write a spelling word to complete each analogy.

1. **Frantically** is to **fearfully** as **honestly** is to _____.
2. **Past** is to **future** as **beforehand** is to _____.
3. **Quietly** is to **softly** as **freely** is to _____.
4. **Back** is to **backward** as **sky** is to _____.
5. **Capable** is to **capably** as **certain** is to _____.
6. **Easily** is to **smoothly** as **entirely** is to _____.
7. **Silent** is to **silently** as **scarce** is to _____.

Complete the Sentences   Write a spelling word to complete each sentence.

8. We looked _____ toward the decorated ceiling.
9. After a long time away from his family, he headed _____.
10. The boat sprung a leak, and water rushed _____.
11. From _____ appearances, she seems confident and capable.
12. The store is _____ located near several apartments.

Complete the Paragraph   Write spelling words from the box to complete the paragraph.

The pilot looked __13.__ toward the field below. This was going to be an __14.__ difficult landing because of the fog. He could just __15.__ make out the field. There was, __16.__, a strong wind from the west and heading __17.__. The people in the control tower helped the pilot as he __18.__ guided the small plane toward the runway. When he __19.__ landed, he said to his co-pilot that this was __20.__ his toughest landing yet.

> carefully
> downward
> eastward
> finally
> barely
> possibly
> especially
> additionally

Spelling and Writing

Proofread a Paragraph

Six words are not spelled correctly in this paragraph that gives directions. Write the words correctly.

Follow Route 94 eastward for two miles. When the road slopes upword, look for a post office on the left. Turn left at the next intersection Proceed carefuly because the street is a dirt road. After bearly a mile, you will come to the lake. Follow the road compleetly around the lake. When you finaly reach the campsite, our blue tent will be dirrectly to your left.

Proofreading Marks

≡ Make a capital.

/ Make a small letter.

∧ Add something.

ℒ Take out something.

⊙ Add a period.

⌗ New paragraph

ⓈⓅ Spelling error

Write a Paragraph

Expository Writing

When you give directions, it is important to give them in sequence. Write the directions from your home or school to another location.

- Refer to familiar sights, such as landmarks and street names, signs, stoplights, and names of stores. This will help make your directions clear.
- Follow the form used in the proofreading sample.

Use as many spelling words as you can.

Proofread Your Writing During

Proofread your writing for spelling errors as part of the editing stage in the writing process. Be sure to check each word carefully. Use a dictionary to check spelling if you are not sure.

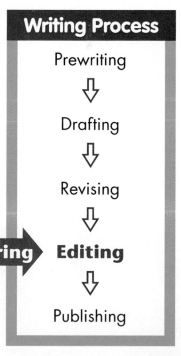

Writing Process

Prewriting

⇩

Drafting

⇩

Revising

⇩

Editing

⇩

Publishing

Vocabulary

Strategy Words

Review Words: Suffixes -ward, -ly

Write words from the box to complete this announcement.

backward	biweekly	proudly	westward	forward

We at *On the Road* __1.__ announce our latest travel magazine. We are moving __2.__ toward our goal of being the leader in the latest travel information. This time we are moving __3.__ from the Midwest to Utah and beyond. We do this without a __4.__ glance. Order your __5.__ subscription today.

Preview Words: Suffixes -ward, -ly

Write a word from the box to complete each sentence.

accurately	economically	historically
initially		usually

6. He was ____ reluctant to speak before such a large group, but later he did it easily.

7. The country has increased its exports; it is striving to be ____ independent.

8. He is late today, but he ____ arrives at work by seven o'clock.

9. The 1700s was ____ a period of great change in our country.

10. She described the accident ____ in every detail.

Connections

Math: Geometry

Write a word from the box to complete each sentence.

congruent	perpendicular	linear
transversal		parallel

1. When two lines meet to form right angles, they are ____.
2. Two triangles that have the same size and shape are ____.
3. Lines that never meet are called ____ lines.
4. The base word of ____ is **line**.
5. A line that intersects two or more other lines is a ____.

Social Studies: International Relations

Write the words from the box that complete the news item.

accord	regional	ally	blockade	sanction

The nation joined with its __6.__ to establish a __7.__ against the country that had broken the peace __8.__. The __9.__ of the harbor will remain in place until all __10.__ neighbors are satisfied that the demands are being met.

Apply the Spelling Strategy

Circle the five content words you wrote that could have an **-ly** ending added to them.

Assessment and Review

Assessment Units 7–11

Each Assessment Word in the box fits one of the spelling strategies you have studied over the past five weeks. Read the spelling strategies. Then write each Assessment Word under the unit number it fits.

Unit 7 _____

I.–4. The /o͞o/ sound is spelled **oo** in **proof**, **ou** in **routine**, **u** in **fluid**, and **vowel-consonant-e** in **assume**. The /o͝o/ sound is spelled **oo** in **goodness**, **ou** in **could've**, and **u** in **bulletin**.

Unit 8 _____

5.–8. This rhyme can often help you decide when to use **ie** and when to use **ei**: Use **i** before **e**, except after **c**, or when sounded as **a**, as in **neighbor** and **weigh**.

Unit 9 _____

9.–I4. The **r**-controlled vowel sounds can be spelled in different ways, including /**ûr**/ spelled **er, ir,** and **ur**; /**är**/ spelled **ar**; /**âr**/ spelled **er;** and /**ôr**/ spelled **or** and **ore**.

Unit 10 _____

I5.–I7. The **schwa** sound (/ə/) often occurs in unstressed final syllables. Think about how /ə/ is spelled in the final syllable in **legal, label, talent,** and **distant**.

Unit 11 _____

I8.–20. The suffix **-ward** means "direction" or "tendency." The suffix **-ly** means "in a specific manner." These suffixes are added to base words to form adverbs.

crooked
mantelpiece
sworn
torrent
windward
simply
pennant
swirl
outfield
gloomy
rooster
infield
original
yearly
hardly
gravel
archery
fiend
prune
mercury

| through | bulletin | introduce | neighborhood | proof |
| routine | assume | understood | goodness | cushion |

Write the spelling words that complete the paragraph.

This week our local __1.__ association sent out a __2.__ about a
picnic. The new mayor wanted to __3.__ himself in person, so he
took the notices to every house. He was __4.__ with the job by noon.
We can __5.__ he got to every house, but there is no __6.__ of that.
Deliveries are not part of his usual __7.__, but we have __8.__ that this
is a new kind of mayor. We hope it's a sign of his generosity and
__9.__ and that he has a good __10.__ for each of his shoes!

| niece | receive | mischief | leisure | thief |
| shriek | relief | fierce | ceiling | seize |

Write the spelling words by adding the missing letters.

11. n __ __ ce
12. misch __ __ f
13. th __ __ f
14. shr __ __ k
15. rel __ __ f

16. f __ __ rce
17. rec __ __ ve
18. c __ __ ling
19. s __ __ ze
20. l __ __ sure

Unit 9: r-Controlled Vowels

carton	circular	purchase	therefore	carpenter
partner	concern	dirty	ignore	curtain

Write a spelling word that completes each group.

1. buy, acquire, _____
2. builder, roofer, _____
3. helper, co-worker, _____
4. box, package, _____
5. drape, shutter, _____
6. neglect, overlook, _____
7. so, then, _____
8. soiled, dusty, _____
9. care, interest, _____
10. round, ring-shaped, _____

Review Unit 10: /ə/ in Final Syllables

ignorant	typical	material	practical	central
label	instant	tunnel	talent	distant

Replace the underlined letters with one or more letters to write a spelling word.

11. cent<u>er</u>
12. practi<u>ce</u>
13. ignor<u>e</u>
14. lab<u>or</u>
15. distan<u>ce</u>
16. inst<u>ea</u>d
17. <u>f</u>unnel
18. <u>s</u>erial
19. typ<u>ist</u>
20. <u>de</u>scent

76

finally	certainly	especially	afterward	carefully
upward	completely	downward	loosely	barely

Form spelling words by adding **-ward** or **-ly** to the underlined word in each sentence.

1. <u>After</u> we went to the movies.
2. She moved <u>down</u> to the bottom of the slide.
3. Joe climbed <u>up</u> to the top of the stairs.
4. You are <u>certain</u> welcome to come with us.
5. He was <u>especial</u> happy to see his grandfather.
6. We <u>final</u> finished the examination!
7. We <u>careful</u> dusted around the glass figurines.
8. We <u>bare</u> had time to catch the bus.
9. They tied the ribbon <u>loose</u> around the kitten's neck.
10. He is <u>complete</u> finished with his homework.

WORD SORT — Spelling Study Strategy

Sorting by Parts of Speech

Sorting words is a good way to help you practice your spelling words. Here is a way to sort the spelling words with a partner.

1. Make four columns on a piece of paper and write **noun, verb, adjective, adverb** at the top of the columns. Write a sample word in each column. For example, you could write **proof** under **noun, adore** under **verb, distant** under **adjective,** and **completely** under **adverb.**

2. Have a partner write a spelling word on the list. Help your partner decide whether the word is in the right list.

3. Take turns filling in the columns.

77

Grammar, Usage, and Mechanics

Prepositions and Prepositional Phrases

A preposition relates a word in a sentence to a noun or pronoun
that follows it. This noun or pronoun is the object of the preposition.
The preposition, its object, and the words in between make a
prepositional phrase.

The cat sleeps <u>under</u> the <u>bed</u>.

preposition   object of the preposition

Practice Activity

A. Write the preposition in each sentence below.

　　1. Birds flew around the trees.

　　2. The package on the table is yours.

　　3. The rocket blasted into space.

　　4. The puppies in the window look so cute!

　　5. Under the branches I found a tunnel.

　　6. Dancers wandered through the building.

　　7. Clouds gathered above our heads.

B. Complete the sentences by adding an object
of the preposition. Try to use spelling words
you reviewed.

　　8. Several families moved into our _____.

　　9. I found a quarter under the middle _____!

　　10. Hang that lamp from the _____.

　　11. Return the hammer to the _____.

　　12. I am standing with my nephew and _____.

　　13. We placed the blankets inside a big _____.

　　14. Is there a window behind that thick _____?

78

WORKSHOP

Circle and Check

Good writers always proofread their writing for spelling errors. Here's a strategy you can use to proofread your papers.

Instead of reading your paper the regular way, look at just the first three or four words. Are they spelled correctly? If you are sure that they are correct, go on and check the next three or four words. If you are not sure of the spelling of a word, circle it and keep going. Look at your whole paper this way—one small group of words at a time.

When you finish, get a dictionary and check the spelling of all the circled words. Looking up several words at once is faster than looking them up one by one. It's also easier. Try it!

Electronic Spelling

Internet Addresses and Terms

You have to tell computers what you want. You do this by typing and clicking. However, you must spell your requests correctly or a computer cannot find what you are looking for.

Some terms are made up from the initial letters of words. For example, the **www** in many Internet addresses stands for **world wide web**. Study these terms:

BBS	**B**ulletin **B**oard **S**ervice
FAQ	**F**requently **A**sked **Q**uestions
HTTP	**H**yper**t**ext **T**ransfer **P**rotocol
URL	**U**niform **R**esource **L**ocator
WAIS	**W**ide **A**rea **I**nformation **S**erver

Which of the following are misspelled? Write them correctly. Write **OK** if a term is correct.

1. FQA   2. BBS   3. WIAS   4. URL   5. HTPT   6. WAIS

Spelling and Thinking

READ THE SPELLING WORDS

1.	fashion	*fashion*	Long skirts are in **fashion** today.
2.	difficult	*difficult*	Cleaning up after a storm is **difficult**.
3.	physician	*physician*	She plans to see a **physician** today.
4.	former	*former*	The mayor is a **former** basketball star.
5.	sophomore	*sophomore*	Max is a **sophomore** in high school.
6.	triumph	*triumph*	The win was a **triumph** for our team.
7.	orphan	*orphan*	The **orphan** was taken in by a family.
8.	effort	*effort*	Running several miles requires **effort**.
9.	phrase	*phrase*	I am fond of the **phrase** "Less is more."
10.	faint	*faint*	He was feeling **faint** after the race.
11.	traffic	*traffic*	She listened to the **traffic** report.
12.	photo	*photo*	He asked me if I had a current **photo**.
13.	golf	*golf*	They played on a public **golf** course.
14.	fulfill	*fulfill*	You can **fulfill** all of your dreams.
15.	phone	*phone*	He kept me on the **phone** for an hour.
16.	officer	*officer*	The **officer** on duty inquired about us.
17.	baffle	*baffle*	The story seems to **baffle** everyone.
18.	suffix	*suffix*	A **suffix** is added to the end of a word.
19.	shelf	*shelf*	We keep the blender on the top **shelf**.
20.	offer	*offer*	I had to turn down her generous **offer**.

SORT THE SPELLING WORDS

1.–6. Write the words that have the /**f**/ sound spelled **f**.

7.–13. Write the words that have the /**f**/ sound spelled **ff**.

14.–20. Write the words that have the /**f**/ sound spelled **ph**.

REMEMBER THE SPELLING STRATEGY

Remember that the **f** sound (/**f**/) can be spelled in different ways:
f in **faint**, **ff** in **baffle**, and **ph** in **phone**.

Spelling ᴬⁿᵈ Vocabulary

Word Groups

Write a spelling word to complete each group of words.

1. hard, laborious, _____
2. victory, success, _____
3. attempt, struggle, _____
4. weak, dim, _____
5. cars, highways, _____
6. clubs, green, _____
7. platform, storage, _____
8. senior, junior, _____
9. affix, prefix, _____
10. nurse, dentist, _____

Word Meanings

Write the spelling word that could replace the underlined word in each sentence.

11. This picture would look nice in an oval frame.
12. The computer problem might puzzle him at first.
13. The chairperson has another plan to suggest.
14. The inventor was able to express his ideas clearly.
15. You can form a lovely wreath out of dried flowers.
16. The previous owner of the house built the addition.

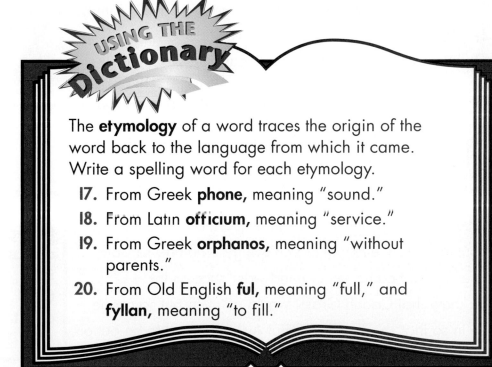

USING THE Dictionary

The **etymology** of a word traces the origin of the word back to the language from which it came. Write a spelling word for each etymology.

17. From Greek **phone,** meaning "sound."
18. From Latin **officium,** meaning "service."
19. From Greek **orphanos,** meaning "without parents."
20. From Old English **ful,** meaning "full," and **fyllan,** meaning "to fill."

Spelling *and* Reading

fashion	difficult	physician	former	sophomore
triumph	orphan	effort	phrase	faint
traffic	photo	golf	fulfill	phone
officer	baffle	suffix	shelf	offer

Solve the Analogies Write a spelling word to complete each analogy.

1. **School** is to **teacher** as **hospital** is to ____.
2. **Write** is to **pencil** as **speak** is to ____.
3. **Painter** is to **painting** as **photographer** is to ____.
4. **Fourth** is to **senior** as **second** is to ____.
5. **Before** is to **after** as **prefix** is to ____.
6. **Boxer** is to **boxing** as **golfer** is to ____.
7. **Conceal** is to **hide** as **bewilder** is to ____.

Complete the Sentences Write a spelling word to complete each sentence.

8. We will need an extra ____ for all of these books.
9. The police ____ asked us if we needed help.
10. As an ____, the young man longed to have a family.
11. Because of the ____ jam, he was late to work.
12. We have vacationed in the mountains and near the ocean, but we prefer the ____.
13. You make quite a ____ statement with those shoes.

Complete the Paragraph Write spelling words from the box to complete the paragraph.

Aisha was exhausted and felt __14.__ as she came off the basketball court after a __15.__ third quarter. Her team was about to __16.__ their goal of achieving a winning season. The __17.__ that came to her mind was "success takes __18.__." She knew that Coach Grassi would __19.__ to put someone else in so that she could rest. But Aisha wanted to be out on the court to see her team eventually __20.__.

phrase
triumph
difficult
faint
fulfill
effort
offer

Spelling and Writing

Proofread a Dialogue

Six words are not spelled correctly in this dialogue. Write the words correctly.

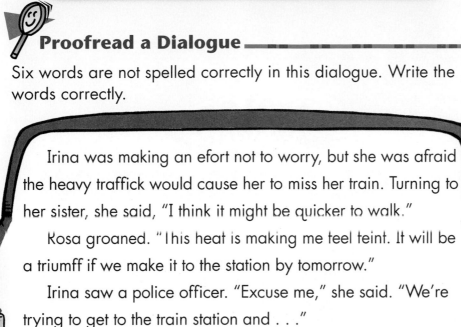

Irina was making an efort not to worry, but she was afraid the heavy traffick would cause her to miss her train. Turning to her sister, she said, "I think it might be quicker to walk."

Rosa groaned. "This heat is making me feel feint. It will be a triumff if we make it to the station by tomorrow."

Irina saw a police officer. "Excuse me," she said. "We're trying to get to the train station and . . ."

"That will be dificult," he interrupted. "You're headed in the direction of its formor location."

BR801

Proofreading Marks

≡ Make a capital.

/ Make a small letter.

∧ Add something.

ℓ Take out something.

⊙ Add a period.

⌗ New paragraph

SP Spelling error

Write a Dialogue

Narrative Writing

A dialogue is a conversation between two or more people. It contains direct quotations that give the speakers' exact words. Write a dialogue between two or more people.

- Remember to indent every time the speaker changes. To make your dialogue believable, use words that your character might actually say.
- Follow the form used in the proofreading sample.

Use as many spelling words as you can.

Writing Process

Prewriting
⬇
Drafting
⬇
Revising
⬇
Editing
⬇
Publishing

Proofread Your Writing During ➤ Editing

Proofread your writing for spelling errors as part of the editing stage in the writing process. Be sure to check each word carefully. Use a dictionary to check spelling if you are not sure.

83

Vocabulary

Strategy Words

Review Words: /f/ Spelled f, ff, ph

Write a word from the box to match each clue.

| beliefs | buffalo | coffee | famous | phosphorus |

1. the bison of North America
2. used in fertilizers and detergents
3. a synonym for **prominent**
4. a drink that comes from the beanlike seeds of a tropical tree
5. strong opinions about something

Preview Words: /f/ Spelled f, ff, ph

Write a word from the box to complete each of these sentences.

| affinity | enforce | folio | manifest | phonics |

6. Our golden retriever has an ____ for people, especially children.
7. It was the officer's job to ____ the speed limits in the county.
8. The study of sounds and letters is called ____.
9. A ____ consists of four pages.
10. The jury took note of the clear and ____ error emphasized by the attorney.

Connections

Content Words

Fine Arts: Photography

Write the words from the box that complete the paragraph.

film	shutterbug	lens	tripod	photograph

Eurie is a ___1.___ who never misses an opportunity to take a ___2.___. She usually uses high-speed ___3.___ to capture action shots. To steady her camera, she attaches it to a ___4.___. When everything is set, she adjusts the camera ___5.___ and shoots.

Social Studies: Government

Write the words from the box that complete the paragraph.

amendment	patriot	candidate
suffrage	nominate	

Women in the early 1900s had to overcome great opposition to gain ___6.___, or the right to vote. In 1920, the nineteenth ___7.___ to the Constitution was passed. This provided women with the right to ___8.___ and vote for the ___9.___ of their choice. Every woman ___10.___ had worked hard toward this goal.

Apply the Spelling Strategy

Circle the letters that spell the /f/ sound in three of the content words you wrote.

Spelling and Thinking

READ THE SPELLING WORDS

1.	magazine	*magazine*	She subscribes to a sports **magazine**.
2.	pessimism	*pessimism*	He is known for his gloomy **pessimism**.
3.	conclusion	*conclusion*	I read the **conclusion** to the story.
4.	optimism	*optimism*	Her cheerful **optimism** sees her through.
5.	television	*television*	I watched a nature special on **television**.
6.	amaze	*amaze*	The gymnast's ability will **amaze** you.
7.	cruise	*cruise*	Ships slowly **cruise** into the harbor.
8.	casual	*casual*	We wore **casual** clothes to the picnic.
9.	husband	*husband*	Her **husband** works for a bus company.
10.	phase	*phase*	He is going through a difficult **phase**.
11.	vision	*vision*	The reading glasses improved his **vision**.
12.	browse	*browse*	I will quickly **browse** through the books.
13.	usual	*usual*	My **usual** lunch is yogurt and fruit.
14.	freeze	*freeze*	The tender plants might **freeze**.
15.	visual	*visual*	Fireworks are a bright **visual** display.
16.	scissors	*scissors*	These **scissors** are not very sharp.
17.	arise	*arise*	Call me if any problems **arise**.
18.	pause	*pause*	There is a dramatic **pause** in the music.
19.	visitor	*visitor*	He invited the **visitor** to stay for lunch.
20.	tease	*tease*	Friends **tease** me about being late.

SORT THE SPELLING WORDS

1.–14. Write the words that have the /**z**/ sound spelled **z, s,** or **ss**. Circle the letters that spell this sound.

15.–20. Write the words that have the /**zh**/ sound spelled **s**. Circle the letters that spell this sound.

REMEMBER THE SPELLING STRATEGY

Remember that the /**z**/ sound can be spelled **z** as in **freeze, s** as in **phase,** and **ss** as in **scissors**. The /**zh**/ sound can be spelled **s** and is often followed by **ual** (**usual**) or **ion** (**vision**).

Spelling and Vocabulary

Word Groups

Write a spelling word to complete each group.

1. bother, taunt, pester, _____
2. guest, caller, company, _____
3. surprise, astonish, flabbergast, _____
4. eraser, tape, stapler, _____
5. periodical, journal, publication, _____
6. oral, auditory, tactile, _____
7. delay, break, rest, _____
8. customary, expected, normal, _____
9. hopelessness, gloom, doubt, _____

Word Analysis

Change the underlined part of each of the following words to write a spelling word.

10. sunrise
11. telephone
12. conference
13. hustle
14. optical
15. freedom
16. castle
17. erase

USING THE Dictionary

When a word has more than one meaning, the dictionary definitions are numbered. Generally, the most common definition is presented first. Write a spelling word to match each less-common definition below.

18. to travel at a constant, efficient speed
19. the sense of sight
20. to feed on leaves

Spelling and Reading

magazine	pessimism	conclusion	optimism	television
amaze	cruise	casual	husband	phase
vision	browse	usual	freeze	visual
scissors	arise	pause	visitor	tease

Solve the Analogies Write a spelling word to complete each analogy.

1. **Scare** is to **shock** as **surprise** is to _____.
2. **Chose** is to **choose** as **froze** is to _____.
3. **Won** is to **win** as **arose** is to _____.
4. **Budge** is to **move** as **pester** is to _____.
5. **Ear** is to **hearing** as **eye** is to _____.
6. **Airplane** is to **fly** as **boat** is to _____.

Complete the Sentences Write a spelling word to complete each sentence.

7. We invited our _____ to have dinner with us.
8. We will _____ for a moment before we continue the tour.
9. His _____ made everyone else gloomy too.
10. We are beginning the next _____ of the space program.
11. She made a _____ remark about meeting for lunch.
12. I like to _____ before I make a decision to buy new jeans.
13. They do not watch _____ during the week.
14. Jane's _____ gave her a ring for their anniversary.

Complete the Paragraph Write spelling words from the box to complete the paragraph.

Yesterday Julio came over to work on our report on world peace. As __15.__, it took us a while to get to work. Mr. Rahad said that we should have a __16.__ presentation with our oral report, so we prepared a poster. Julio borrowed my __17.__ to cut pictures from a __18.__. At the __19.__ of the report, we will give reasons for our __20.__ about world peace.

scissors
optimism
visual
magazine
usual
conclusion

88

Spelling and Writing

Proofread a Paragraph

Six words are not spelled correctly in this persuasive paragraph. Write the words correctly.

> Of all the trips you could take, a cruize on a paddle-wheel boat might be the most memorable. As you floated down the river at a cashual pace, the sights would amaze you. One of the most impressive is the vishion of the enormous wheel as it churns the water. Aside from the ussual relaxing activities of a pleasure trip, you could listen to a lecture on river lore or brouse through shops at the various stops. So step back into the past to an era powered by steam, and you too will come to the conclusun that this is the best way to spend a vacation.

Proofreading Marks

≡	Make a capital.
/	Make a small letter.
∧	Add something.
ℓ	Take out something.
⊙	Add a period.
#	New paragraph
SP	Spelling error

Write a Paragraph

Persuasive Writing

A persuasive paragraph expresses an opinion and tries to convince the reader that the opinion is correct. Write a persuasive paragraph.

- Write about something that you feel strongly about. State your opinion in the topic sentence. Then write detail sentences that support your opinion.
- Follow the form used in the proofreading sample.

Use as many spelling words as you can.

Proofread Your Writing During

Writing Process

Prewriting
⇩
Drafting
⇩
Revising
⇩
Editing
⇩
Publishing

Proofread your writing for spelling errors as part of the editing stage in the writing process. Be sure to check each word carefully. Use a dictionary to check spelling if you are not sure.

Spelling ᴬⁿᵈ Thinking

READ THE SPELLING WORDS

1.	complained	*complained*	He **complained** that his leg hurt.
2.	permitting	*permitting*	Are you **permitting** us to go now?
3.	remained	*remained*	The store **remained** open until six.
4.	profiting	*profiting*	She is **profiting** from the book sale.
5.	excelling	*excelling*	The team is **excelling** this season.
6.	obtaining	*obtaining*	He is **obtaining** his fishing license.
7.	remaining	*remaining*	Food is **remaining** from the picnic.
8.	permitted	*permitted*	Swimming is **permitted** in the lake.
9.	complaining	*complaining*	He is **complaining** about the heat.
10.	directed	*directed*	A police officer **directed** traffic.
11.	resulted	*resulted*	His fall **resulted** in a broken arm.
12.	admitted	*admitted*	I **admitted** to having lost the book.
13.	excelled	*excelled*	Lin **excelled** in foreign languages.
14.	obtained	*obtained*	He **obtained** two tickets to the play.
15.	differing	*differing*	We are **differing** over where to eat.
16.	profited	*profited*	The client **profited** from our advice.
17.	admitting	*admitting*	He is finally **admitting** his mistake.
18.	differed	*differed*	Our taste in music **differed** greatly.
19.	directing	*directing*	He will be **directing** the school play.
20.	resulting	*resulting*	Heavy rains are **resulting** in floods.

SORT THE SPELLING WORDS

1.–6. Write the spelling words in which the final consonant in the base word is doubled when **-ed** or **-ing** is added. Circle the base words.

7.–20. Write the spelling words in which the base word does not change when **-ed** or **-ing** is added. Circle the base words.

REMEMBER THE SPELLING STRATEGY

Remember that the suffixes **-ed** and **-ing** can be added to some base words to form new words. In other words, the final consonant is doubled when **-ed** or **-ing** is added.

Word Groups

Write a spelling word to complete each sequence.

I. getting, gaining, securing, _____

2. accused, grumbled, railed, _____

3. acknowledged, conceded, revealed, _____

4. gaining, reaping, earning, _____

5. enduring, lasting, residing, _____

6. allowing, authorizing, tolerating,

Word Replacement

Write spelling words that could replace the underlined words.

7. The worker was <u>protesting</u> about the long hours.

8. Only a few people <u>stayed</u> in the theater after the play.

9. The campers <u>got</u> a permit to pitch their tent.

10. The witness was finally <u>confessing</u> what he saw.

II. Swimming is not <u>allowed</u> in the pond.

12. I <u>benefited</u> from having an excellent swim coach.

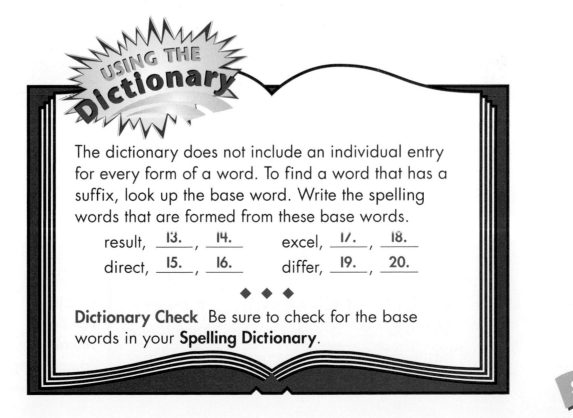

USING THE Dictionary

The dictionary does not include an individual entry for every form of a word. To find a word that has a suffix, look up the base word. Write the spelling words that are formed from these base words.

result, 13. , 14.   excel, 17. , 18.

direct, 15. , 16.   differ, 19. , 20.

◆ ◆ ◆

Dictionary Check Be sure to check for the base words in your **Spelling Dictionary**.

Spelling and Reading

complained	remaining	excelled	directing
obtaining	admitted	differed	excelling
profited	admitting	profiting	directed
resulted	remained	complaining	differing
permitting	permitted	obtained	resulting

Solve the Analogies Write a spelling word to complete each analogy.

1. **Player** is to **coached** as **actor** is to _____.
2. **Inquired** is to **replied** as **praised** is to _____.
3. **Agreeing** is to **contradicting** as **denying** is to _____.
4. **Omitting** is to **including** as **failing** is to _____.
5. **Questioning** is to **replying** as **agreeing** is to _____.
6. **Bothered** is to **pestered** as **benefited** is to _____.

Complete the Sentences Write a spelling word to complete each sentence.

7. There was not one piece of birthday cake _____.
8. Robert Frost _____ in writing poems about nature.
9. Our opinion _____ on what time the party should end.
10. Job seekers are _____ from the strong economy.
11. They are _____ a permit for their home addition.
12. His constant watering is _____ in a green lawn.
13. The principal is not _____ us to use the gym after school.

Complete the Paragraph Write spelling words from the box to complete the paragraph.

As a result of road reconstruction, only one lane __14.__ open, and trucks were not __15.__ to get on the highway. These restrictions __16.__ in a traffic jam during rush hour. Motorists were __17.__ to a police officer who was __18.__ traffic. He __19.__ that this was not the best time of day for the construction, but the company had not __20.__ permission to work at night.

admitted
directing
permitted
obtained
resulted
remained
complaining

Spelling and Writing

Proofread a Paragraph

Six words are not spelled correctly in this paragraph. Write the words correctly.

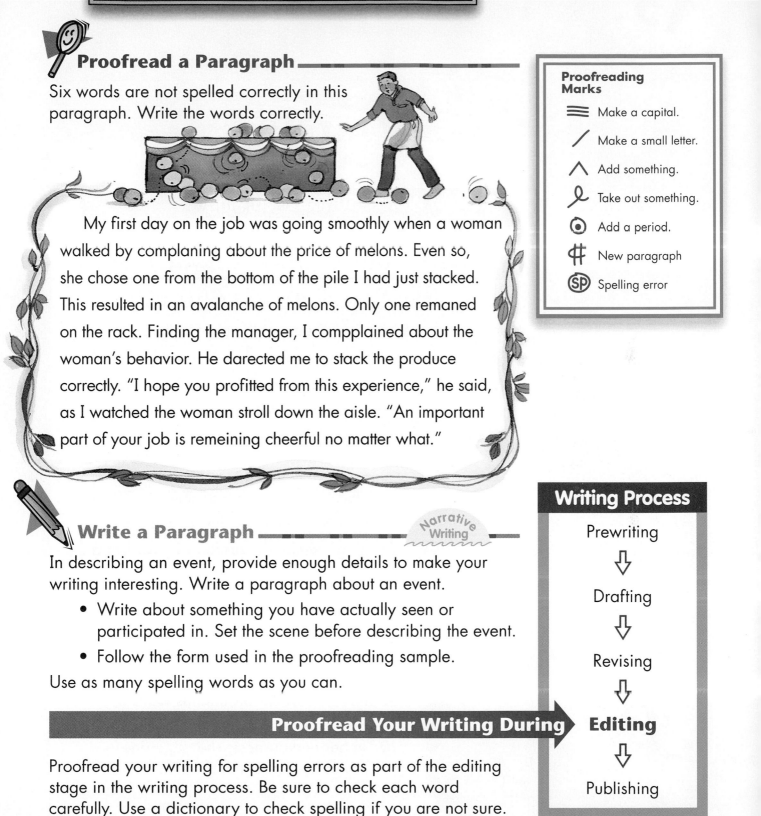

My first day on the job was going smoothly when a woman walked by complaning about the price of melons. Even so, she chose one from the bottom of the pile I had just stacked. This resulted in an avalanche of melons. Only one remaned on the rack. Finding the manager, I compplained about the woman's behavior. He darected me to stack the produce correctly. "I hope you profitted from this experience," he said, as I watched the woman stroll down the aisle. "An important part of your job is remeining cheerful no matter what."

Proofreading Marks

≡	Make a capital.
/	Make a small letter.
∧	Add something.
℮	Take out something.
⊙	Add a period.
#	New paragraph
SP	Spelling error

Write a Paragraph

Narrative Writing

In describing an event, provide enough details to make your writing interesting. Write a paragraph about an event.

- Write about something you have actually seen or participated in. Set the scene before describing the event.
- Follow the form used in the proofreading sample.

Use as many spelling words as you can.

Proofread Your Writing During

Writing Process

Prewriting
⇩
Drafting
⇩
Revising
⇩
Editing
⇩
Publishing

Proofread your writing for spelling errors as part of the editing stage in the writing process. Be sure to check each word carefully. Use a dictionary to check spelling if you are not sure.

95

Vocabulary

Review Words: Suffixes -ed, -ing

Write words from the box to complete the paragraph.

| gleaming | interesting | removed | supplying | trimmed |

Mario had created an ___1.___ menu for his new restaurant. He had ___2.___ some of the old furniture and waxed the floors until they were ___3.___ . The company ___4.___ Mario with equipment had already delivered the table linens. Mario ___5.___ the bushes outside the restaurant and hung the sign. He was ready for business.

Preview Words: Suffixes -ed, -ing

Write words from the box to complete the sentences.

| compelling | obliging | omitted | preferred | recurring |

6. Al liked baseball but _____ soccer.

7. The speaker's first point kept _____ throughout his speech.

8. The lawyer presented a very _____ argument.

9. The _____ waiter brought us water three times.

10. In her nervousness, she _____ one whole section of her speech.

Connections

Science: Computers

Write the words from the box that complete the paragraph.

| debugging   output   flow chart   programming   input |

One of the jobs of a programmer is to provide the computer with a set of instructions for problem solving. This is called __1.__. The information that programmers put into a system is __2.__. The information that a computer sends out is called __3.__. Sometimes this is in the form of a __4.__, or a diagram showing the sequence of operations. Another important job for a programmer is removing errors from, or __5.__, a program.

Language Arts: Linguistics

Write the words from the box that complete the paragraph.

| consonant   vibrate   linguistics   voiced   unvoiced |

The study of __6.__ includes understanding how the vocal system works. Saying the __7.__ letter **v** causes the vocal cords to __8.__, which in turn produces a __9.__ sound. The letter **f,** however, produces an __10.__ sound.

Apply the Spelling Strategy

Circle the suffix **-ed** or **-ing** in four of the content words you wrote.

Spelling AND Thinking

READ THE SPELLING WORDS

1.	handkerchief	*handkerchief*	He bought a red silk **handkerchief**.
2.	plumber	*plumber*	A **plumber** repaired the leaky pipe.
3.	knowledge	*knowledge*	He gained **knowledge** from books.
4.	cupboard	*cupboard*	The **cupboard** is filled with cans.
5.	almond	*almond*	The cookie has an **almond** flavor.
6.	crumb	*crumb*	A bird pecked at the bread **crumb**.
7.	knack	*knack*	He has a **knack** for cooking.
8.	solemn	*solemn*	It was a very **solemn** ceremony.
9.	knob	*knob*	This **knob** controls the volume.
10.	autumn	*autumn*	My favorite season is **autumn**.
11.	palm	*palm*	We sat in the shade of a **palm** tree.
12.	aisle	*aisle*	At the movies, I prefer an **aisle** seat.
13.	numb	*numb*	The cold made my hands **numb**.
14.	salmon	*salmon*	The **salmon** is a freshwater fish.
15.	column	*column*	Ivy will grow up the porch **column**.
16.	isle	*isle*	Take a ferry to get to the **isle**.
17.	kneel	*kneel*	I will **kneel** down to untie the boat.
18.	hymn	*hymn*	Let's sing a **hymn** to praise nature.
19.	tomb	*tomb*	That pyramid was a king's **tomb**.
20.	debt	*debt*	He paid the **debt** he owed his dad.

SORT THE SPELLING WORDS

1.–7. Write the spelling words whose first consonant is silent.

8.–14. Write the spelling words with a silent final consonant.

15.–20. Write the spelling words with a silent consonant that is neither the first nor the last consonant.

REMEMBER THE SPELLING STRATEGY

Remember that some words have more consonant letters than consonant sounds. If a consonant is not pronounced, it is considered silent: **k** in **knob** and **b** in **tomb**.

Spelling and Vocabulary

Word Clues

1. It is a homophone for **him**.

2.–3. They are homophones for **I'll**.

4. It can refer to a kind of tree or a part of your hand.

5. It ends with **er**.

6. It is a piece of cloth that you hold in your hand.

7. You do this when you get down on your knees.

8. It is a nut that grows on a tree.

9. It is a fish with pink flesh.

Word Meanings

Write a spelling word to replace the underlined word or words.

10.–11. To open the <u>cabinet</u>, turn the <u>handle</u> to the right.

12.–13. In the <u>fall</u> I will pay off my <u>financial obligation</u>.

14. I dropped a <u>little piece</u> of bread.

15. This <u>burial place</u> dates back to the twelfth century.

16. She writes a weekly <u>article</u> for the school paper.

17. He has a special <u>talent</u> for many puns.

USING THE Thesaurus

A thesaurus provides synonyms and antonyms for words. When you use a thesaurus, be sure that the word you choose is used in the way you intend. Write a spelling word that is a synonym for each set of words.

18. serious, sedate, critical

19. dull, insensitive

20. comprehension, insight, understanding

Spelling and Reading

handkerchief	plumber	knowledge	cupboard	almond
crumb	knack	solemn	knob	autumn
palm	aisle	numb	salmon	column
isle	kneel	hymn	tomb	debt

Solve the Analogies Write a spelling word to complete each analogy.

1. **Board** is to **plank** as **pillar** is to _____.
2. **Hammer** is to **carpenter** as **wrench** is to _____.
3. **Vegetable** is to **lettuce** as **nut** is to _____.
4. **Recite** is to **poem** as **sing** is to _____.
5. **Bird** is to **robin** as **fish** is to _____.
6. **Cheerful** is to **depressed** as **lively** is to _____.
7. **Ocean** is to **sea** as **island** is to _____.

Complete the Sentences Write a spelling word to complete each sentence.

8. Leaves of deciduous trees turn color in _____.
9. Her fingers felt _____ from the frigid air.
10. Norma brushed a _____ from the side of her mouth.
11. King Tut's treasures were discovered inside his _____.
12. Charles felt relieved after he paid off his _____.
13. Tasha has a _____ for always saying the right thing.
14. Fire laws prohibit anyone from sitting in the _____ at the theater.
15. Kyle has a lot of _____ about old cars.

Complete the Paragraph Write spelling words from the box to complete the paragraph.

Maria carefully turned the __16.__ of the old door and tiptoed into the attic. She had to __17.__ in order to peek under the wooden __18.__. Suddenly, there it was in the __19.__ of her hand. Wrapped in an old linen __20.__ was the lost ring.

cupboard
handkerchief
knob
kneel
palm

Spelling AND Writing

Proofread a Paragraph

Six words are not spelled correctly in this paragraph. Write the words correctly.

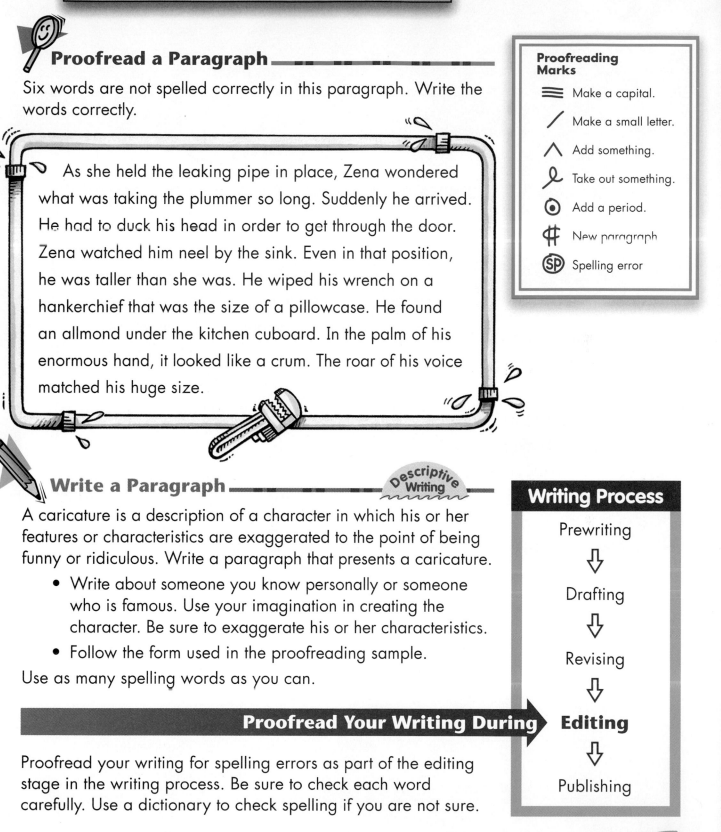

As she held the leaking pipe in place, Zena wondered what was taking the plummer so long. Suddenly he arrived. He had to duck his head in order to get through the door. Zena watched him neel by the sink. Even in that position, he was taller than she was. He wiped his wrench on a hankerchief that was the size of a pillowcase. He found an allmond under the kitchen cuboard. In the palm of his enormous hand, it looked like a crum. The roar of his voice matched his huge size.

Write a Paragraph

Descriptive Writing

A caricature is a description of a character in which his or her features or characteristics are exaggerated to the point of being funny or ridiculous. Write a paragraph that presents a caricature.

- Write about someone you know personally or someone who is famous. Use your imagination in creating the character. Be sure to exaggerate his or her characteristics.
- Follow the form used in the proofreading sample.

Use as many spelling words as you can.

Writing Process

Prewriting

⇩

Drafting

⇩

Revising

⇩

Proofread Your Writing During ▶ Editing

⇩

Publishing

Proofread your writing for spelling errors as part of the editing stage in the writing process. Be sure to check each word carefully. Use a dictionary to check spelling if you are not sure.

Vocabulary

Strategy Words

Review Words: Silent Consonants

Write words from the box that complete the paragraph.

bowl	calmer	knapsack	unknown	writer

Asad took a __1.__ from his __2.__ and filled it with cereal and milk. Then he grabbed his notebook and started to jot down some notes. He had been feeling much __3.__ since he had left the hectic toy store where he used to work. I may be __4.__ now, he thought, but someday I am going to be a successful __5.__.

Preview Words: Silent Consonants

Write words from the box that complete the paragraph.

gnarled	herb	honesty	hustle	knoll

Asad was writing an essay about truth and __6.__. He had chosen to sit on a little __7.__ overlooking the quiet valley below. He leaned against the twisted and __8.__ branch of a huge chestnut tree. Smelling a leaf of a nearby plant, he wondered if it was an __9.__. Suddenly, he realized it was getting late. He decided to __10.__ before it got dark.

Connections

Social Studies: The Law

Write words from the box that complete the paragraph.

corrupt	indict	demonstrate	verdict	defend

Sometimes officials are accused of being __1.__ . It is the job of the grand jury to determine whether or not to charge them with a crime, or __2.__ them. Lawyers __3.__ their clients and present evidence to __4.__ that their clients are not guilty. After listening to all of the testimony, the grand jury delivers its __5.__ .

Math: Geometry

Write a word from the box that matches each clue.

decagon	rhombus	parallelogram
trapezoid	quadrilateral	

6. a geometric figure with four sides and four angles
7. a four-sided figure with opposite sides parallel
8. a geometric figure with ten sides and ten angles
9. a four-sided plane figure with opposite sides parallel and all sides equal
10. a four-sided plane figure with one pair of parallel sides

Apply the Spelling Strategy

Circle the silent consonant in two of the content words you wrote.

103

Spelling and Thinking

READ THE SPELLING WORDS

1. accident	*accident*	I was involved in a minor car **accident**.
2. horrible	*horrible*	The skunk left a **horrible** odor.
3. announce	*announce*	They are about to **announce** the winner.
4. impress	*impress*	His knowledge will **impress** you.
5. possess	*possess*	They **possess** a large book collection.
6. innocent	*innocent*	He is **innocent** of the crime.
7. occasion	*occasion*	Tuesday will be a special **occasion**.
8. express	*express*	I would like to **express** my thanks.
9. banner	*banner*	I hung the **banner** from the railing.
10. terrible	*terrible*	He feels **terrible** about the accident.
11. success	*success*	The party was a huge **success**.
12. manner	*manner*	The students left in an orderly **manner**.
13. assist	*assist*	The salesperson said she could **assist** us.
14. error	*error*	You made one **error** on this test.
15. process	*process*	He described the filmmaking **process**.
16. tissue	*tissue*	Trace the picture on this **tissue**.
17. mirror	*mirror*	He saw his reflection in the **mirror**.
18. connect	*connect*	Now, **connect** the brace to the frame.
19. issue	*issue*	The coach will **issue** new uniforms.
20. recess	*recess*	We play basketball during **recess**.

SORT THE SPELLING WORDS

1.–11. Write the spelling words that have a double **c** or double **s**, or both. Circle these letters in the words you write.

12.–20. Write the spelling words that have a double **r** or double **n**. Circle these letters in the words you write.

REMEMBER THE SPELLING STRATEGY

Remember that double consonants usually represent a single sound: **banner, mirror**.

Spelling and Vocabulary

Word Replacement

Write a spelling word that could replace each underlined word.

1. You should send the letter by <u>fast</u> mail.
2. Her family used to <u>own</u> a small farm.
3. He apologized for making the <u>mistake</u>.
4. The baker explained his bread-making <u>system</u>.
5. Students went outside during their morning <u>break</u>.
6. The principal will <u>distribute</u> new report cards soon.
7. He performs his job in a quiet and formal <u>way</u>.
8. She attributes her <u>achievement</u> in science to hard work.

Word Analysis

Change the underlined part of these words to write spelling words.

9. hor<u>net</u>
10. ter<u>minal</u>
11. <u>rec</u>ent
12. <u>in</u>sist
13. oct<u>opus</u>
14. ac<u>tual</u>
15. <u>in</u>spect
16. imp<u>oster</u>

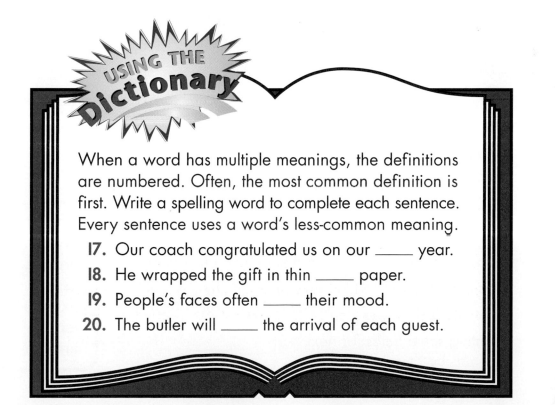

USING THE Dictionary

When a word has multiple meanings, the definitions are numbered. Often, the most common definition is first. Write a spelling word to complete each sentence. Every sentence uses a word's less-common meaning.

17. Our coach congratulated us on our _____ year.
18. He wrapped the gift in thin _____ paper.
19. People's faces often _____ their mood.
20. The butler will _____ the arrival of each guest.

Spelling and Reading

accident	horrible	announce	impress	possess
innocent	occasion	express	banner	terrible
success	manner	assist	error	process
tissue	mirror	connect	issue	recess

Solve the Analogies Write a spelling word to complete each analogy.

1. **Echo** is to **surface** as **image** is to _____.
2. **Sign** is to **poster** as **flag** is to _____.
3. **Terror** is to **terrible** as **horror** is to _____.
4. **Donate** is to **accept** as **detach** is to _____.
5. **Assemble** is to **gather** as **distribute** is to _____.
6. **Speech** is to **present** as **news** is to _____.

Complete the Sentences Write a spelling word to complete each sentence.

7. His fine drawing will _____ you.
8. The holiday party was a happy _____.
9. They _____ many albums of photographs.
10. The waiter had a very friendly _____.
11. The judge announced a two-hour _____.
12. The scientist examined the _____ under the microscope.
13. His friends congratulated him on his _____.

Complete the Letter Write spelling words from the box to complete the letter.

Dear Mr. Greenthumb,

I would like to __14.__ my regret for the __15.__ yesterday. I feel __16.__ about cutting your prize tulips. It was an __17.__ __18.__. I know what a lengthy __19.__ it is to grow these flowers, so I would like to __20.__ you in planting some bulbs for next year.

Sincerely,

Your former gardener

innocent
accident
process
assist
express
terrible
error

106

Spelling and Writing

Proofread a Letter

Six words are not spelled correctly in this letter. Write the words correctly.

> Dear Advice Giver,
>
> I often have ocassion to expres my opinion to friends, but I am afraid that they might disagree with my ideas. Maybe I am trying too hard to empress them. Or perhaps it's the manner in which I present my opinions. I posess a good sense of humor, but I rarely use it. What is the secret to sucess? Is there a prosess that you would recommend?
>
> Gratefully,
>
> B. Cranky

Proofreading Marks

≡ Make a capital.

/ Make a small letter.

∧ Add something.

℘ Take out something.

⊙ Add a period.

⌗ New paragraph

SP Spelling error

Write a Letter

Expository Writing

Opinions and feelings are not always easy to express. Write a response to B. Cranky's letter.

- Include answers to the questions that B. Cranky asks. Explain how a person can disagree with another person and still be friends. Also explain the importance of constructive criticism.
- Follow the form used in the proofreading sample.

Use as many spelling words as you can.

Proofread Your Writing During

Proofread your writing for spelling errors as part of the editing stage in the writing process. Be sure to check each word carefully. Use a dictionary to check spelling if you are not sure.

Writing Process

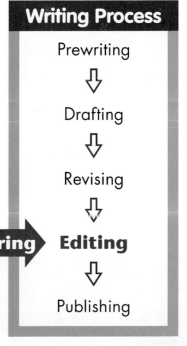

Prewriting

⇩

Drafting

⇩

Revising

⇩

Editing

⇩

Publishing

Vocabulary

Strategy Words

Review Words: Double Consonants

Write a word from the box to complete each of these sentences.

arrival	cinnamon	hiccupped	possible	stirrups

1. The flight _____ has been delayed by an hour.
2. As a puppy, Roscoe _____ after eating his food too fast.
3. Your cheery card arrived at the best _____ time.
4. She sprinkled a little _____ on the applesauce.
5. The rider climbed onto the horse and put his feet into the _____.

Preview Words: Double Consonants

Write words from the box to complete the following paragraph.

afford	assumption	challenge	corrode	embarrass

While he struggled to start his new business, Sal had another __6.__. He could not __7.__ a new car, but the finish on his car had begun to rust and __8.__. It was his __9.__ that if he took care of his car it would last another few years. He would not allow his rusty old car to __10.__ him. In fact, he was proud of it.

Connections

Content Words

Language Arts: Nouns

Write a word from the box to complete each sentence.

collective	proper	plural	singular	possessive

1. The word **family** is a _____ noun because it refers to a group as a whole.
2. The word **families** is a _____ noun; it refers to more than one person, place, or thing.
3. A _____ noun, such as **family's,** shows ownership.
4. **Child** is a _____ noun, referring to a single person, place, or thing.
5. A _____ noun, such as **Murphy,** is a formal name.

Social Studies: Australia

Write the words from the box that complete the paragraph.

outback	drought	paddock	mutton	grazing

Much of the western part of Australia is desert. The summer dry spell, or __6.__, can be severe. In the dry central plains, called the __7.__, there are huge sheep farms. People often see sheep __8.__ on grass in an enclosed area, or __9.__. Meat from these sheep is called __10.__.

Apply the Spelling Strategy

Circle the double consonants in four of the content words you wrote.

Assessment and Review

Assessment / Units 13–17

Each Assessment Word in the box fits one of the spelling strategies you have studied over the past five weeks. Read the spelling strategies. Then write each Assessment Word under the unit number it fits.

Unit 13

1.–4. The **f** sound (/**f**/) can be spelled in different ways: **f** in **faint, ff** in **baffle,** and **ph** in **phone.**

Unit 14

5.–8. The /**z**/ sound can be spelled: **z** as in **freeze, s** as in **phase,** and **ss** as in **scissors.** The /**zh**/ sound can be spelled **s** and is often followed by **ual** (**usual**) or **ion** (**vision**).

Unit 15

9.–12. The suffixes **-ed** and **-ing** can be added to some base words to form new words. In other words, the final consonant is doubled when **-ed** or **-ing** is added.

Unit 16

13.–16. Some words have more consonant letters than consonant sounds. If a consonant is not pronounced, it is considered silent: **k** in **knob** and **b** in **tomb.**

Unit 17

17.–20. Double consonants usually represent a single sound: **banner, mirror.**

scuffle
illusion
patrolling
dumb
glossary
intellect
salve
patrolled
dispose
gopher
chef
hazel
frightened
knelt
surround
suggest
knead
frightening
hazy
fatal

Review — Unit 13: /f/ Spelled f, ff, ph

| effort | fulfill | physician | sophomore | faint |
| difficult | phone | offer | phrase | officer |

Write a spelling word for each clue.

1. another word for **doctor**
2. last year's freshman
3. person in a position of authority

Use spelling words to complete each sentence.

4.–5. I will make an ____ to ____ your wish.

6. It took me an hour to solve that ____ math problem.

7.–9. The ____ was too ____ to hear on the ____.

10. I will sell it if you will make me a fair ____.

Review — Unit 14: Consonant Sounds /z/, /zh/

| optimism | scissors | usual | conclusion | amaze |
| tease | pause | husband | visitor | television |

Write the spelling word that matches the definition.

11. a person who visits
12. a tool that cuts
13. the end
14. a male spouse
15. to surprise or astonish
16. to stop briefly
17. routine
18. a hopeful disposition
19. to bother by making jokes or gestures
20. a set that receives images and sounds

Review — Unit 15: Suffixes -ed, -ing

directed	complaining	differed	admitting	directing
resulted	profiting	remained	remaining	permitted

Write the spelling word that is the opposite of the word or words given.

1. praising
2. refused to allow
3. agreed
4. losing money
5. departed

6. denying
7. took orders
8. departing
9. following orders
10. had no effect

Review — Unit 16: Silent Consonants

aisle	column	knowledge	handkerchief	knob
palm	numb	kneel	solemn	autumn

Write the spelling word that completes each sentence.

11. The knight was forced to _____ before his captors.
12. After walking in the snow, my toes became _____.
13. He wore a tie and carried a matching _____.
14. The runner placed the baton firmly in the _____ of her teammate's hand.
15. It is a lovely day and quite warm for _____.
16. It was a sad and _____ ceremony.
17. We have seats in section A, _____ 13.
18. He writes a _____ for the daily newspaper.
19. I tried to open the cabinet door, but the _____ fell off.
20. Ask Sally who has a lot of _____ about that topic.

connect	occasion	possess	recess	announce
terrible	mirror	horrible	success	accident

Write a spelling word for each clue.

1. This is a good part of the school day.
2. This is an event that wasn't planned.
3. Look in this to see yourself.
4. When you join two things, you do this to them.
5. When an event goes very well, it is this.
6. This is a particular event or happening.
7.–8. These words might describe a wicked monster.
9. If you own a bicycle, you could say this about owning it.
10. If you tell something, you do this to it.

GAME Spelling Study Strategy

Spelling Tic-Tac-Toe

Practicing spelling words can be fun if you make it into a game. Play this game with a partner.

1. Both you and your partner write spelling words on lists. Trade lists.

2. Draw a tic-tac-toe board on a piece of paper. Decide who will use **O** and who will use **X**.

3. Ask your partner to call the first word on your spelling list to you. Spell it out loud. If you spell it correctly, make an **X** or an **O** on the tic-tac-toe board. If you misspell the word, ask your partner to spell it out loud for you. You miss your turn.

4. Now you call a word from your partner's spelling list.

5. Keep playing until one of you makes tic-tac-toe. Keep starting over until you both have practiced all your spelling words.

WRITER'S

Grammar, Usage, and Mechanics

Direct Objects

The direct object is the noun or pronoun that receives the action of the verb. Only action verbs have a direct object.

The goalie kicked the **ball**.

Practice Activity

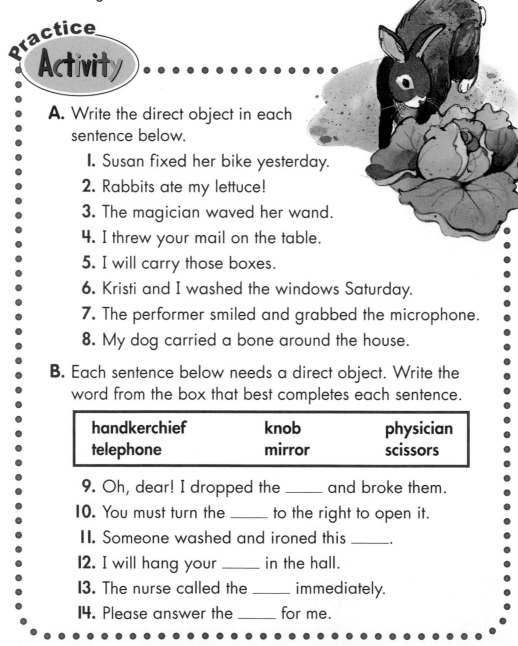

A. Write the direct object in each sentence below.

   I. Susan fixed her bike yesterday.

   2. Rabbits ate my lettuce!

   3. The magician waved her wand.

   4. I threw your mail on the table.

   5. I will carry those boxes.

   6. Kristi and I washed the windows Saturday.

   7. The performer smiled and grabbed the microphone.

   8. My dog carried a bone around the house.

B. Each sentence below needs a direct object. Write the word from the box that best completes each sentence.

handkerchief	knob	physician
telephone	mirror	scissors

   9. Oh, dear! I dropped the _____ and broke them.

  10. You must turn the _____ to the right to open it.

  II. Someone washed and ironed this _____.

  12. I will hang your _____ in the hall.

  13. The nurse called the _____ immediately.

  14. Please answer the _____ for me.

WORKSHOP

Proofreading Strategy

Box It Up!

Good writers always proofread their work for spelling errors. Here's a strategy that you can use to proofread your papers.

Cut a small hole or box in a piece of paper. Slide it over your work so that one or two words appear inside the box. You won't be able to see a whole sentence at one time. Instead of reading **The rider jumped onto the horse and galloped away!** you might see **rider jumped** or **and galloped**.

This may sound like a strange thing to do, but this strategy helps you focus on word spelling, not meaning. Try it!

Electronic Spelling

Spell Checkers

Computers have many programs and tools that help you proofread. Many have spell checkers that signal misspelled words. But even the best spell checker won't find every mistake, so you must be alert for problems.

Sometimes the misspelling of one word will spell a different word. For example, you might mean to write the word **dessert** and write **desert** instead. Since both words are spelled correctly, a spell checker would not catch the mistake.

A spell checker was used to correct the misspelled words in these sentences. Find the words it missed and write them correctly.

1. Hang the pitcher on the wall.
2. You will need allot of wrapping paper.
3. At the party well see many of our friends.
4. I one first prize in the writing contest!
5. Dry your hands before you doe that.
6. Their were many people in the room.

Spelling and Thinking

READ THE SPELLING WORDS

1.	responsible	*responsible*	I am **responsible** for the accident.
2.	approachable	*approachable*	My friendly boss is **approachable**.
3.	reversible	*reversible*	Her new rain jacket is **reversible**.
4.	changeable	*changeable*	Our weather is often **changeable**.
5.	acceptable	*acceptable*	That silly answer is not **acceptable**.
6.	adorable	*adorable*	The baby's teddy bear is **adorable**.
7.	sensible	*sensible*	We all like your **sensible** ideas.
8.	profitable	*profitable*	Her store had a **profitable** year.
9.	forcible	*forcible*	Was entry into the house **forcible**?
10.	favorable	*favorable*	He wrote a **favorable** play review.
11.	edible	*edible*	Some wild mushrooms are **edible**.
12.	visible	*visible*	Cars were not **visible** in the fog.
13.	flexible	*flexible*	The doctor's schedule is **flexible**.
14.	notable	*notable*	DaVinci was a **notable** painter.
15.	legible	*legible*	I hope you find my writing **legible**.
16.	available	*available*	It is **available** for your use.
17.	probable	*probable*	I tried to find the **probable** cause.
18.	valuable	*valuable*	Be careful with that **valuable** vase.
19.	invisible	*invisible*	The star is **invisible** in the daylight.
20.	capable	*capable*	You are a very **capable** writer.

SORT THE SPELLING WORDS

1.–7. Write the words in which the spelling of the base word does not change when **-able** or **-ible** is added.

8.–14. Write the spelling words in which the **silent e** is dropped from the base word when **-able** or **-ible** is added.

15.–20. Write the spelling words in which the suffix **-able** or **-ible** is added to a root word.

REMEMBER THE SPELLING STRATEGY

Remember that the suffixes **-able** and **-ible** can be added to base words and root words to form new words: **favor<u>able</u>** and **vis<u>ible</u>**.

Word Meanings

Write a spelling word to match each definition.

1. able to be seen
2. able to be forced
3. worthy of notice
4. able to be approached
5. able to be reversed
6. able to be bent
7. likely to change
8. worthy of acceptance
9. likely to happen
10. of great value

Word Replacements

Write a spelling word that could replace each underlined word.

11. They have two <u>lovable</u> puppies.
12. The apartment is <u>obtainable</u> for rent.
13. The doctor gave the patient a very <u>encouraging</u> report about his health.
14. These berries are <u>safe for eating</u>.
15. Selling the land was <u>moneymaking</u> for the company.
16. Winslow Homer was a gifted and <u>skillful</u> artist.

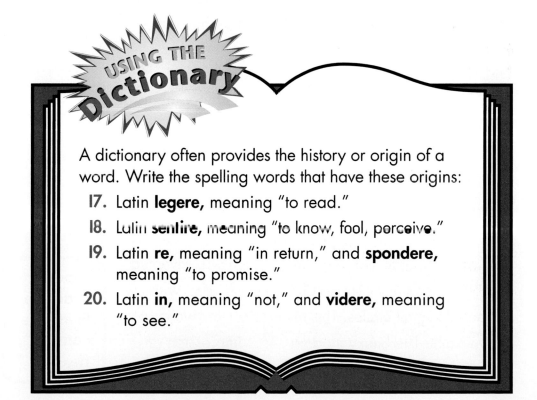

USING THE Dictionary

A dictionary often provides the history or origin of a word. Write the spelling words that have these origins:

17. Latin **legere,** meaning "to read."
18. Latin **sentire,** meaning "to know, feel, perceive."
19. Latin **re,** meaning "in return," and **spondere,** meaning "to promise."
20. Latin **in,** meaning "not," and **videre,** meaning "to see."

Spelling and Reading

responsible	approachable	reversible	changeable
acceptable	adorable	sensible	profitable
forcible	favorable	edible	visible
flexible	notable	legible	available
probable	valuable	invisible	capable

Solve the Analogies Write a spelling word to complete each analogy.

1. **Speech** is to **understandable** as **handwriting** is to _____.

2. **Water** is to **drinkable** as **food** is to _____.

3. **Seldom** is to **often** as **worthless** is to _____.

4. **Dull** is to **shiny** as **concealed** is to _____.

5. **Grateful** is to **appreciative** as **delightful** is to _____.

6. **Knowledgeable** is to **ignorant** as **unreliable** is to _____.

7. **Cautious** is to **careful** as **variable** is to _____.

Complete the Sentences Write a spelling word to complete each sentence.

8. Police officers made a _____ entry into the building.

9. Your test scores were not great, but they were _____.

10. The salesperson's smile made her seem _____.

11. Once the judge makes a decision, it is not _____.

12. The counselor offered a _____ solution to the problem.

13. I think a lightning strike was the _____ cause of the fire.

14. The lighthouse beam was nearly _____ in the fog.

15. The family is pleased with the _____ sale of the house.

Complete the Paragraph Write spelling words from the box to complete the paragraph.

One __16.__ fad was the Slinky, which was invented in 1945. The Slinky consists of 87 feet of __17.__ wire coiled into small circles. This toy is __18.__ of "walking" down stairs. The Slinky made a __19.__ impression on millions. It is still __20.__ in stores today.

capable
available
favorable
notable
flexible

118

Spelling and Writing

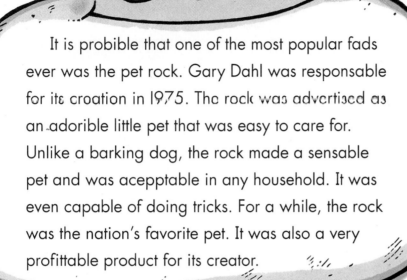

Proofread a Paragraph

Six words are not spelled correctly in this paragraph. Write the words correctly.

It is probible that one of the most popular fads ever was the pet rock. Gary Dahl was responsable for its croation in 1975. The rock was advertised as an adorible little pet that was easy to care for. Unlike a barking dog, the rock made a sensable pet and was acepptable in any household. It was even capable of doing tricks. For a while, the rock was the nation's favorite pet. It was also a very profittable product for its creator.

Write a Paragraph

Persuasive Writing

Sometimes the simplest idea, like the pet rock, can become very popular. Choose something you think could become a fad. This can be an object that already exists or something from your imagination. Try to persuade others that they need this object.

- Write about a fad that you are starting.
- Use details about your fad to persuade others to follow the fad.

Use as many spelling words as you can.

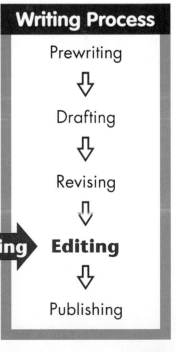

Writing Process

Prewriting

⇩

Drafting

⇩

Revising

⇩

Proofread Your Writing During ➤ **Editing**

⇩

Publishing

Proofread your writing for spelling errors as part of the editing stage in the writing process. Be sure to check each word carefully. Use a dictionary to check spelling if you are not sure.

Vocabulary

Strategy Words

Review Words: Suffixes -able, -ible

Write words from the box to complete the sentences. Use the underlined words as clues.

divisible	force	impossible	inflate	suit

1. You can _____ this ball. It is <u>inflatable</u>.
2. Your idea is _____. It is <u>not possible</u>.
3. The project is _____. It is <u>capable of being divided into separate tasks</u>.
4. I think this dress will _____ you. You will find it <u>suitable</u> to your tastes.
5. He had to _____ the window open. The entry was <u>forcible</u>.

Preview Words: Suffixes -able, -ible

Write words from the box to replace the underlined words.

admirable	eligible	incredible
noticeable	remarkable	

6.–10. The makers of Smile announce a new toothpaste. You will see <u>observable</u> differences in the whiteness of your teeth. Enter a contest to describe your experience with our <u>memorable</u> new product. All <u>praiseworthy</u> contributions will be rewarded with a free tube of Smile. This is an <u>unbelievable</u> offer that you should not pass up. Anyone over the age of twelve is <u>qualified</u> to enter.

120

Connections

Content Words

Social Studies: Agriculture

Write words from the box to complete the paragraph.

| agriculture | irrigate | arable | scarcity | famine |

As a nation's population increases, the availability of __1.__ land decreases. The construction of new buildings and roadways also adds to a possible __2.__ of land in the future. Today, efforts are being made in the field of __3.__ to teach people how to __4.__ their land and maintain rich soil. Such planning can help prevent a major __5.__.

Science: Digestion

Write the words from the box that complete the paragraph.

| digestive | pancreas | enzyme | saliva | liver |

The __6.__ juices play an important role in digestion. An __7.__ such as __8.__, which is produced in the mouth, helps break down food. The __9.__, a gland behind the stomach, also secretes juices into the small intestine to aid in the process. The __10.__ is a large organ near the stomach that transfers nutrients into the blood.

Apply the Spelling Strategy

Circle the suffixes **-able** and **-ive** in two of the content words you wrote.

Spelling and Thinking

READ THE SPELLING WORDS

1.	antifreeze	*antifreeze*	Does your car need **antifreeze**?
2.	nonreturnable	*nonreturnable*	We recycle **nonreturnable** cans.
3.	misbehave	*misbehave*	Try not to **misbehave** in class.
4.	misfortune	*misfortune*	I am sorry for your **misfortune**.
5.	irresistible	*irresistible*	I find these cookies **irresistible**.
6.	illiterate	*illiterate*	He teaches **illiterate** adults.
7.	misinform	*misinform*	Juan did not **misinform** you.
8.	irrational	*irrational*	Some fears are totally **irrational**.
9.	nonprofit	*nonprofit*	Charities are **nonprofit** groups.
10.	antisocial	*antisocial*	He is **antisocial,** so he sits alone.
11.	mistrust	*mistrust*	I **mistrust** his motives.
12.	illegible	*illegible*	She rewrote her **illegible** paper.
13.	misplace	*misplace*	Dad tends to **misplace** his keys.
14.	misread	*misread*	I **misread** the map and got lost.
15.	illogical	*illogical*	Your argument is **illogical**.
16.	irregular	*irregular*	The dog's heartbeat is **irregular**.
17.	misuse	*misuse*	The toy broke from **misuse**.
18.	nonfat	*nonfat*	I bought a gallon of **nonfat** milk.
19.	illegal	*illegal*	It is **illegal** to park here.
20.	mislead	*mislead*	False headlines **mislead** readers.

SORT THE SPELLING WORDS

1.–7. Write the spelling words with the prefixes **il-** or **ir-**.

8.–15. Write the spelling words with the prefix **mis-**.

16.–18. Write the spelling words with the prefix **non-**.

19.–20. Write the spelling words with the prefix **anti-**.

REMEMBER THE SPELLING STRATEGY

Remember that the prefixes **ir-, anti-, il-, non-,** and **mis-** can be added to base words to form new words. These new words mean the opposite of the base word.

Word Structure

Replace the first word in each pair with a prefix and write the spelling word.

1. badly + lead
2. badly + inform
3. badly + read
4. not + legal

5. not + rational
6. not + profit
7. not + returnable
8. not + social

Word Replacement

Write a spelling word that could replace each underlined word.

9. His handwriting is nearly <u>unreadable</u>.
10. I am concerned about the dog's <u>unusual</u> behavior.
11. If you <u>mistreat</u> the violin strings, they might break.
12. He is <u>uneducated</u> in the subject of modern art.
13. If you <u>disobey</u> once more, you will have to leave.
14. I had an <u>overwhelming</u> urge to open the gift early.

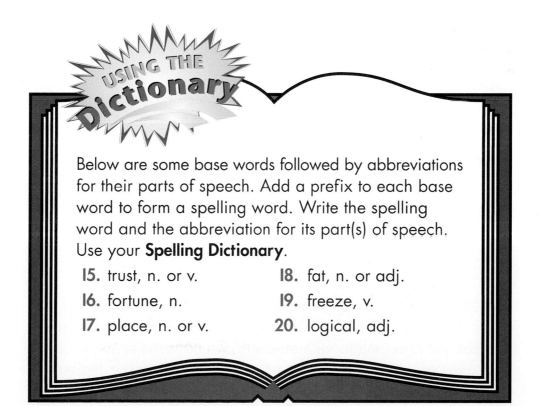

USING THE Dictionary

Below are some base words followed by abbreviations for their parts of speech. Add a prefix to each base word to form a spelling word. Write the spelling word and the abbreviation for its part(s) of speech. Use your **Spelling Dictionary**.

15. trust, n. or v.
16. fortune, n.
17. place, n. or v.

18. fat, n. or adj.
19. freeze, v.
20. logical, adj.

Spelling *and* Reading

antifreeze	nonreturnable	misbehave	misfortune
irresistible	illiterate	misinform	irrational
nonprofit	antisocial	mistrust	illegible
misplace	misread	illogical	irregular
misuse	nonfat	illegal	mislead

Solve the Analogies   Write a spelling word to complete each analogy.

1. **High** is to **low** as **literate** is to _____.
2. **Accept** is to **unacceptable** as **return** is to _____.
3. **Reasonable** is to **unreasonable** as **rational** is to _____.
4. **Enjoyment** is to **misery** as **confidence** is to _____.
5. **Include** is to **exclude** as **inform** is to _____.
6. **Little** is to **none** as **low fat** is to _____.
7. **Strong** is to **powerful** as **unlawful** is to _____.
8. **Summer** is to **coolant** as **winter** is to _____.

Complete the Sentences   Write a spelling word to complete each sentence.

9. It took him five years to recover from his _____.
10. Our _____ organization holds an annual fundraiser.
11. I hope you will not _____ while I am gone.
12. Try not to _____ your book. We do not have any extras.
13. I got lost when I _____ a sign on the highway.
14. Some people tend to _____ a word if they have never seen or heard it used properly.
15. The angry neighbors thought we had tried to _____ them.

Correct the Paragraph   Correct the paragraph by adding prefixes to the underlined words. Write the spelling words.

16.–20. Julian finds coin collecting an <u>resistible</u> pursuit. Some people say coin collectors are <u>social</u>, but Julian claims that this is <u>logical</u>. He often meets with others to compare the <u>regular</u> markings on old coins. Because some of the lettering is <u>legible</u>, he frequently consults experts.

Spelling and Writing

Proofread a Paragraph

Six words are not spelled correctly in this paragraph. Write the words correctly.

> Because stamps rarely come in irreguler shapes, they can be easily placed in special albums so collectors will not misplace them. Unused stamps are the most valuable, since the cancellation mark on a stamped envelope may make the stamp's words ilegible. If you buy old stamps in a store, they are often nonreturnible. It is illegle to reuse a cancelled stamp; the U.S. Postal Service, a nonproffit government-owned corporation, does not tolerate this missuse of stamps.

Proofreading Marks

≡ Make a capital.

/ Make a small letter.

∧ Add something.

℘ Take out something.

⊙ Add a period.

⌗ New paragraph

SP Spelling error

Write a Paragraph

Expository Writing

There are all kinds of hobbies. Some involve sports. Others, like stamp collecting, require research. Write a paragraph about a hobby.

- Describe a hobby that you have or would like to have. Tell why it is an interesting hobby.
- Follow the form used in the proofreading sample.

Use as many spelling words as you can.

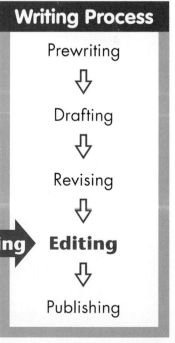

Writing Process

Prewriting

⇩

Drafting

⇩

Revising

⇩

Editing

⇩

Publishing

Proofread Your Writing During

Proofread your writing for spelling errors as part of the editing stage in the writing process. Be sure to check each word carefully. Use a dictionary to check spelling if you are not sure.

125

Vocabulary

Strategy Words

Review Words: Prefixes ir-, anti-, il-, non-, mis-

Write the word from the box that completes each sentence. Circle the prefix in each word you write.

antislavery	misjudge	miscalculate
	nonfiction	nonviolent

1. Abolitionists were against slavery. They were _____.
2. The protest must not be violent. It should be _____.
3. We do not want to badly calculate this math problem. We do not want to _____ it.
4. Biographies are not fiction. Because they are about real people, like Dr. Martin Luther King, Jr., they are _____.
5. I do not want to judge him wrongly. Because he may be a nice person, I do not want to _____ him.

Preview Words: Prefixes ir-, anti-, il-, non-, mis-

Add the correct prefix to each underlined word. You will write words from the box. The prefix turns the meaning of each word into its opposite.

nontoxic	nonconsumable	inexpensive
	mistaken	misunderstanding

6. I apologize for our <u>understanding</u>.
7. I had <u>taken</u> your meaning badly.
8. I thought the flowers were <u>toxic</u>.
9. You knew they were <u>consumable</u>.
10. We both knew, however, that they were <u>expensive</u>.

Content Words

Social Studies: Insurance

Write words from the box to complete the paragraph.

collect	policy	insure	provision	nonrenewal

The job of an insurance agency is to __1.__ you in the event of accident or injury. The agency will __2.__ payments from you on a regular basis. This is a __3.__ of the written contract, or __4.__, that covers you against loss. Sometimes a __5.__ clause will be included to protect the insurance company against risk.

Language Arts: Usage

The underlined words in the sentences are examples of each term in the box. Write the words from the box that match the underlined words.

appositive	modifier	grammar	tense	linking verb

6. Jill, a sixth grader, will be twelve in April.
7. She laughed, laughs, will laugh all the way home.
8. He is feeling lighthearted today.
9. I only want advice. I want only advice.
10. all of the above

Apply the Spelling Strategy

Circle the prefix that means "not" in one of the content words you wrote.

127

Spelling and Thinking

READ THE SPELLING WORDS

1. advancement	*advancement*	I hope to get a job **advancement**.
2. advantage	*advantage*	Studying is to your **advantage**.
3. development	*development*	What is the latest **development**?
4. marriage	*marriage*	Their **marriage** was a surprise.
5. measurement	*measurement*	His height **measurement** is six feet.
6. appointment	*appointment*	She has a doctor's **appointment**.
7. carriage	*carriage*	I pushed the baby's **carriage**.
8. excitement	*excitement*	Their victory caused **excitement**.
9. bandage	*bandage*	The **bandage** will protect that cut.
10. assignment	*assignment*	Your **assignment** is a book report.
11. passage	*passage*	A secret **passage** leads to the attic.
12. experiment	*experiment*	The **experiment** led to a discovery.
13. mileage	*mileage*	We kept track of the trip **mileage**.
14. postage	*postage*	Your package has enough **postage**.
15. instrument	*instrument*	He plays a musical **instrument**.
16. equipment	*equipment*	We set up our camera **equipment**.
17. garage	*garage*	The **garage** holds two cars.
18. courage	*courage*	That firefighter has great **courage**.
19. document	*document*	Ina's lawyer signed the **document**.
20. garbage	*garbage*	Please take out the **garbage**.

SORT THE SPELLING WORDS

1.–11. Write the spelling words that have the suffix **-age** or **-ment** added to a base word. Circle the base word.

12.–20. Write the spelling words that have the suffix **-age** or **-ment** added to a root word.

REMEMBER THE SPELLING STRATEGY

Remember that the suffixes **-age** and **-ment** can be added to root words and base words to form new words. These new words are nouns: **courage, equipment**.

Spelling and Vocabulary

Word Clues

Write a spelling word for each clue.

1. the collective term for **supplies**
2. the process of determining dimensions
3. the result of setting a time for a meeting
4. a means by which people are carried
5. the process of conducting a test
6. the collective term for **miles covered**
7. movement forward

Word Groups

Write a spelling word to complete each group of words.

8. letter, envelope, address, _____
9. bravery, valor, fearlessness, _____
10. certificate, license, diploma, _____
11. thrill, adventure, agitation, _____
12. peelings, trash, leftovers, _____
13. homework, chore, duty, _____
14. benefit, upper hand, asset, _____

USING THE Dictionary

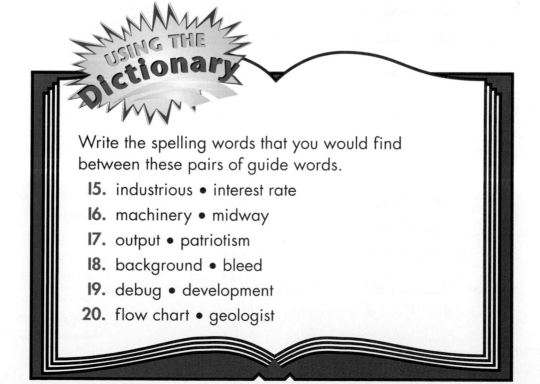

Write the spelling words that you would find between these pairs of guide words.

15. industrious • interest rate
16. machinery • midway
17. output • patriotism
18. background • bleed
19. debug • development
20. flow chart • geologist

Spelling and Reading

advancement	advantage	development	marriage
measurement	appointment	carriage	excitement
bandage	assignment	passage	experiment
mileage	postage	instrument	equipment
garage	courage	document	garbage

Solve the Analogies Write a spelling word to complete each analogy.

1. **Airplane** is to **hangar** as **car** is to _____.
2. **Surgeon** is to **operation** as **scientist** is to _____.
3. **Rake** is to **tool** as **violin** is to _____.
4. **Indecision** is to **certainty** as **retreat** is to _____.
5. **Supermarket** is to **groceries** as **post office** is to _____.

Complete the Sentences Write a spelling word to complete each sentence.

6. The young mother pushed the baby _____ down the street.
7. I would like to read you a _____ from this book.
8. We should check the car _____ before we start on our trip.
9. The tailor took a final _____ before hemming the skirt.
10. You should take _____ of the wonderful sale.
11. The parents were pleased with the baby's _____.
12. I am afraid I will be late for my dentist _____.
13. The lawyer asked me to sign the legal _____.

Complete the Paragraph Write spelling words from the box to complete the paragraph.

During their first year of __14.__, the Fischers bought an old horse farm. When Alex got up enough __15.__ to ask for a part-time job, they hired her. She cleaned all the __16.__ and broken __17.__ out of the old barn. Her major __18.__ was to groom the horses. She even had to change the __19.__ on a lame horse. Alex loved the __20.__ of being around horses.

excitement
garbage
assignment
marriage
courage
bandage
equipment

Spelling and Writing

Proofread a Paragraph

Six words are not spelled correctly in this paragraph. Write the words correctly.

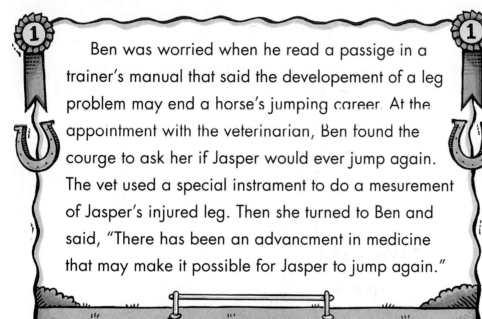

Ben was worried when he read a passige in a trainer's manual that said the developement of a leg problem may end a horse's jumping career. At the appointment with the veterinarian, Ben found the courge to ask her if Jasper would ever jump again. The vet used a special instrament to do a mesurement of Jasper's injured leg. Then she turned to Ben and said, "There has been an advancment in medicine that may make it possible for Jasper to jump again."

Proofreading Marks

≡   Make a capital.

/   Make a small letter.

∧   Add something.

℮   Take out something.

⊙   Add a period.

New paragraph

SP   Spelling error

Write a Paragraph

Descriptive Writing

There are many kinds of jobs. Most workers are paid for doing the job, but sometimes the job experience itself is their "pay." Write about a job you have had or would like to have.

- Describe the job and its responsibilities. Describe the best part and the challenges.
- Follow the form used in the proofreading sample.

Use as many spelling words as you can.

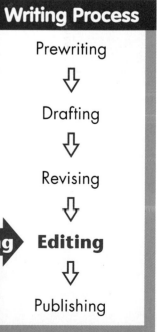

Writing Process

Prewriting

⇩

Drafting

⇩

Revising

⇩

Proofread Your Writing During ➤ **Editing**

⇩

Publishing

Proofread your writing for spelling errors as part of the editing stage in the writing process. Be sure to check each word carefully. Use a dictionary to check spelling if you are not sure.

Vocabulary

Strategy Words

Review Words: Suffixes -age, -ment

Write words from the box to complete this advertisement.

amusement	employment	judgment
prepackage		voyage

Looking for a vacation that offers a lot of excitement and ___1.___? Come to Wendall Island. In our ___2.___, this is the best vacation spot for the entire family. We will even ___3.___ your entire trip so that your stay will be paid for before you arrive. Included in the package is a five-day ___4.___ on a clipper ship.

We have ___5.___ opportunities available, too.

Preview Words: Suffixes -age, -ment

Write words from the box to complete the paragraph.

acreage	amazement	coverage
encouragement		management

The governor watched the television ___6.___ of the forest fire with shock and ___7.___. He had no idea that the fire had destroyed so much ___8.___. He was pleased to learn about the effective ___9.___ of the fire so that it would not spread farther. He immediately placed a call to fire-fighting headquarters to add his words of ___10.___.

Connections

Math: Percentages

Write words from the box to complete this advertisement.

discount	**percentage**	**interest rate**
	portion	**percent**

Adco Mortgage Company has just lowered its __1.__ from eight to seven __2.__. You will not find this low a __3.__ rate anywhere else. We will even pay a __4.__ of your closing costs. We also offer a __5.__ for first-time home buyers.

Science: Atmosphere

Write the words from the box that complete the paragraph.

nitrogen	**pollution**	**carbon dioxide**
	environment	**water vapor**

The effects of __6.__ can be seen in our __7.__. The automobile engine is the major cause of this problem in cities. Earth's atmosphere is made up of oxygen, __8.__, and __9.__. When car fumes mix with __10.__, the balance of these elements is upset, producing acid rain.

Apply the Spelling Strategy

Circle the suffixes **-age** and **-ment** in two of the content words you wrote.

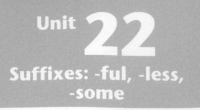
Spelling and Thinking

READ THE SPELLING WORDS

1.	successful	*successful*	She is a **successful** and skilled artist.
2.	thoughtless	*thoughtless*	I apologized for being **thoughtless**.
3.	wholesome	*wholesome*	Eat a **wholesome** breakfast daily.
4.	wonderful	*wonderful*	We had a **wonderful** vacation.
5.	worthless	*worthless*	Throw out this **worthless** item.
6.	worrisome	*worrisome*	It is **worrisome** that he is so late.
7.	delightful	*delightful*	The warm weather was **delightful**.
8.	lonesome	*lonesome*	He was **lonesome** without his family.
9.	priceless	*priceless*	Your friendship is **priceless** to me.
10.	fanciful	*fanciful*	The child made **fanciful** drawings.
11.	eventful	*eventful*	The weekend was busy and **eventful**.
12.	fruitless	*fruitless*	Our search for the ring was **fruitless**.
13.	forgetful	*forgetful*	Were you always so **forgetful**?
14.	senseless	*senseless*	That joke was cruel and **senseless**.
15.	doubtful	*doubtful*	It is **doubtful** that I will be there.
16.	tiresome	*tiresome*	To recopy his work was **tiresome**.
17.	tireless	*tireless*	She is a **tireless** worker.
18.	dutiful	*dutiful*	He is a **dutiful** parent.
19.	fearless	*fearless*	She performed a **fearless** rescue.
20.	pitiful	*pitiful*	The injured bird was a **pitiful** sight.

SORT THE SPELLING WORDS

1.–9. Write the spelling words that have the suffix **-ful**.

10.–16. Write the spelling words that have the suffix **-less**.

17.–20. Write the spelling words that have the suffix **-some**.

REMEMBER THE SPELLING STRATEGY

Remember that the suffixes **-ful, -less,** and **-some** can be added to base words to form adjectives such as **wonderful, priceless,** and **worrisome**.

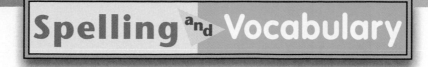

Spelling ^{and} Vocabulary

Word Clues

Use the clues to write spelling words by adding a suffix to the underlined words. You may have to change the spelling of the base word before adding the suffix.

1. full of <u>pity</u>
2. without <u>worth</u>
3. full of <u>fancy</u>
4. full of <u>success</u>
5. inclined to <u>worry</u>
6. full of <u>delight</u>
7. full of <u>doubt</u>
8. inclined to <u>forget</u>
9. full of <u>duty</u>

Word Meanings

Write the spelling word that could best replace the underlined word or words.

10. He prepared a delicious and <u>healthy</u> meal.
11. She thanked them for their <u>never-ending</u> efforts.
12. They showed their guests their <u>invaluable</u> art collection.
13. The day was <u>filled with important happenings</u>.
14. Several people fell asleep during the <u>boring</u> speech.
15. Our search for the missing papers was <u>unsuccessful</u>.

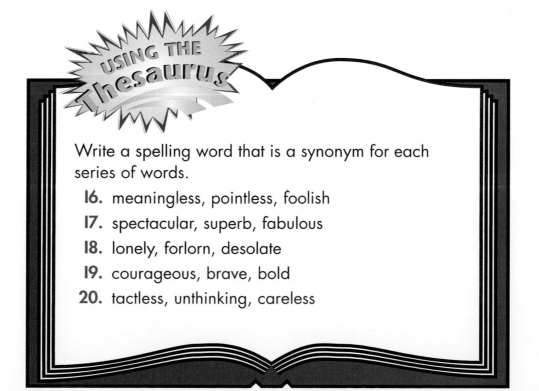

USING THE Thesaurus

Write a spelling word that is a synonym for each series of words.

16. meaningless, pointless, foolish
17. spectacular, superb, fabulous
18. lonely, forlorn, desolate
19. courageous, brave, bold
20. tactless, unthinking, careless

Spelling and Reading

successful	thoughtless	wholesome	wonderful
worthless	worrisome	delightful	lonesome
priceless	fanciful	eventful	fruitless
forgetful	senseless	doubtful	tiresome
tireless	dutiful	fearless	pitiful

Solve the Analogies   Write a spelling word to complete each analogy.

1. **Agreeable** is to **pleasant** as **imaginative** is to _____.
2. **Lively** is to **inactive** as **worthless** is to _____.
3. **Hope** is to **hopeful** as **wonder** is to _____.
4. **Careful** is to **careless** as **fruitful** is to _____.
5. **Generous** is to **greedy** as **certain** is to _____.
6. **Inaccurate** is to **incorrect** as **industrious** is to _____.
7. **Meaningful** is to **meaningless** as **sensible** is to _____.
8. **Awkward** is to **graceful** as **considerate** is to _____.
9. **Lazy** is to **energetic** as **disobedient** is to _____.
10. **Beauty** is to **beautiful** as **delight** is to _____.

Complete the Sentences   Write the spelling word to complete each sentence.

11. I am sorry to say that your broken clock is now _____.
12. Frank Lloyd Wright was a _____ architect.
13. Answering the phone all day was boring and _____.
14. If I were not so _____, I would not have misplaced my lunch.
15. We will keep busy during this very _____ weekend.
16. How _____ our garden looked after the storm.
17. Her illness made for a _____ situation.
18. The lion tamer seemed _____ as he entered the cage.
19. With everyone gone, she spent the _____ evening reading.
20. Everyone benefits from a _____ diet.

Spelling and Writing

Proofread a Paragraph

Six words are not spelled correctly in this paragraph. Write the words correctly.

Hamsters make wonderfull pets. These four-ounce creatures enjoy a diet of such holesome foods as dandelion leaves and fruit. It is doutful that you will find it difficult to care for a hamster. All a hamster needs is a wire cage and an exercise wheel. You might think the small cage would become tirsome, but a hamster finds ways to make each day eventful. As long as you play with your hamster, it will not become lonsome. You will enjoy many deliteful hours with this pocket-sized pet.

Proofreading Marks

≡	Make a capital.
/	Make a small letter.
∧	Add something.
ℓ	Take out something.
⊙	Add a period.
⌗	New paragraph
⒮⒫	Spelling error

Write a Paragraph

Expository Writing

People own pets for many different reasons. Think about a pet you have owned or would like to own. Write a paragraph about this pet.

- Describe the pet and its needs.
- Discuss the best part about owning this pet.
- Follow the form used in the proofreading sample.

Use as many spelling words as you can.

Writing Process

Prewriting

⇩

Drafting

⇩

Revising

⇩

Editing

⇩

Publishing

Proofread Your Writing During → Editing

Proofread your writing for spelling errors as part of the editing stage in the writing process. Be sure to check each word carefully. Use a dictionary to check spelling if you are not sure.

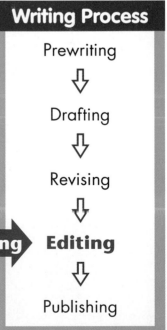

137

Vocabulary

Strategy Words

Review Words: Suffixes -ful, -less, -some

Replace the underlined word or words in this poster with words from the box.

| awful | beauty | delight | handsome | homeless |

Give a Hoot About the Owls

I.–5. Some of these <u>attractive</u> birds, including the spotted owl, are <u>without a home</u>. Help them escape their <u>dreadful</u> situation. They prefer a home in a huge old tree in the evergreen forest of the Pacific Northwest. The <u>loveliness</u> of their surroundings is important to them. They work nights and keep to themselves, so they would be a <u>pleasure</u> to have as neighbors.

Preview Words: Suffixes -ful, -less, -some

Complete each of these sentences with a word from the box.

| distasteful | fearlessness | adventuresome |
| thoughtlessness | | regardless |

6. Max does what he wants, _____ of the rules.

7. He is always seeking adventure. He is _____.

8. Don't you think those green scrambled eggs are _____?

9. His _____ caused us great disappointment.

10. The movie hero's _____ helps him conquer the villain.

Connections

Content Words

Fine Arts: Crafts

Write words from the box to complete the paragraph.

ceramics	kiln	pewter	glaze	pottery

The art of making __1.__ is called __2.__. Porcelain is a very fine clay to which a __3.__ is applied before the object is fired in a __4.__. Porcelain dishes and __5.__ candlesticks can make a simple meal a festive occasion.

Science: Astronomy

Write the word from the box that fits each definition.

astronomy	nebula	constellation	stellar	galaxy

6. a hazy patch of light visible in the sky
7. the science that deals with the universe beyond Earth
8. an easily recognized group of stars that appear close together in the sky, like Ursa Minor
9. a large, self-contained mass of stars, like the Milky Way
10. an adjective that means "having to do with a star"

Apply the Spelling Strategy

Circle the two content words you wrote with the **short a** sound. Underline the two content words you wrote with the **long a** sound.

Spelling and Thinking

READ THE SPELLING WORDS

1.	thunderstorm	*thunderstorm*	The **thunderstorm** was loud.
2.	self-addressed	*self-addressed*	Send a **self-addressed** card.
3.	background	*background*	She stood in the **background**.
4.	cross-country	*cross-country*	We drove **cross-country**.
5.	post office	*post office*	The **post office** sells stamps.
6.	weatherproof	*weatherproof*	My coat is **weatherproof**.
7.	throughout	*throughout*	Listen **throughout** the day.
8.	sister-in-law	*sister-in-law*	Ollie is my **sister-in-law**.
9.	bill of sale	*bill of sale*	Here is your **bill of sale**.
10.	everybody	*everybody*	He told **everybody** the news.
11.	checkbook	*checkbook*	She balanced her **checkbook**.
12.	skyscraper	*skyscraper*	How tall is that **skyscraper**?
13.	overcast	*overcast*	It is **overcast,** not sunny.
14.	all right	*all right*	It is **all right** to call.
15.	passerby	*passerby*	A **passerby** stopped to help.
16.	wristwatch	*wristwatch*	I like my new **wristwatch**.
17.	campsite	*campsite*	The **campsite** is near a river.
18.	campfire	*campfire*	We sat around the **campfire**.
19.	bookstore	*bookstore*	Arno works at a **bookstore**.
20.	grown-up	*grown-up*	Ask a **grown-up** to help.

SORT THE SPELLING WORDS

1.–13. Write the spelling words that are closed compounds (written as a single word).

14.–17. Write the spelling words that are hyphenated compounds.

18.–20. Write the spelling words that are open compounds (made up of two or more words).

REMEMBER THE SPELLING STRATEGY

Remember that a compound word is formed from two or more words that make a new word or group of words, such as **bookstore, all right,** and **grown-up.**

Spelling **and** Vocabulary

Word Meanings

Write a spelling word that could replace the underlined words.

1. A <u>person who walked by</u> helped untangle the dog from its leash.

2. Trees protected the <u>site where we chose to set up camp</u>.

3. I bought a novel at a <u>store that sells books</u>.

4. We went inside during the <u>storm that raged with thunder</u>.

5. <u>The fire at our camp</u> went out during the night.

6. Enclose an envelope that is <u>addressed to yourself</u>.

7. She went shopping with her <u>husband's sister</u>.

8. He checked his <u>clock he wears on his wrist</u>.

9. They planned a trip <u>across the country</u>.

Word Structure

Change the underlined parts of these compound words to write spelling words.

10. back<u>pack</u>   12. <u>out</u>cast   14. bill of <u>fare</u>   16. every<u>one</u>

11. <u>with</u>out   13. <u>sky</u>light   15. <u>fire</u>proof

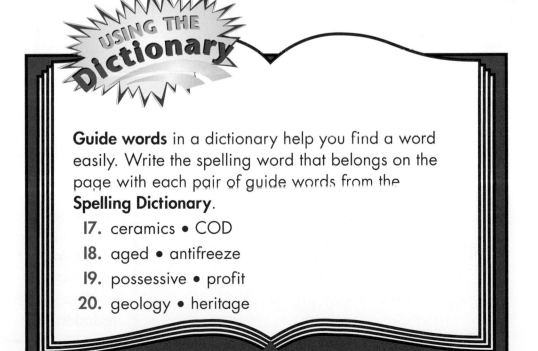

USING THE Dictionary

Guide words in a dictionary help you find a word easily. Write the spelling word that belongs on the page with each pair of guide words from the **Spelling Dictionary**.

17. ceramics • COD

18. aged • antifreeze

19. possessive • profit

20. geology • heritage

Spelling and Reading

thunderstorm	self-addressed	background	cross-country
post office	weatherproof	throughout	sister-in-law
bill of sale	everybody	checkbook	skyscraper
overcast	all right	passerby	wristwatch
campsite	campfire	bookstore	grown-up

Solve the Analogies Write a spelling word to complete each analogy.

1. **Neck** is to **necklace** as **wrist** is to _____.
2. **Recipe** is to **cookbook** as **check** is to _____.
3. **Permanent** is to **unstable** as **clear** is to _____.
4. **Child** is to **young** as **adult** is to _____.
5. **Book** is to **bookstore** as **stamp** is to _____.
6. **None** is to **all** as **no one** is to _____.
7. **Tour** is to **self-guided** as **envelope** is to _____.

Complete the Sentences Write a spelling word to complete each sentence.

8. The _____ stopped to help the man with the flat tire.
9. I hope it will be _____ if we park here.
10. The invention of the elevator made it realistic to build a _____.
11. When my brother got married, his wife became my _____.
12. When we sold our house, we were given a _____.
13. We gathered wood and kindling to build a _____.
14. The lonely dog howled _____ the night.

Complete the Paragraph Write the spelling words from the box to complete the paragraph.

The photographers planned their __15.__ trip well. They bought guidebooks in a __16.__, rented equipment, and arranged to stay at a different __17.__ each night. Their __18.__ clothing would protect them from a __19.__. They planned to photograph animals against the __20.__ of national parks.

campsite
cross-country
weatherproof
background
bookstore
thunderstorm

Spelling and Writing

Proofread a Paragraph

Six words are not spelled correctly in this paragraph. Write the words correctly.

It had rained threwout the night, so when the photographers woke up, the day was over cast. They made sure their campfire was out and headed toward the postoffice. They mailed film back to their studio and enclosed a self addressed envelope to have some prints sent back to their homes. Jim suddenly realized that he did not have his ristwatch. As he searched for it, some people stopped to see if he was alright. Jim found his missing watch in, of all places, his camera case.

Write a Paragraph

Descriptive Writing

Exploring your natural environment can be an adventure. Even a walk in the rain can be fun. Write a paragraph about an outdoor adventure you have had.

- Describe the purpose of your adventure and any preparations you made.
- Relate any problems that you encountered.
- Follow the form used in the proofreading sample.

Use as many spelling words as you can.

Proofread Your Writing During ▶

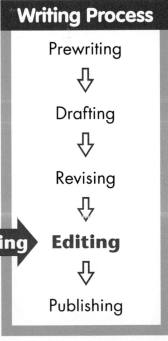

Writing Process

Prewriting
⇩
Drafting
⇩
Revising
⇩
Editing
⇩
Publishing

Proofread your writing for spelling errors as part of the editing stage in the writing process. Be sure to check each word carefully. Use a dictionary to check spelling if you are not sure.

Vocabulary

Strategy Words

Review Words: Compound Words

Write a word from the box to match each clue.

home run	make-believe	peanut butter
sweatshirt	waterproof	

1. a spread that was created by a scientist as a health food
2. the opposite of factual
3. what most baseball batters strive for
4. capable of keeping water from coming through
5. a heavy, long-sleeved jersey worn especially by athletes

Preview Words: Compound Words

Write words from the box to complete the paragraph.

briefcase	classmate	newsstand
well-known	word processing	

As Tai stood at the ___6.___ looking for a magazine on ___7.___, she noticed a man nearby holding a leather ___8.___. Although she had not seen him since high school, Tai recognized her old ___9.___. She knew that he was now a ___10.___ writer of children's books.

Connections

Content Words

Science: Machines

Write the words from the box to complete the paragraph.

automation	machinery	horsepower
mechanize	hydraulic	

Before automatic __1.__ was invented, it would take a farmer weeks to plow several acres. The __2.__ of farm work brought tremendous changes in agriculture. Oxen and horses were replaced by machines with engines whose strength is measured in __3.__. Today's plows use __4.__ power to raise and lower the blades. Efforts are continuing to be made to __5.__ farming techniques.

Science: Light

Write the words from the box that complete the paragraph.

medium	spectrum	reflect	wavelength	refract

Light waves __6.__, or bend, as they pass through mist. Fine raindrops can create the __7.__ through which all the sun's colors can be seen. The water separates the light into a __8.__ of colors. The colors that the sky will __9.__ are different because they each have a different __10.__.

Apply the Spelling Strategy

Circle the two compound content words you wrote.

Assessment Units 19–23

Each Assessment Word in the box fits one of the spelling strategies you have studied over the past five weeks. Read the spelling strategies. Then write each Assessment Word under the unit number it fits.

Unit 19

1.–4. The suffixes -**able** and -**ible** can be added to base words and root words to form new words: **favorable, visible**.

Unit 20

5.–8. The prefixes **ir-, anti-, il-, non-,** and **mis-** can be added to base words to form new words. These new words mean the opposite of the base word.

Unit 21

9.–12. The suffixes -**age** and -**ment** can be added to root words and base words to form new words. These new words are nouns: **courage, equipment**.

Unit 22

13.–16. The suffixes -**ful, -less,** and -**some** can be added to base words to form adjectives such as **wonderful, priceless,** and **worrisome**.

Unit 23

17.–20. A compound word is formed from two or more words that make a new word or group of words, such as **bookstore, all right,** and **grown-up**.

indivisible
attachment
misprint
motionless
contact lens
worn-out
bothersome
ailment
misspell
audible
imaginable
nonverbal
usage
plentiful
birthstone
typewriter
fearful
wreckage
antibody
enjoyable

Review — Unit 19: Suffixes -able, -ible

acceptable	changeable	valuable	responsible	favorable
available	sensible	visible	invisible	flexible

Write the spelling words by adding the missing letters.

1. __ ccept __ ble
2. chang _____ ble
3. r __ sp __ ns __ ble
4. __ avora __ le
5. vis __ __ __ e

6. __ nvisi __ __ __
7. fle __ ib __ __
8. s __ ns __ ble
9. __ vail __ ble
10. val __ __ ble

Review — Unit 20: Prefixes ir-, anti-, il-, non-, mis-

irresistible	illiterate	nonreturnable	misbehave	irregular
antifreeze	illegal	nonfat	mislead	misfortune

Write the spelling words for these clues.

11. might describe something very tempting
12. bad luck
13. unusual or uneven
14. one way is to disobey a teacher
15. deceive
16. It has the suffix **-able**.
17. It means "without fat."
18. It begins with the prefix **anti-**.
19. needing instruction in reading
20. against the law

anti-
non-
il-
mis-

Review | Unit 21: Suffixes -age, -ment

mileage	marriage	equipment	document	garage
development	garbage	excitement	courage	experiment

Write the spelling word that completes the sentence.

1. Our old car has a lot of (mileage, marriage).
2. Ken and Barb's (mileage, marriage) was in June.
3. The lab has expensive computer (courage, equipment).
4. Park the car in the (garbage, garage).
5. There's been an interesting (development, equipment) in the case.
6. The child squealed with (experiment, excitement).
7. It takes (garage, courage) to face your mistakes.
8. Today we'll do a science (experiment, excitement).
9. Take this important (excitement, document) to the office.
10. The cafeteria throws out many cans of (courage, garbage) every day.

Review | Unit 22: Suffixes -ful, -less, -some

successful	pitiful	thoughtless	wholesome	wonderful
doubtful	delightful	fearless	worthless	lonesome

Write the spelling word for each meaning.

11. full of pity
12. full of success
13. healthy
14. full of wonder
15. inconsiderate
16. full of delight
17. full of doubt
18. without fear
19. without worth
20. lonely

all right	self-addressed	everybody	throughout
bookstore	background	campfire	skyscraper
	thunderstorm	grown-up	

The underlined part of each compound word below is also part of a spelling word. Write each spelling word.

1. every<u>one</u>
2. <u>sky</u>writing
3. <u>book</u>end
4. <u>back</u>bone
5. bon<u>fire</u>
6. <u>through</u>way

Write the spelling words for these clues.

7.–8. They have hyphens.
9. It means "satisfactory" or "yes."
10. It involves rain and lightning.

WORD SORT Spelling Study Strategy

Sorting by Prefixes and Suffixes

One good way to practice spelling is to place words into groups according to some spelling pattern. Here is a way to practice some of the words you studied in the past few weeks.

1. Make two columns on a large piece of paper or on the chalkboard.

2. At the top of one column write **Prefixes: ir-, anti-, il-, non-, mis-**. At the top of the other column write **Suffixes: -able, -ible, -age, -ment, -ful, -less, -some**.

3. Have a partner choose a spelling word from Units 19 through 22 and say it aloud.

4. Write the spelling word under the prefix or suffix column.

Grammar, Usage, and Mechanics

Action Verbs and Linking Verb

An action verb shows action. A linking verb does not show action. Instead, it connects the subject of a sentence to one or more words that describe or rename the subject. Common linking verbs include **am, is, are, was, were,** and **will be**. The verbs **become, seem, appear,** and **look** can also be used as linking verbs.

Action Verb: The men **painted** the barn.

Linking Verb: I **am** hungry, but you **seem** thirsty.

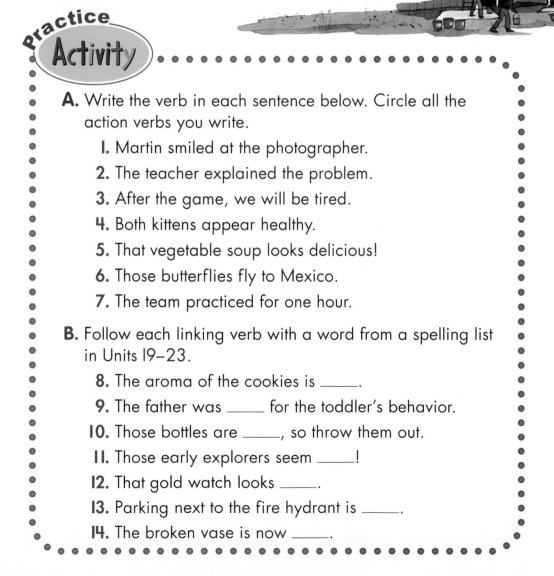

Practice Activity

A. Write the verb in each sentence below. Circle all the action verbs you write.

   1. Martin smiled at the photographer.

   2. The teacher explained the problem.

   3. After the game, we will be tired.

   4. Both kittens appear healthy.

   5. That vegetable soup looks delicious!

   6. Those butterflies fly to Mexico.

   7. The team practiced for one hour.

B. Follow each linking verb with a word from a spelling list in Units 19–23.

   8. The aroma of the cookies is _____.

   9. The father was _____ for the toddler's behavior.

  10. Those bottles are _____, so throw them out.

  11. Those early explorers seem _____!

  12. That gold watch looks _____.

  13. Parking next to the fire hydrant is _____.

  14. The broken vase is now _____.

150

WORKSHOP

Proofreading Strategy

First and Last

Good writers always proofread their work for spelling errors. Here's a strategy you can use to proofread your papers.

Instead of reading in the regular way, look at one sentence at a time. Pay close attention to the first and last word. Make sure that the first word starts with a capital letter. Then make sure that the last word is followed by a punctuation mark.

This way of looking at a paper helps you focus on details, such as capital letters and punctuation, instead of ideas. It may sound funny, but it works. Try it!

Electronic Spelling

Technical Language

Computers have created a whole new language. We often see words like **diskettes** and **icons**.

Much of this technical language is not found by spell checkers, so you need to learn the spelling yourself. You can do this by making a personal dictionary of such words and their meanings. How many of these terms do you know?

byte: a unit of memory on a computer

cache: a type of computer memory

digitize: to put into a form that a computer can read

hypertext: text that is connected to other text

morph: to change from one form to another

FAQ: frequently asked questions

Which of the following are misspelled? Write the misspelled words correctly. Write **OK** if a term is correct.

1. cashe	3. digitize	5. hypertext
2. morf	4. bite	6. FAQ

Spelling and Thinking

READ THE SPELLING WORDS

1.	unfortunate	*unfortunate*	It is **unfortunate** that he is sick.
2.	approximate	*approximate*	What is your **approximate** height?
3.	momentary	*momentary*	The game delay was **momentary**.
4.	imaginary	*imaginary*	The child has an **imaginary** friend.
5.	immediate	*immediate*	She wants an **immediate** response.
6.	temporary	*temporary*	The power outage was **temporary**.
7.	customary	*customary*	It is **customary** to tip a cab driver.
8.	desperate	*desperate*	He was **desperate** to find his dad.
9.	secondary	*secondary*	For her, fun is **secondary** to work.
10.	necessary	*necessary*	It is **necessary** that I leave soon.
11.	accurate	*accurate*	She drew an **accurate** map.
12.	voluntary	*voluntary*	My decision to quit was **voluntary**.
13.	delicate	*delicate*	Be careful with the **delicate** plate.
14.	solitary	*solitary*	One **solitary** car was in the lot.
15.	ultimate	*ultimate*	His **ultimate** goal is to succeed.
16.	moderate	*moderate*	Drive at a **moderate** rate of speed.
17.	ordinary	*ordinary*	My dress is plain and **ordinary**.
18.	honorary	*honorary*	He is an **honorary** club member.
19.	fortunate	*fortunate*	I am **fortunate** to have friends.
20.	desolate	*desolate*	The street was dark and **desolate**.

SORT THE SPELLING WORDS

1.–10. Write the spelling words with the **-ate** suffix. Circle the words with a double consonant in their spelling.

11.–20. Write the spelling words with the **-ary** suffix. Circle the words in which the suffix has been added to a base word.

REMEMBER THE SPELLING STRATEGY

Remember that the suffixes **-ate** and **-ary** can be added to root words and base words to form adjectives such as **delicate** and **honorary**.

Spelling ᴬⁿᵈ Vocabulary

Word Replacement

Write spelling words to replace the underlined words.

1. She made a <u>frantic</u> attempt to score a goal in the final moments of the game.
2. Your decision to join the club should be <u>by choice</u>.
3. The <u>final</u> cost of the job is one hundred dollars.
4. His degree from the university is <u>a token of honor</u>.
5. It was a <u>favorable</u> day when we moved here.
6. It is <u>traditional</u> to take off your hat at the door.

Synonyms and Antonyms

Write the spelling words that are synonyms or antonyms for these words.

Synonyms

7. uninhabited
8. required
9. brief; taking only a moment
10. without delay
11. correct

Antonyms

12. excessive
13. exact
14. tough
15. permanent
16. lucky

USING THE Dictionary

Write the spelling words for these respellings.

17. /ôr′ dn ĕr′ē/
18. /sĕk′ ən dĕr′ē/
19. /sŏl′ ĭ tĕr′ē/
20. /ĭ măj′ ə nĕr′ē/

In the words you wrote:

- Circle the syllable with the primary stress, shown in boldface and followed by an accent mark.
- Underline the syllable with the secondary stress, shown in regular type and followed by an accent mark.

Spelling and Reading

unfortunate	approximate	momentary	imaginary
immediate	temporary	customary	desperate
secondary	necessary	accurate	voluntary
delicate	solitary	ultimate	moderate
ordinary	honorary	fortunate	desolate

Solve the Analogies Write a spelling word to complete each analogy.

1. **First** is to **second** as **primary** is to _____.
2. **Reckless** is to **careless** as **fragile** is to _____.
3. **Loyal** is to **faithful** as **single** is to _____.
4. **Tragic** is to **comic** as **forced** is to _____.
5. **Definite** is to **vague** as **exact** is to _____.
6. **Difficult** is to **troublesome** as **common** is to _____.
7. **Caution** is to **cautionary** as **moment** is to _____.

Complete the Sentences Write a spelling word to complete each sentence.

8. It was _____ that you could not see the wonderful play.
9. The politician was given an _____ position on the board.
10. It is _____ in Chan's home to eat with chopsticks.
11. The landscape was _____ after the tornado swept through.
12. Every detail of the plan must be _____ before I begin to build.
13. Her _____ approach to the crisis kept everyone calm.
14. The survivors of the hurricane were _____ for food and water.

Complete the Paragraph Write spelling words from the box to complete the paragraph.

Ice skaters were __15.__ in 1817 when Joseph Merlin, a Belgian, dreamed up skates that could move on dry land. To make his __16.__ skates into real ones, it was __17.__ to replace ice-skate blades with wheels. Merlin's roller skates became an __18.__ success and not just a __19.__ fad. Roller-skating became the __20.__ summer sport for ice skaters.

> necessary
> ultimate
> immediate
> temporary
> fortunate
> imaginary

Spelling and Writing

Proofread a Paragraph

Six words are not spelled correctly in this paragraph.
Write the words correctly.

Until the early 1900s, the customery method of travel was a horse-drawn buggy. Then Henry Ford began to manufacture the ultamate driving machine, a car called the Model T. Its low price made it affordable to the ordinary wage earner. The aproximate cost in 1924 was $290. There were problems, however. Lack of driving experience and poor roads led to unfortunite accidents, even when the drivers were traveling at a modorate rate of speed. Still, people soon began to believe that owning a car was absolutely neccesary.

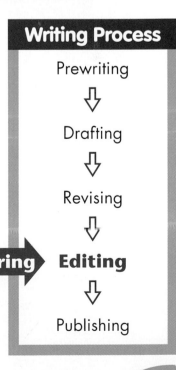

Proofreading Marks

≡	Make a capital.
/	Make a small letter.
∧	Add something.
ℓ	Take out something.
⊙	Add a period.
#	New paragraph
SP	Spelling error

Write a Paragraph

Expository Writing

Many inventions change life as we know it. Write about a real invention or use your imagination to create an invention.

- Describe how this invention changed or could change people's lives.
- Did people accept the invention immediately?
- Were there any problems with the invention?
- Follow the form used in the proofreading sample.

Use as many spelling words as you can.

Proofread Your Writing During ▶

Writing Process

Prewriting
⬇
Drafting
⬇
Revising
⬇
Editing
⬇
Publishing

Proofread your writing for spelling errors as part of the editing stage in the writing process. Be sure to check each word carefully. Use a dictionary to check spelling if you are not sure.

Vocabulary

Strategy Words

Review Words: Suffixes -ate, -ary

Write words from the box to complete this news article.

circulate	cooperate	legislate	operate	populate

Conservationists are working hard to persuade Congress to __1.__ with their efforts to save the fish in southern waters. They are urging their representatives to __2.__ restrictions for oil and gas companies that __3.__ offshore drilling equipment. It also may be necessary to __4.__ the waters with more shrimp and fish. The conservationists will soon begin to __5.__ a flier promoting their efforts.

Preview Words: Suffixes -ate, -ary

Write a word from the box to complete each sentence.

anniversary	contemplate	frustrate
	initiate	precautionary

6. It was the first _____ of the opening of their bookstore.

7. The difficult homework assignment seemed to _____ him.

8. Before the storm, she gathered supplies as a _____ measure.

9. I need to _____ your request before I respond.

10. We will soon _____ a different way of resolving disagreements.

Connections

Content Words

Language Arts: The Media

Write a word from the box to complete each sentence.

broadcast	journalist	columnist	literate	expert

1. If you can read and write, you are ___1.___.
2. If you write and publish the news, you are a ___2.___.
3. If you are knowledgeable about a certain subject, you are an ___3.___.
4. If you write a magazine column, you are a ___4.___.
5. The transmission of a television program is a ___5.___.

Social Studies: Cultures

Write each scrambled word from the box correctly.

heritage	taboo	kinsman	tribe	mores

6. A male relative is a <u>maskinn</u>.
7. When several villages share a common ancestry, language, culture, and name, the result is a <u>brite</u>.
8. The customs accepted by a particular social group are considered this group's <u>romes</u>.
9. When a society forbids the use or even the mention of something, that subject or object is <u>tooba</u>.
10. Our <u>gearithe</u> is passed on through the generations.

Apply the Spelling Strategy

Circle the suffix **-ate** in one of the content words you wrote.

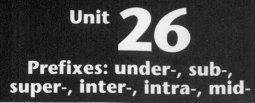

Spelling and Thinking

READ THE SPELLING WORDS

1.	underground	*underground*	A mole lives **underground**.
2.	interchange	*interchange*	It was an **interchange** of ideas.
3.	intramural	*intramural*	He plays **intramural** soccer.
4.	submarine	*submarine*	The **submarine** is underwater.
5.	underneath	*underneath*	Dust is **underneath** the bed.
6.	midsummer	*midsummer*	Our picnic is in **midsummer**.
7.	interstate	*interstate*	Is this an **interstate** highway?
8.	supersonic	*supersonic*	He pilots a **supersonic** aircraft.
9.	undercover	*undercover*	She is an **undercover** officer.
10.	intrastate	*intrastate*	Our **intrastate** taxes rose.
11.	interact	*interact*	Some toddlers **interact** well.
12.	midway	*midway*	We plan to meet **midway**.
13.	underpass	*underpass*	A car stalled in the **underpass**.
14.	superstar	*superstar*	He is a baseball **superstar**.
15.	subway	*subway*	Did you travel by **subway**?
16.	intersect	*intersect*	Those two streets **intersect**.
17.	supervise	*supervise*	She will **supervise** the project.
18.	interface	*interface*	Will all the software **interface**?
19.	subtotal	*subtotal*	Add tax to the bill's **subtotal**.
20.	interview	*interview*	A reporter will **interview** you.

SORT THE SPELLING WORDS

Write the word with the prefix that means:
- 1.–2. "middle."
- 3.–9. "under" or "beneath."
- 10.–12. "above."
- 13.–18. "between."
- 19.–20. "within."

REMEMBER THE SPELLING STRATEGY

Remember that the prefix **mid-** means "middle," **under-** and **sub-** mean "under" or "beneath," **super-** means "above," **inter-** means "between," and **intra-** means "within."

Spelling and Vocabulary

Word Meanings

Write the spelling word that could best replace each underlined word or phrase.

1. The puppies did not <u>cooperate</u> well with each other.
2. The heat in <u>the middle of the summer</u> can be unbearable.
3. Parts of an electrical system must <u>connect at a common point</u> smoothly.
4. We are supposed to meet them where the two roads <u>cross</u>.
5. The mutual <u>exchange</u> of ideas at the meeting helped us all.
6. He asked us to <u>oversee</u> the building project.
7. Add the tip to the <u>partial total</u> of our dinner check.

Word Clues

Write the spelling words that match these definitions.

8. middle distance
9. below ground
10. beneath cover
11. below sea
12. above the speed of sound
13. road beneath a railroad
14. train beneath the ground
15. between one state and another

USING THE Dictionary

16.–20. Knowing how to alphabetize easily will help you find words in a dictionary. When words have the same first letter, use the second letter. If the first two letters are the same, continue looking until you find the first letters that are different before you arrange the words in alphabetical order. Write these spelling words in alphabetical order.

superstar   interview   intramural
underneath   intrastate

Spelling and Reading

underground	interchange	intramural	submarine
underneath	midsummer	interstate	supersonic
undercover	intrastate	interact	midway
underpass	superstar	subway	intersect
supervise	interface	subtotal	interview

Solve the Analogies   Write a word to complete each analogy.

1. **Alert** is to **attentive** as **secret** is to _____.
2. **Over** is to **above** as **below** is to _____.
3. **Author** is to **writer** as **celebrity** is to _____.
4. **Bridge** is to **tunnel** as **overpass** is to _____.
5. **Above** is to **ocean liner** as **below** is to _____.

Complete the Sentences   Write a spelling word that completes each sentence.

6. The rates for both out-of-state and _____ calls will rise.
7. I must get these two software programs to _____.
8. There is a disabled car where the roads _____.
9. The first _____ flight occurred in 1947.
10. He is organizing an _____ basketball league after school.
11. The senator answered many questions during the _____.
12. Because he was low on cash, he asked the cashier for a _____ before she rang up all of his groceries.
13. One _____ highway extends from California to Florida.
14. You can _____ the parts of these two machines.

Complete the Paragraph   Write spelling words from the box to complete the paragraph.

Work is going forward on the city's new __15.__. The __16.__ heat made the work difficult for those working in small __17.__ spaces. "Thanks to your hard work," the foreman told his workers, "we are at the __18.__ point in the project. You have shown that you can __19.__ well together. It is a pleasure to __20.__ you."

midsummer
midway
interact
underground
supervise
subway

Spelling and Writing

Proofread a Paragraph

Six words are not spelled correctly in this paragraph. Write the words correctly.

Proofreading Marks

≡ Make a capital.
/ Make a small letter.
∧ Add something.
℘ Take out something.
⊙ Add a period.
⌗ New paragraph
(SP) Spelling error

Roads allow people in different communities to intteract. Yesterday's dirt roads are today's multilane highways. The large volume of traffic has made it necessary to construct expressways undergrownd. It is not unusual to see an intersteate highway underneeth a building or park. To avoid traffic hazards at points where roads intercect, an underpass is often constructed. In addition, signs clearly mark an intirchange, avoiding confusion and accidents.

Write a Paragraph

Expository Writing

Public participation is important in planning a highway construction project. Write a paragraph about the construction of a road, a commercial building, or a new home in your community.

- How did the construction affect life in your community?
- Was there opposition to the project?
- Follow the form used in the proofreading sample.

Use as many spelling words as you can.

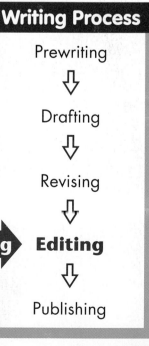

Writing Process

Prewriting
⇩
Drafting
⇩
Revising
⇩
Editing
⇩
Publishing

Proofread Your Writing During ➤

Proofread your writing for spelling errors as part of the editing stage in the writing process. Be sure to check each word carefully. Use a dictionary to check spelling if you are not sure.

Vocabulary

Unit 26 enrichment

Strategy Words

Review Words: Prefixes

Write words from the box to complete the paragraph.

midnight underline subhead internal midafternoon

The reporter had asked for a two-hour extension on his 10 p.m. deadline. His article on __1.__ politics was now due at __2.__. It was already __3.__, and he had not even stopped for lunch. Thus far he had written an introduction and a __4.__, which he decided to __5.__ for emphasis. It was going to be a long day.

Preview Words: Prefixes

Write the word from the box that could best replace the underlined word or words.

intermission midpoint subterranean superficial underestimate

6. The play will have a ten-minute <u>break</u>.
7. Fortunately, she sustained only <u>surface</u> cuts in the accident.
8. Do not <u>undervalue</u> his potential as a hard worker.
9. The bus stops for a break near the <u>halfway mark</u> of the trip.
10. A long <u>underground</u> passage led from one castle to another.

Connections

Content Words

Language Arts: Sentences

Write a word from the box to identify each sentence or phrase.

declarative	imperative	interrogative
fragment	exclamatory	

1. Proper manners are easy to learn.
2. Watch out for that car!
3. The bright blue sky
4. Why is your dog chewing the TV remote?
5. Call home by six o'clock.

Social Studies: Maps

Write words from the box to complete the paragraph.

boundary	local	real estate	settlement	subdivide

The neighbors had been feuding for years. A __6.__ broker was encouraging them to sell their land to a developer, who would __7.__ it and build several homes. But the neighbors disagreed over the __8.__ between their two parcels of land. Finally, they hired a __9.__ attorney whom they all knew from neighborhood get-togethers. A __10.__ was reached that was agreeable to all parties.

Apply the Spelling Strategy

One of the content words you wrote has a prefix that indicates position. Circle that word.

Spelling and Thinking

READ THE SPELLING WORDS

1. mountainous	*mountainous*	The terrain was **mountainous**.
2. tremendous	*tremendous*	She has a **tremendous** workload.
3. courageous	*courageous*	What a **courageous** girl she is!
4. industrious	*industrious*	Ants are **industrious** creatures.
5. continuous	*continuous*	A **continuous** rain caused floods.
6. gorgeous	*gorgeous*	The view from here is **gorgeous**.
7. wondrous	*wondrous*	Sunsets at sea are **wondrous**!
8. nutritious	*nutritious*	Eat a **nutritious** breakfast daily.
9. cautious	*cautious*	Be **cautious** on the icy roads.
10. precious	*precious*	Rubies are **precious** gems.
11. fabulous	*fabulous*	He accumulated **fabulous** wealth.
12. jealous	*jealous*	The dog is **jealous** of the baby.
13. glorious	*glorious*	We spent a **glorious** day at sea.
14. obvious	*obvious*	His embarrassment was **obvious**.
15. tedious	*tedious*	The **tedious** chores tired me out.
16. curious	*curious*	Ask questions if you are **curious**.
17. nervous	*nervous*	I get **nervous** in front of a crowd.
18. furious	*furious*	He gets **furious** when we are late.
19. studious	*studious*	The **studious** girl got good grades.
20. various	*various*	We sell **various** types of boots.

SORT THE SPELLING WORDS

1.–2. Write the spelling words in which the spelling of the base word does not change when **-ous** is added.

Write the other spelling words in which

3.–13. **-ous** was added to a base word whose spelling changed.

14.–20. **-ous** was added to a root word.

REMEMBER THE SPELLING STRATEGY

Remember that the suffix **-ous** can be added to base words or root words to form adjectives such as **mountainous, nervous,** and **obvious**.

Spelling and Vocabulary

Word Meanings

Write the spelling word that could best replace each underlined word.

1. One <u>unbroken</u> chalk line marked mid-field.
2. Even the steam shovel seemed to struggle as it moved the <u>enormous</u> boulder.
3. The answer was <u>clear</u> to all of us.
4. She is getting <u>anxious</u> about giving her speech.
5. I am <u>envious</u> of people who finish their homework early.
6. I am <u>interested</u> to know how you made those pancakes.

Word Clues

Write the spelling word that matches each clue.

7. of high elevation
8. full of intense anger
9. full of diligence
10. devoted to study
11. full of bravery
12. full of glory
13. of diverse kinds
14. full of wonder
15. full of nutrition

USING THE Dictionary

English has borrowed many words from other languages. Write the spelling words that match these word histories.

16. from Latin **cautio,** meaning "taking care"
17. from Latin **taedium,** meaning "weariness"
18. from Latin **pretium,** meaning "price"
19. from Middle English **gorgayse,** meaning "elegant"
20. from Latin **fabula,** meaning "fable"

165

Spelling and Reading

mountainous	tremendous	courageous	industrious
continuous	gorgeous	wondrous	nutritious
cautious	precious	fabulous	jealous
glorious	obvious	tedious	curious
nervous	furious	studious	various

Solve the Analogies   Write a spelling word to complete each analogy.

1. **Simple** is to **elaborate** as **unattractive** is to _____.
2. **Indifferent** is to **enthusiastic** as **lazy** is to _____.
3. **Miserable** is to **wretched** as **wholesome** is to _____.
4. **Virtue** is to **virtuous** as **glory** is to _____.
5. **Grace** is to **gracious** as **wonder** is to _____.
6. **Miniature** is to **tiny** as **valuable** is to _____.

Complete the Sentences   Write the spelling word that completes each sentence.

7. A _____ line of cars stretched as far as the eye could see.
8. He was _____ at me for forgetting to pick him up on time.
9. She does not study on weekends, yet she is very _____.
10. I enjoy _____ types of movies, but I prefer action films.
11. I am _____ to know where you bought that heavy sweater.
12. Sherman is _____ when we pay attention to another dog.
13. Near the sea the land was flat, but inland it was _____.

Complete the Paragraph   Write spelling words from the box to complete the paragraph.

Most ski resorts rely on the __14.__ efforts of their brave ski patrol to keep skiers safe. Ski patrol members are trained to be __15.__ when moving injured skiers. They are a __16.__ help to __17.__ skiers who need encouragement. Ski patrol members show an __18.__ enthusiasm for their job. They say that their job never becomes __19.__, and they tell some __20.__ tales of daring rescue missions.

nervous
cautious
courageous
tedious
tremendous
fabulous
obvious

Spelling and Writing

Proofread a Paragraph

Six words are not spelled correctly in this paragraph. Write the words correctly.

An obvius alternative to downhill skiing is cross-country, or Nordic, skiing. Unlike downhill skiing, this sport does not require mountainous terrain. Instead, the skier hikes over snow-covered ground that is flat or slightly hilly. A Nordic skier should be sure to eat a nutricious breakfast, because this sport demands tramendous physical endurance. Some downhill skiers find this skiing tedeous, but enthusiastic Nordic skiers enjoy the georgeous views as they glide comfortably along the varyous trails.

Proofreading Marks

☰	Make a capital.
/	Make a small letter.
∧	Add something.
ℓ	Take out something.
⊙	Add a period.
⌗	New paragraph
(SP)	Spelling error

Write a Paragraph

Persuasive Writing

Today there are many outdoor activities for people of all ages and abilities. Write a paragraph to persuade others that your favorite outdoor sport is the best.

- Describe the equipment needed.
- Write about the challenges and rewards of this sport.
- Follow the form used in the proofreading sample.

Use as many spelling words as you can.

Writing Process

Prewriting
⇩
Drafting
⇩
Revising
⇩
Editing
⇩
Publishing

Proofread Your Writing During ➤ **Editing**

Proofread your writing for spelling errors as part of the editing stage in the writing process. Be sure to check each word carefully. Use a dictionary to check spelling if you are not sure.

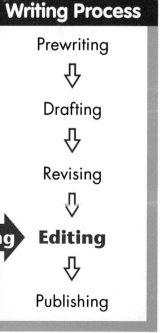

Vocabulary

Strategy Words

Review Words: Suffix -ous

1.–5. Write words from the box that could replace the underlined words in this book review.

dangerous	generous	humorous	joyous	mysterious

The Incredible Cat Tale describes the <u>funny</u> adventures of two sisters who smuggle a cat named Simon into their parents' apartment, where pets are restricted. The girls' escapades are more silly than they are <u>risky</u>. The landlord discovers Simon but, in a <u>charitable</u> mood, allows the girls to keep their cat. In fact, he is even responsible for the <u>puzzling</u> appearance of another cat who keeps Simon company. This book will make you feel <u>happy</u>.

Preview Words: Suffix -ous

Write the adjective from the box that best completes each description.

ambitious	copious	spacious	superfluous	vivacious

6. Eli's goal is to become a famous doctor. Eli is _____.

7. Lucy is lively and very animated. Lucy is _____.

8. The rooms in the old house were large, and the ceilings were high. The house was _____.

9. He has many art books. Another one will be _____.

10. The secretary recorded every word that was said during the meeting. She took _____ notes.

Connections

Content Words

Science: Geology

Write the words from the box that will complete the sentences.

avalanche	sediment	debris	shale	delta

1.–2. After an _____, there is a lot of _____ to clean up.

3.–4. At the _____ of a river, _____ collects.

5. A rock composed of fine-grained sediments is _____.

Social Studies: The Desert

Write words from the box to complete the paragraph.

caravan	sultan	oasis	traveler	turban

In days gone by, a __6.__ from Persia sent a small __7.__ of nomads in search of a new, temporary home. Loading their belongings onto their camels, they set off. Each __8.__ wore a __9.__ for protection from the desert's scorching sun. By midday, they had settled at a fertile __10.__, where they found a welcoming water supply. Caravans continue even today.

Apply the Spelling Strategy

A word inventor made up two words: **middeltaous** and **antiturbaneous**. Circle their base words in two of the content words you wrote.

Spelling and Thinking

READ THE SPELLING WORDS

1.	restaurant	*restaurant*	He dined at a fine **restaurant**.
2.	appreciate	*appreciate*	I **appreciate** your help with the chores.
3.	probably	*probably*	We will **probably** be home by noon.
4.	different	*different*	Each room had **different** wallpaper.
5.	bargain	*bargain*	Those shoes are a **bargain** at that price.
6.	victory	*victory*	The team celebrated after the **victory**.
7.	bureau	*bureau*	The top drawer in my **bureau** is stuck.
8.	surely	*surely*	I thought that **surely** he would be here.
9.	perspire	*perspire*	I am beginning to **perspire** in this heat.
10.	rhythm	*rhythm*	We enjoyed the **rhythm** of the music.
11.	sauce	*sauce*	She makes a special **sauce** for pasta.
12.	jewelry	*jewelry*	I bought a watch at the **jewelry** store.
13.	captain	*captain*	Team members chose a new **captain**.
14.	pigeon	*pigeon*	A **pigeon** flew over to the park bench.
15.	athlete	*athlete*	The talented **athlete** plays four sports.
16.	amateur	*amateur*	The **amateur** artist shows great talent.
17.	license	*license*	She just received her driver's **license**.
18.	muscle	*muscle*	The tennis player pulled a leg **muscle**.
19.	villain	*villain*	The **villain** stole the money and ran.
20.	similar	*similar*	We have **similar** taste in clothes.

SORT THE SPELLING WORDS

1. Write the spelling word that has one syllable.

2.–12. Write the spelling words that have two syllables. Draw a line between the syllables.

13.–20. Write the spelling words that have three or more syllables. Draw a line between the syllables.

REMEMBER THE SPELLING STRATEGY

Remember that it is important to learn the spellings of words that writers often misspell.

Word Meanings

Write a spelling word to complete each sequence.

1. nonprofessional, hobbyist, _____
2. undoubtedly, certainly, _____
3. triumph, success, _____
4. agreement, deal, _____
5. scoundrel, wicked person, _____
6. movement, beat, _____

Word Replacement

Write the spelling word that could best replace the underlined word or words.

7. I am thankful for your efforts in organizing the party.
8. We will likely go to a lake for our vacation.
9. It is so hot in here, I am beginning to sweat.
10. Our tastes in music are not alike.
11. She went to the passport office to fill out a form.
12. He got his driver's document of permission last week.
13. The women's dresses were nearly alike.

USING THE Dictionary

Words are often misspelled because the pronunciation differs from the spelling. Write the spelling words that match these dictionary respellings.

14. /sôs/
15. /rĕs' tər ənt/
16. /pĭj' ən/
17. /jo͞o' əl rē/
18. /ăth' lēt'/
19. /kăp' tən/
20. /mŭs' əl/

Spelling and Reading

restaurant	appreciate	probably	different
bargain	victory	bureau	surely
perspire	rhythm	sauce	jewelry
captain	pigeon	athlete	amateur
license	muscle	villain	similar

Solve the Analogies   Write a spelling word to complete each analogy.

1. **Carefully** is to **cautiously** as **definitely** is to _____.
2. **Flour** is to **bread** as **tomato** is to _____.
3. **Fish** is to **trout** as **bird** is to _____.
4. **Movie** is to **theater** as **meal** is to _____.
5. **Airplane** is to **pilot** as **ship** is to _____.
6. **Hammer** is to **tool** as **necklace** is to _____.
7. **Markdown** is to **discount** as **sale** is to _____.

Complete the Sentences   Write the spelling word that completes each sentence.

8. She carefully folded her sweaters and put them in the _____.
9. The story ends when the nasty _____ surrenders to the hero.
10. All this exercise is making me _____.
11. The game ended in a _____ for our team.
12. The two windows are not identical in size, but they are _____.
13. Although he is an _____, he is a very good golfer.
14. The police officer asked to see her driver's _____.

Complete the Paragraph   Write spelling words from the box to complete the paragraph.

> muscle
> appreciate
> probably
> rhythm
> different
> athlete

   If you have ever seen gymnasts perform, then you __15.__ can __16.__ what a beautiful sport gymnastics is to watch. One particularly artful form of gymnastics is a routine that an __17.__ performs to the __18.__ of music. Rhythmic gymnasts perform with __19.__ pieces of equipment, such as hoops, ribbons, and jump ropes. Over time, gymnasts develop __20.__ strength, a sense of balance, and flexibility.

Spelling and Writing

Proofread a Paragraph

Six words are not spelled correctly in this paragraph about gymnastics. Write the words correctly.

Gymnastics dates back to 2000 B.C., when an Egyptian athalete used his body to perform balancing stunts. Although today's events are probly simalar to those of ancient Egypt, the sport has expanded. There are many diffrent events for amature and professional gymnasts. When a gymnast's hands or feet perspire, chalk helps keep them dry. Each muscel in the legs, arms, and stomach is used in performing.

Proofreading Marks

≡ Make a capital.

/ Make a small letter.

∧ Add something.

℮ Take out something.

⊙ Add a period.

⌗ New paragraph

SP Spelling error

Write a Paragraph

Expository Writing

Expository writing is informative and based on facts. Most newspaper articles use expository writing. Write a paragraph about a sports-related topic.

- Explain how a sport is played or performed.
- Another option is to describe the details of a sports event.
- Follow the form used in the proofreading sample.

Use as many spelling words as you can.

Proofread Your Writing During ➤

Proofread your writing for spelling errors as part of the editing stage in the writing process. Be sure to check each word carefully. Use a dictionary to check spelling if you are not sure.

Writing Process

Prewriting

⇩

Drafting

⇩

Revising

⇩

Editing

⇩

Publishing

Vocabulary

Strategy Words

Review Words: Words Writers Use

Write the word from the box that best completes each sentence.

business	career	delicious	polite	remember

1. She has started her own computer _____.
2. It is _____ to give up your bus seat to a senior citizen.
3. She prepared a _____ meal of meatballs and spaghetti.
4. He retired from a thirty-year _____ as an electrician.
5. I will always _____ the day I learned how to ride a bike.

Preview Words: Words Writers Use

Write words from the box to complete this sign posted in a storefront window.

cafeteria	potatoes	privilege	sufficient	schedule

Annie's Place

It is our __6.__ to announce the opening of our new __7.__ on the first day of May. The __8.__ of hours will be posted soon. Annie's Place will feature home-cooked dishes, such as roast chicken and mashed __9.__ . Our menu choices will be __10.__ for every appetite!

Connections

Language Arts: Research

Which reference book would you use to answer each of the following questions? Write a word from the box.

> encyclopedia guidebook thesaurus almanac atlas

1. What is the history of the Olympic games?
2. Which country won the most medals in the Olympics?
3. Where can you find a map of Finland?
4. What is a synonym for **athletic**?
5. Where do you find out about sights to see in Tokyo?

Science: Computers

Write words from the box to complete the paragraph.

> floppy disk printer diskette terminal hardware

In some businesses, several people share a single computer system by means of a piece of __6.__ called a __7.__. Users store their files on a __8.__, or __9.__. When they finish preparing a document, they signal the __10.__ to print the information on paper.

Apply the Spelling Strategy

Circle the following three content words you wrote: the one with the **y** pronounced **long i,** the one with the double consonant in the second syllable, and the one with the /ô/ sound spelled **au.**

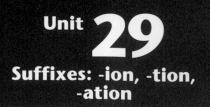

Spelling and Thinking

READ THE SPELLING WORDS

1.	consideration	*consideration*	I appreciate your **consideration**.
2.	introduction	*introduction*	The book's **introduction** was brief.
3.	satisfaction	*satisfaction*	My work gives me **satisfaction**.
4.	permission	*permission*	I have **permission** to leave early.
5.	completion	*completion*	He carried his plan to **completion**.
6.	information	*information*	We will mail you the **information**.
7.	expression	*expression*	His **expression** was sad and lonely.
8.	population	*population*	Our city has a growing **population**.
9.	discussion	*discussion*	We had a lively class **discussion**.
10.	suggestion	*suggestion*	Your **suggestion** was excellent.
11.	decision	*decision*	It was his **decision** to stay home.
12.	action	*action*	The firefighter sprang into **action**.
13.	position	*position*	Get into a comfortable **position**.
14.	location	*location*	The store moved to a new **location**.
15.	direction	*direction*	He is going in the wrong **direction**.
16.	tension	*tension*	I sense **tension** between the rivals.
17.	attention	*attention*	Pay **attention** to the instructions.
18.	operation	*operation*	He needs an **operation** on his foot.
19.	condition	*condition*	My old car is in great **condition**.
20.	invention	*invention*	Describe your latest **invention**.

SORT THE SPELLING WORDS

1.–8. Write the words that add **-ion** or **-ation** to a base word.

9.–18. Write the words in which the spelling of the base word changes before the suffix **-ion** or **-tion** is added.

19.–20. Write the words that are not formed from base words.

REMEMBER THE SPELLING STRATEGY

Remember that the suffixes **-ion, -tion,** and **-ation** can be added to a base word or root to form a noun, such as **action, introduction,** and **information.**

176

Spelling and Vocabulary

Word Replacement

Write spelling words that best replace the underlined words.

1. The windsurfer is a recent <u>creation</u>.
2. It is important to keep your windsurfer in good <u>shape</u>.
3. Be sure to get accurate weather <u>data</u>.
4. Your hand and body <u>stance</u> on the windsurfer is important.
5. Check the <u>path</u> of the wind.
6. Pay <u>heed</u> to safety rules for water sports.
7. The <u>beginning</u> of windsurfing added a new sport for surfers.
8. It takes practice to master the <u>working</u> of a windsurfer.

Word Structure

When the suffix **-ion** is added to a verb root or base word, a noun is formed. Follow the directions and write the spelling words.

9. locate – e + ion = _____
10. populate – e + ion = _____
11. permit – t + ss + ion = _____
12. express + ion = _____
13. tense – e + ion = _____
14. discuss + ion = _____

USING THE Dictionary

A dictionary often provides other forms of an entry word. By changing prefixes and suffixes, several words can be formed from one stem. Add and subtract prefixes and suffixes to the words below to write spelling words.

15. inactivity
16. indecisive
17. suggestible
18. inconsiderate
19. incomplete
20. unsatisfactory

Spelling and Reading

consideration	introduction	satisfaction	permission
completion	information	expression	population
discussion	suggestion	decision	action
position	location	direction	tension
attention	operation	condition	invention

Solve the Analogies Write a spelling word to complete each analogy.

1. **Approval** is to **acceptance** as **thoughtfulness** is to _____.
2. **Builder** is to **construction** as **surgeon** is to _____.
3. **Digest** is to **digestion** as **invent** is to _____.
4. **Narrate** is to **narration** as **complete** is to _____.
5. **Receive** is to **gift** as **obtain** is to _____.

Complete the Sentences Write a spelling word to complete each sentence.

6. He had a relieved _____ on his face.
7. Look on the map for the exact _____ of Hill Road.
8. I will go to the picnic on the _____ that you will come, too.
9. There was _____ between the friends after their argument.
10. She asked the librarian for _____ on tornadoes.
11. China has the highest _____ of any other country.
12. The movie is full of adventure and _____.
13. We must devote more _____ to our new puppy.

Complete the Paragraph Write spelling words from the box to complete the paragraph.

Lee Kravitz, a surfboarding instructor, gives a basic ___14.___ to surfing while beginner students are still on shore. First, he holds a ___15.___ about surfing safety. Then he gives a ___16.___ about selecting a surfboard. This lesson includes learning the correct foot ___17.___ for standing and balancing. The ___18.___ to ride a wave is up to the surfer. There is great ___19.___ in catching a wave in the right ___20.___ and riding all the way to shore.

satisfaction
introduction
decision
direction
suggestion
discussion
position

Spelling and Writing

Proofread an Advertisement

Six words are not spelled correctly in this advertisement. Write the words correctly.

BLAKE'S

If you are in the market for a mountain bike, give concideration to buying one of Blake's Bikes. You will appreciate its easy oporation. Come in and have a discushion with one of our specialists, who will help you with your desision about the best model for you. We guarantee your satisfactshun. We will even provide you with an introduction to biking safety. Our mountain bike will take you where you want to go under any condishion.

Proofreading Marks

≡ Make a capital.

/ Make a small letter.

∧ Add something.

℮ Take out something.

⊙ Add a period.

⌗ New paragraph

ⓢⓟ Spelling error

Write an Advertisement

Persuasive Writing

Advertising uses special techniques to try to persuade you to buy something. Some ads use endorsements from famous people. Write a magazine advertisement for a sports product.

- Explain why your product is superior to others.
- What special qualities does it have?
- Follow the form used in the proofreading sample.

Use as many spelling words as you can.

Proofread Your Writing During ➤

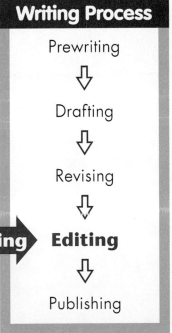

Writing Process

Prewriting

⬇

Drafting

⬇

Revising

⬇

Editing

⬇

Publishing

Proofread your writing for spelling errors as part of the editing stage in the writing process. Be sure to check each word carefully. Use a dictionary to check spelling if you are not sure.

Vocabulary

Strategy Words

Review Words: Suffixes -ion, -tion, -ation

Write a word from the box to complete each sentence.

companion	composition	fiction	mention	onion

1. Although the book is _____, it is based on a true story.
2. Peeling an _____ always makes me cry.
3. My little sister has an imaginary _____.
4. Our teacher asked us to write a _____ about a heroic person in our family.
5. Please _____ my name if you call the plumber.

Preview Words: Suffixes -ion, -tion, -ation

Write words from the box to complete this review for a television show.

compassion	condensation	hesitation
omission	recognition	

Do not miss tonight's one-hour __6.__ of the key events of the most recent summer Olympics. The events are told with __7.__ and humor. The producer gives proper __8.__ to those athletes who did not win a medal but revealed their talents in other ways. The only flaw that I noticed was the __9.__ of coverage of the diving event, which I always enjoy. In spite of this, I would recommend this show without __10.__.

Connections

Language Arts: Mechanics

Write a word from the box to complete each sentence.

| abbreviation | punctuation | apostrophe |
| quotation | capitalization | |

1. Use _____ at the beginning of every sentence.
2. Periods and commas are examples of _____.
3. **Dr.** is the _____ for **doctor**.
4. In a contraction, put an _____ where letters have been omitted.
5. Use _____ marks to show someone's exact words.

Math: Estimating

Write the words from the box that complete the paragraph.

| computation | estimation | difference |
| trillion | rounding | |

When engineers bid on a project, they give an ___6.___ of the cost. There should not be a large ___7.___ between the estimate and the actual costs. Engineers usually use a computer to do the ___8.___ of expenses. It is common to give an estimate by ___9.___ off to the nearest hundred. No single project has yet cost one ___10.___ dollars.

Apply the Spelling Strategy

Circle the six content words you wrote with the suffix **-ation**.

181

Assessment — Units 25–29

Each Assessment Word in the box fits one of the spelling strategies you have studied over the past five weeks. Read the spelling strategies. Then write each Assessment Word under the unit number it fits. You will not write any words from Unit 28.

Unit 25

1.–6. The suffixes **-ate** and **-ary** can be added to root words and base words to form adjectives such as **delicate** and **honorary**.

Unit 26

7.–10. The prefix **mid-** means "middle," **under-** and **sub-** mean "under" or "beneath," **super-** means "above," **inter-** means "between," and **intra-** means "within."

Unit 27

11.–15. The suffix **-ous** can be added to base words or root words to form adjectives such as **mountainous, nervous,** and **obvious.**

Unit 28

It is important to learn the spellings of words that writers often misspell.

Unit 29

16.–20. The suffixes **-ion, -tion,** and **-ation** can be added to a base word or root to form a noun, such as **action, introduction,** and **information.**

veterinary
understanding
hilarious
transfusion
exclamation
glamorous
intermediate
sanitary
inadequate
midweek
nonpoisonous
exception
instruction
poisonous
subtitle
inaccurate
intercept
affectionate
outrageous
appreciation

immediate	fortunate	necessary	temporary	accurate
delicate	unfortunate	ordinary	desperate	imaginary

Write spelling words to complete the sentences.

1. It is _____ to speak up if you want to be heard.
2. I am _____ to have so many friends.
3. My absence will be only _____.
4. Her account of the sales is always _____.

Add the missing letters to write spelling words.

5. _mag_n_ry
6. del_c_t_
7. unf_r_un_te
8. d_sp_r_te
9. _rd_n_ry
10. im__d_ate

underneath	supervise	interview	intramural	midsummer
underground	subway	submarine	interstate	interchange

Write a spelling word for each clue.

11. an underground transportation system
12. to switch the place of
13. questions asked of one person by another
14. contest between teams within the school
15. middle of summer
16. beneath
17. sea vessel that travels under the water
18. to direct the work of others
19. connecting states
20. beneath the ground

continuous	tremendous	industrious	courageous	nervous
various	glorious	curious	precious	cautious

Complete the sentence by adding the suffix **-ous** to the underlined word.

1. The victory was filled with <u>glory</u>. It was a _____ day.
2. Her actions took great <u>courage</u>. She is a _____ person.
3. Our city has much <u>industry</u>. We live in an _____ city.
4. The weather will <u>vary</u>. I enjoy the _____ types of weather.

Write the spelling word for these meanings.

5. excited
6. ongoing
7. huge; great
8. dear
9. careful
10. interested

Review Unit 28: Words Writers Use

different	athlete	probably	license	similar
pigeon	captain	surely	muscle	sauce

Find the misspelled word in each sentence and write it correctly.

11. It takes strong mussle to lift this box.
12. David just got his driver's lisense.
13. We probly won't go early to the game.
14. Our new jackets are simmilar, aren't they?
15. You surley will learn the music piece by Monday.
16. Saira has a diffrent outfit for each role in the play.
17. She showed great talent as an athelete.
18. Do you know how he makes that lemon sause?
19. We saw the same pijon at the park every day.
20. The captin of the ship spoke to the crew.

suggestion	expression	decision	completion	action
direction	information	population	position	attention

Write a spelling word that ends with the same letters as the underlined part of the words below.

1. inten<u>tion</u>
2. excla<u>mation</u>
3. circul<u>ation</u>
4. q<u>uestion</u>
5. del<u>etion</u>
6. compre<u>ssion</u>
7. in<u>cision</u>
8. subtrac<u>tion</u>
9. impo<u>sition</u>
10. el<u>ection</u>

GAME Spelling Study Strategy

Spelling Questions

Practicing spelling can be fun if you make it into a game. Here's an idea you can try with a friend.

1. Swap spelling lists with your friend. Be sure you can each read the other's list.

2. Your friend should pick one of the words on your list but not say it.

3. You may ask your friend three questions about the word. For example, you could ask, "Does it end with **ion**?" If you guess the word with your three questions, you get two points. Write the word.

4. Ask your friend to check the spelling. If you have the word spelled correctly, you get two points. If not, ask one question. If you get the spelling right this time, you get one point. If not, your friend will tell you the spelling, but you don't get any points.

5. If you don't guess the word, ask your friend to tell you the word. You don't get any points just now.

6. Now it's your friend's turn to guess a word and write it.

7. Keep going until you have both practiced all the words.

Grammar, Usage, and Mechanics

Conjunctions

Coordinating conjunctions, such as **and, but,** and **or,** connect words or groups of words (including independent clauses) that are similar.

Jenny **and** I wanted to go, **but** we were too late.

Subordinating conjunctions, such as **although, because, since, so, if,** and **before,** show how one clause is related to another. Subordinating conjunctions are often used at the beginning of dependent clauses.

Since Jamal was on time, he caught the bus.

Practice Activity

A. Write the conjunction in each sentence below. Circle it if it is a subordinating conjunction.

1. We can call ahead, or we can just arrive.

2. This trail is easy, but it is long.

3. Although I speak Spanish, I do not speak it well.

4. If Lori comes, we will have eight people.

5. Because it's a school night, I can't go.

B. Complete each sentence with a conjunction from the box. Capitalize the conjunction if it begins a sentence.

but	or	because	if	before

6. You may come, _____ you may stay at home.

7. _____ it rained earlier, puddles were everywhere.

8. _____ Alexis left, she had walked the dog.

9. I see Dan's bike, _____ I don't see him.

10. _____ more snow falls, we can go sledding.

WORKSHOP

Read it Backwards!

Good writers always proofread their writing for spelling errors. Here's a strategy that you can use to proofread your papers.

Usually, you read a paper from the first word to the last. This time, try reading it backwards. In other words, read it from the last word to the first. You would read the sentence **I finished my homework.** like this: **homework. my finished I**

It sounds like a funny way to proofread, but reading backwards helps you think about the spelling of each word instead of the meaning of the sentence. Try it!

Electronic Spelling

Foreign Spellings

Although the people of England and the United States both speak and write English, they do not always speak and write it the same way. They also do not spell everything the same way.

When you visit British sites on the Internet, you may notice spelling differences. Unless you are quoting, you should use the American spelling rather than the British.

Try doing that now. Below are six words that you might see on a British site. Write the American spelling of each word.

1. honour
2. theatre
3. organisation
4. realise
5. colour
6. labour

Spelling and Thinking

READ THE SPELLING WORDS

1.	lieutenant	*lieutenant*	The **lieutenant** saluted.
2.	superintendent	*superintendent*	She is our **superintendent**.
3.	merchant	*merchant*	This **merchant** sells jewelry.
4.	volunteer	*volunteer*	He is a hospital **volunteer**.
5.	participant	*participant*	Each **participant** had a turn.
6.	electrician	*electrician*	The **electrician** fixed the bell.
7.	comedian	*comedian*	We laughed at the **comedian**.
8.	opponent	*opponent*	She debated her **opponent**.
9.	applicant	*applicant*	He is a college **applicant**.
10.	attendant	*attendant*	An **attendant** moved her car.
11.	engineer	*engineer*	He is chief project **engineer**.
12.	custodian	*custodian*	A **custodian** cleans the office.
13.	assistant	*assistant*	Dr. Ito hired an **assistant**.
14.	resident	*resident*	He is a **resident** of our town.
15.	servant	*servant*	A mayor is a public **servant**.
16.	agent	*agent*	The singer fired her **agent**.
17.	guardian	*guardian*	Who is the child's **guardian**?
18.	musician	*musician*	The **musician** plays piano.
19.	tenant	*tenant*	A new **tenant** just moved in.
20.	librarian	*librarian*	The **librarian** has the book.

SORT THE SPELLING WORDS

1.–2. Write the spelling words that end in the suffix **-eer**.

3.–8. Write the spelling words that end in the suffix **-ian**.

9.–16. Write the spelling words that end in the suffix **-ant**.

17.–20. Write the spelling words that end in the suffix **-ent**.

REMEMBER THE SPELLING STRATEGY

Remember that the suffixes **-eer, -ian, -ant,** and **-ent** can be used to form nouns. These nouns often name people: **engineer, librarian, assistant,** and **resident.**

Spelling and Vocabulary

Related Meanings

Write a spelling word that is related in meaning to each word.

1. apply
2. voluntary
3. agency
4. reside
5. library
6. engine

Word Clues

Write the spelling word that matches each clue.

7. the person in charge
8. installs electrical equipment
9. composes or performs music
10. makes people laugh
11. takes care of a building
12. a rival or competitor
13. a military officer
14. a renter or boarder

USING THE Dictionary

Write the spelling word that goes with each origin.

15. from Latin **mercari** (to trade)
16. from Old French **garder** (to guard)
17. from Latin **participare** (to take part)
18. from Latin **ad** (near to) and **sistere** (to stand)
19. from Latin **attendere** (to heed)
20. from Old French **servir** (to serve)

Spelling and Reading

lieutenant	superintendent	merchant	volunteer
participant	electrician	comedian	opponent
applicant	attendant	engineer	custodian
assistant	resident	servant	agent
guardian	musician	tenant	librarian

Solve the Analogies Write a word to complete each analogy.

1. **Friend** is to **foe** as **teammate** is to _____.
2. **Head** is to **chief** as **parent** is to _____.
3. **Help** is to **helper** as **serve** is to _____.
4. **Occupy** is to **occupant** as **reside** is to _____.
5. **Teacher** is to **instructor** as **aide** is to _____.
6. **Immigrate** is to **immigrant** as **attend** is to _____.
7. **General** is to **colonel** as **captain** is to _____.
8. **Hotel** is to **guest** as **apartment** is to _____.

Complete the Descriptions Write a spelling word to match each job description.

9. Wanted: a _____ to make people laugh.
10. Book lover needed to assist a _____.
11. Band will hold auditions for a _____.
12. Hospital seeks a _____ to visit patients.
13. An _____ needed to rewire building.
14. New school system looking for school _____.

Complete the Paragraph Write spelling words from the box to complete the paragraph.

As a __15.__ in the job search process, Mr. Arnold needed assistance. So he talked to an __16.__ at an employment office. He described his goal to be an __17.__ of bridges. Then, Mr. Arnold described his work as head __18.__ in a school and his work with a local __19.__ who owned a computer store. Mr. Arnold feels that he is a qualified __20.__ for a better job.

engineer
merchant
applicant
participant
agent
custodian

Spelling and Writing

Proofread a Paragraph

Six words are not spelled correctly in this paragraph. Write the words correctly.

Someday you will be a particapant in the world of work. Do what you enjoy! If you love music, consider being a musicien in an orchestra. Do math and science challenge you? Then consider a career as an engineer or electrishian. People who like people should consider a job as a travel agant or a liberarian. Are you funny? TV can always use a good comedien. The possibilities are endless.

Proofreading Marks

≡	Make a capital.
/	Make a small letter.
∧	Add something.
ℓ	Take out something.
⊙	Add a period.
⌗	New paragraph
(SP)	Spelling error

Write a Paragraph

Expository Writing

What kind of career appeals to you? What are your interests and how can you apply them to a job? Write a description of a job that you would like.

- Explain why you think you would enjoy this job.
- What skills do you already have that you would need to perform this job?
- What skills would you need to acquire?
- Follow the form used in the proofreading sample.

Use as many spelling words as you can.

Proofread Your Writing During ➤ Editing

Proofread your writing for spelling errors as part of the editing stage in the writing process. Be sure to check each word carefully. Use a dictionary to check spelling if you are not sure.

Writing Process

Prewriting
⇩
Drafting
⇩
Revising
⇩
Editing
⇩
Publishing

Vocabulary

Strategy Words

Review Words: Suffixes -eer, -ian, -ant, -ent

Write a word from the box to match each clue.

amphibian	impatient	patient	rodent	sergeant

1. not willing to put up with delay or trouble
2. a soldier's rank
3. willing to put up with delay or trouble; also, someone being treated by a doctor
4. an animal characterized by large front teeth for gnawing
5. an animal that breathes water when it is young

Preview Words: Suffixes -eer, -ian, -ant, -ent

Write words from the box to complete this book review.

consistent	descendant	detergent
proficient		vegetarian

Chef Claude is a direct __6.__ of the famous cook, Paul Plouffe. A strict __7.__, Chef Claude presents his vegetable dishes with delightful originality. One lesson this writer learned in reading the book was to wash all vegetables well before cooking. There is no need to use __8.__; plain water will do. Chef Claude's book is __9.__ with his previous books in its creativity and beautiful pictures. The chef is as __10.__ in writing as he is in cooking.

Connections

Content Words

Social Studies: The Military

Write words from the box to complete the paragraph.

| civilian | military | defense | protection | endanger |

The armed forces include all of the groups that might fight in ___1.___ of our country. Every United States citizen helps to support the armed forces through taxes. When threats of foreign invasion ___2.___ our freedom, the armed forces prepare to provide ___3.___ for us. A citizen not serving in the ___4.___ is referred to as a ___5.___.

Fine Arts: Music

Write words from the box to complete the sentences.

| cellist | flutist | violinist | pianist | composer |

6. George Gershwin was a _____ of both popular and classical music.

7. Gershwin began his career as a _____, playing the piano for musicals and shows.

8. A _____ must control her breathing in order to play well.

9.–10. Before the performance, both the _____ and _____ repaired the broken strings on their instruments.

Apply the Spelling Strategy

Circle the content word you wrote that ends in the suffix **-ian**.

Spelling and Thinking

READ THE SPELLING WORDS

1.	performance	*performance*	Did you like our **performance**?
2.	experience	*experience*	I had a frightening **experience**.
3.	appearance	*appearance*	He disguised his **appearance**.
4.	ambulance	*ambulance*	Call an **ambulance** at once!
5.	attendance	*attendance*	He recorded class **attendance**.
6.	excellence	*excellence*	She performed with **excellence**.
7.	importance	*importance*	This clue has great **importance**.
8.	obedience	*obedience*	Our parents expect **obedience**.
9.	inheritance	*inheritance*	The house was his **inheritance**.
10.	innocence	*innocence*	I will prove my **innocence**.
11.	clearance	*clearance*	The bridge has a low **clearance**.
12.	insurance	*insurance*	Car **insurance** is expensive.
13.	absence	*absence*	I am in charge in her **absence**.
14.	balance	*balance*	He lost his **balance** on the stairs.
15.	sequence	*sequence*	Follow the steps in **sequence**.
16.	distance	*distance*	She ran the **distance** in an hour.
17.	residence	*residence*	Her legal **residence** is in Utah.
18.	instance	*instance*	He is excused in this **instance**.
19.	silence	*silence*	The audience sat in **silence**.
20.	patience	*patience*	Have **patience** while you wait.

SORT THE SPELLING WORDS

Write the spelling words in which

1.–6. the suffix **-ance** is added to a base word that does not change spelling. Circle the base words.

7. the final consonant of the base word is doubled.

8.–20. the suffixes **-ance** or **-ence** were added to a root.

REMEMBER THE SPELLING STRATEGY

194

Remember that the suffixes **-ance** and **-ence** can be used to form nouns: **clearance, experience**.

Spelling and Vocabulary

Word Meanings

Write spelling words to complete the sentences. Use the underlined words as clues.

1. I am sending my <u>disobedient</u> dog to _____ school.
2. Let's <u>clear</u> out the shelves with a _____ sale.
3. When stars <u>appear</u> in the sky, I welcome their _____.
4. If you are <u>absent</u>, bring a note explaining your _____.
5. Any <u>imbalance</u> will be corrected when you _____ the wheels.
6. The <u>distant</u> city was only a short _____ from the border.
7. A <u>sequential</u> set of directions make the _____ easy to follow.
8. If the injured are not <u>ambulatory</u>, they may need an _____.
9. If you <u>inherit</u> money, taxes will take part of that _____.
10. The goal of _____ is to <u>insure</u> you against major losses.

Word Structure

Write the spelling words that are homophones for these words.

11. patients
12. residents
13. attendants
14. innocents
15. instants
16. excellents

USING THE Thesaurus

Replace the underlined words in the sentences below with synonyms from the spelling list.

17. A paper route provides valuable <u>training</u>.
18. There was complete <u>quiet</u> when Mom spoke.
19. The captain praised the soldier's <u>accomplishment</u>.
20. We all understand the <u>significance</u> of getting to school on time.

Spelling and Reading

performance	experience	appearance	ambulance
attendance	excellence	importance	obedience
inheritance	innocence	clearance	insurance
absence	balance	sequence	distance
residence	instance	silence	patience

Solve the Analogies   Write a spelling word to complete each analogy.

1. **Sincerity** is to **honesty** as **stability** is to _____.
2. **Cowardice** is to **courage** as **guilt** is to _____.
3. **Loud** is to **noise** as **quiet** is to _____.
4. **Confidence** is to **certainty** as **image** is to _____.
5. **Perform** is to **performance** as **clear** is to _____.
6. **Disturb** is to **disturbance** as **obey** is to _____.

SSHHHH!

Complete the Sentences   Write spelling words to complete these interview questions. The first letter of each word is provided.

7. What past e_____ qualifies you for this job?
8. Tell me about your previous employment in s_____, starting with your first job.
9. Can you explain your a_____ from your last job?
10. How far is your current r_____ from R and B Vehicle Services?
11. Have you ever driven an a_____?
12. Are you comfortable driving a long d_____?
13. Describe an i_____ that shows you can think quickly.

Complete the Paragraph   Write spelling words from the box to complete the paragraph.

Jack Kramer's __14.__ of the family __15.__ business is a great opportunity. He realizes the __16.__ of customer service, so he insists on faithful __17.__. In turn, Jack's staff appreciates his __18.__ with their questions and his fairness in evaluating their daily __19.__. Kramer Insurance is known for its excellent record, and Jack plans to continue this __20.__.

attendance
patience
insurance
performance
inheritance
importance
excellence

Spelling ᴬⁿᵈ Writing

Proofread a Letter

Six words are not spelled correctly in this letter. Write the words correctly.

Dear Mr. McKee,

    Please make me editor of the school paper. I have experiance as a writer, and know the importance ot meeting deadlines. There has not been one instence when I have turned in work late. I have a good atendance record, too, with only one day of abcence in two years. I will prove my excellance through my job performance.

        Sincerely,

        Jason Workhard

Write a Letter — *Persuasive Writing*

Imagine that you are trying to persuade an employer to hire you. Write a letter that describes your job qualifications.

- Describe your experience, your skills, and your ability to work with others.
- Follow the form used in the proofreading sample.

Use as many spelling words as you can.

Proofread Your Writing During ➤ Editing

Writing Process

Prewriting

⇩

Drafting

⇩

Revising

⇩

Editing

⇩

Publishing

Proofread your writing for spelling errors as part of the editing stage in the writing process. Be sure to check each word carefully. Use a dictionary to check spelling if you are not sure.

Vocabulary

Strategy Words

Review Words: Suffixes -ance, -ence

Write words from the box to complete the paragraph.

allowance	audience	entrance
	nuisance	ordinance

Ernest decided to spend part of his weekly __1.__ on a movie ticket. Not wanting to leave his new puppy home alone, however, he brought Shadow with him. At the theater __2.__, he was told that an __3.__ prohibits dogs. "I promise that Shadow will not be a __4.__," Ernest pleaded. "The __5.__ will not even know that she is there."

Preview Words: Suffixes -ance, -ence

Write a word from the box to complete each sentence.

conscience	endurance	ignorance
	insistence	maintenance

6. Quality control standards at the factory ensure that your new washing machine will need little ____.

7. At our mother's ____, we wrote a note of apology.

8. Running a marathon requires great ____.

9. She did not intentionally break the rules. Her ____ of the restrictions caused the problem.

10. His ____ told him that what he was about to do was not right.

Connections

Math: Measurement

Write words from the box to complete the paragraph.

arc	pi	chord	radius	circumference

The distance around a circle is called its __1.__. This can be determined by multiplying __2.__, or 3.14, times the __3.__ times 2. An __4.__ is a part of a circle. A __5.__ is a line segment joining two points on a circle.

Social Studies: Banking

Write a word from the box to complete each sentence.

finance	invest	fiscal	stockbroker	partnership

6. The study of money management is the study of _____.
7. A business of two or more individuals is a _____.
8. A _____ buys and sells stocks for a living.
9. A _____ matter pertains to the subject of money.
10. When you put money into something to make a profit, you _____ it.

Apply the Spelling Strategy

Circle the suffix **-ance** or **-ence** in two of the content words you wrote.

Spelling and Thinking

READ THE SPELLING WORDS

1. progress	*progress*	He has made **progress** in school.
2. compound	*compound*	Try not to **compound** the problem.
3. aged	*aged*	The toy is for babies **aged** one.
4. conduct	*conduct*	Try to **conduct** yourselves properly.
5. present	*present*	She bought a small **present**.
6. minute	*minute*	We will be ready in one **minute**.
7. console	*console*	She tried to **console** the sad child.
8. primer	*primer*	I read a **primer** on how to play golf.
9. rebel	*rebel*	She will **rebel** if she has to work late.
10. convict	*convict*	The **convict** sat in a jail cell.
11. content	*content*	We were **content** to just sit and read.
12. wound	*wound*	Your **wound** will heal in a few days.
13. compact	*compact*	A **compact** car will fit in that space.
14. buffet	*buffet*	We enjoyed the **buffet** dinner.
15. extract	*extract*	My dentist had to **extract** my tooth.
16. refuse	*refuse*	Please do not **refuse** this gift.
17. contract	*contract*	The writer signed a book **contract**.
18. invalid	*invalid*	Her driver's license is **invalid**.
19. convert	*convert*	I will **convert** dollars to pesos.
20. object	*object*	Do you **object** to wearing uniforms?

SORT THE SPELLING WORDS

1. Write the spelling word that has either one or two syllables depending on its meaning.

2. Write the spelling word that has only one syllable.

3.–19. Write the spelling words that have two syllables.

20. Write the spelling word that has three syllables.

REMEMBER THE SPELLING STRATEGY

Remember that **homographs** are words that are spelled the same but have different meanings, origins, or pronunciations.

Spelling and Vocabulary

Word Meanings

Write the spelling word that matches both definitions.

1. thing inside; satisfied
2. textbook; paint
3. pull out; flavoring
4. reduce; agreement
5. type of meal; knock about
6. reject; garbage
7. combine; enclosed area
8. advance; improvement

Word Replacements

Write a spelling word that could be used twice in each sentence to replace the underlined words.

9. He <u>wrapped</u> the bandage around the <u>injury</u>.
10. The prosecutor will <u>prove</u> the <u>guilt</u> of the <u>prisoner</u>.
11. I tried to <u>comfort</u> him when his TV <u>cabinet</u> broke.
12. The sick, <u>weak person</u> has a will that is <u>not legally enforceable</u>.
13. This machine will <u>compress</u> your trash into a <u>tightly packed</u> bundle.

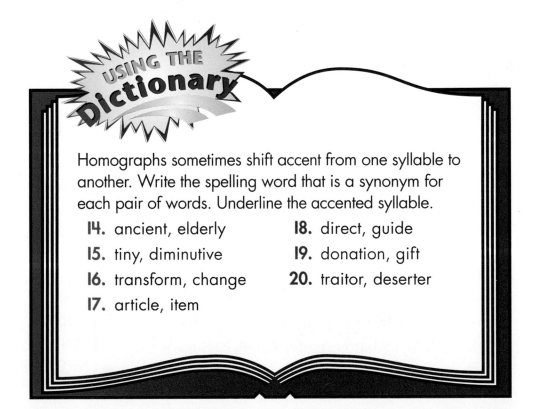

Homographs sometimes shift accent from one syllable to another. Write the spelling word that is a synonym for each pair of words. Underline the accented syllable.

14. ancient, elderly
15. tiny, diminutive
16. transform, change
17. article, item
18. direct, guide
19. donation, gift
20. traitor, deserter

progress	compound	aged	conduct	present
minute	console	primer	rebel	convict
content	wound	compact	buffet	extract
refuse	contract	invalid	convert	object

Solve the Analogies Write the spelling word that completes each analogy.

1. **Grind** is to **ground** as **wind** is to _____.
2. **Traveler** is to **wanderer** as **prisoner** is to _____.
3. **Big** is to **expand** as **small** is to _____.
4. **Wide** is to **narrow** as **spacious** is to _____.
5. **In** is to **inject** as **out** is to _____.
6. **Agree** is to **endorse** as **oppose** is to _____.

Complete the Sentences For each sentence, write one spelling word that would make the sentence complete.

7. I am not _____ with the _____ of the package.
8. The _____ senior citizen walked with a child _____ six.
9. They will _____ the problem if they move inmates from the prison _____.
10. I expect good _____ from you as I _____ the tour.
11. I _____ to dispose of their _____.
12. The child will _____ the birthday _____ to the mayor.
13. This _____ on painting suggests using a _____ coat.
14. While waves _____ the boat, we serve a _____ lunch.

Complete the Paragraph Write spelling words from the box to complete the paragraph.

Why be a __15.__ when it is time to visit the dentist? Any excuses are __16.__. A receptionist sits at a computer __17.__ and keeps track of each patient's checkup date. The dentist scolds me if I am even a __18.__ late. I have made __19.__ in taking care of my teeth and have become a __20.__ to proper dental care.

| minute |
| invalid |
| convert |
| rebel |
| console |
| progress |

202

Spelling and Writing

Proofread a Paragraph

Six words are not spelled correctly in this paragraph. Write the words correctly.

Benjy was a food reble. He used to refuze to eat even minutte bits of food. Then we discovered "a-little-of-everything pizza." Now it is difficult to extrakt Benjy from his chair after a meal. He does not abject to vegetables or aged cheese, as long as it is on his own pizza. My parents are cintent now that Benjy eats healthy food.

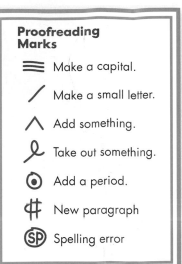

Proofreading Marks

≡ Make a capital.

/ Make a small letter.

∧ Add something.

℮ Take out something.

⊙ Add a period.

⌗ New paragraph

㏚ Spelling error

Write a Paragraph

Narrative Writing

Sometimes creativity can solve a problem. Write a paragraph about a problem that was solved in a clever way.

- Describe the problem.
- Then describe how you or someone you know solved it creatively.
- Describe any failed attempts to solve the problem, too.
- Follow the form used in the proofreading sample.

Use as many spelling words as you can.

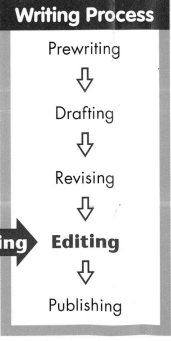

Writing Process

Prewriting

⇩

Drafting

⇩

Revising

⇩

Editing

⇩

Publishing

Proofread Your Writing During → Editing

Proofread your writing for spelling errors as part of the editing stage in the writing process. Be sure to check each word carefully. Use a dictionary to check spelling if you are not sure.

Vocabulary

Strategy Words

Review Words: Homographs

Write words from the box to complete the paragraph.

alternate	estimate	separate	contest	subject

We have decided to enter the essay __1.__ . We can write about any __2.__ that has to do with an endangered animal, such as the bald eagle. An __3.__ topic is to write about endangered plants. If we write more than one essay, we are to mail each one in a __4.__ envelope. The officials __5.__ that it will take about a month to process all the entries.

Preview Words: Homographs

Write one word from the box to complete each sentence.

annex	combine	complex	excuse	suspect

6. I _____ that the robbery _____ is hiding somewhere.

7. You are going to give me a _____ about my math ability if you continue to give me such _____ problems to solve.

8. Please _____ me, but I have an _____ for being late.

9. The university is planning to _____ the library _____ to its main building.

10. The farmer will drive the _____ through the field and then _____ the grain he cuts with the rest of the grain in the barn.

Connections

Social Studies: Government

Write words from the box to complete the paragraph.

bilingual	premier	cabinet	province	parliament

Quebec is Canada's largest __1.__. Many people here are __2.__, speaking both French and English. The __3.__ of Quebec is the head of the provincial government. However, the chief executive for all of Canada is the prime minister. A __4.__ of about forty ministers helps govern. Canada's legislative body is a __5.__, which is divided into two sections.

Social Studies: Russia

Write words from the box to complete the paragraph.

czar	steppes	peasant	tyrant	serf

For hundreds of years, Russia was ruled by a king called a __6.__. The first one was Ivan IV, known as Ivan the Terrible because he was a __7.__. During his reign, a hired farm worker, or __8.__, was often bound to the landlord as a __9.__, or slave. Farm workers planted grain on the __10.__, the flat, treeless plains in southern Russia.

Apply the Spelling Strategy

Circle the two content words you wrote that are homographs.

Spelling and Thinking

READ THE SPELLING WORDS

1.	autobiographer	autobiographer	I am an **autobiographer**.
2.	speedometer	speedometer	Check the **speedometer**.
3.	thermometer	thermometer	The **thermometer** says zero.
4.	photography	photography	I took a **photography** class.
5.	oceanographer	oceanographer	She is an **oceanographer**.
6.	biographer	biographer	His **biographer** was truthful.
7.	paragraph	paragraph	Write a brief **paragraph**.
8.	geographer	geographer	A **geographer** read the map.
9.	thermostat	thermostat	A **thermostat** regulates heat.
10.	geography	geography	The land's **geography** is hilly.
11.	diameter	diameter	What is the circle's **diameter**?
12.	thermal	thermal	The skier's socks are **thermal**.
13.	autograph	autograph	The star signed an **autograph**.
14.	graphic	graphic	Sue is a **graphic** designer.
15.	barometer	barometer	Check the **barometer**.
16.	geology	geology	Jim studied Alaska's **geology**.
17.	biology	biology	We studied insects in **biology**.
18.	geologist	geologist	A **geologist** studied the rocks.
19.	telegraph	telegraph	He sent a **telegraph** message.
20.	geometry	geometry	I study shapes in **geometry**.

SORT THE SPELLING WORDS

1.–5. Write the spelling words that end in **-meter** or **-metry**.

6.–15. Write the spelling words that have the root **graph** in them.

16.–18. Write the spelling words that end in **-ology** or **-ologist**.

19.–20. Write the spelling words that end with **-al** or **-stat**.

REMEMBER THE SPELLING STRATEGY

Remember that many English words have Greek roots. For example, the words **thermometer, barometer,** and **speedometer** all share the root **meter,** meaning "measure."

Spelling and Vocabulary

Word Meanings

Write spelling words to match these clues.

1. one who studies the earth, its features, and inhabitants
2. the study of the composition of the earth's structure
3. an instrument that measures air pressure
4. the study of solid and plain figures
5. an instrument that measures speed
6. one who writes the story of someone else's life
7. the process of taking pictures
8. one who studies the composition of the earth's structure
9. the study of the earth, its features, and inhabitants

Word Structure

Match a word part from Group A with one from Group B to write spelling words.

10.–14. **A.** para   bio   dia   therm   ocean
        B. meter   al   graph   logy   ographer

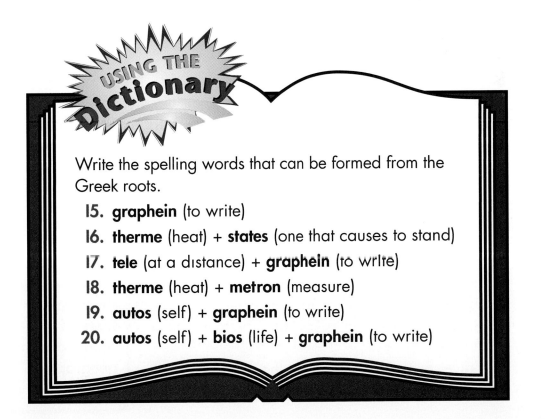

USING THE Dictionary

Write the spelling words that can be formed from the Greek roots.

15. **graphein** (to write)
16. **therme** (heat) + **states** (one that causes to stand)
17. **tele** (at a distance) + **graphein** (to write)
18. **therme** (heat) + **metron** (measure)
19. **autos** (self) + **graphein** (to write)
20. **autos** (self) + **bios** (life) + **graphein** (to write)

Spelling and Reading

autobiographer	speedometer	thermometer	photography
oceanographer	biographer	paragraph	geographer
thermostat	geography	diameter	thermal
autograph	graphic	barometer	geology
biology	geologist	telegraph	geometry

Solve the Analogies Write a spelling word to complete each analogy.

1. **Water** is to **faucet** as **heat** is to ____.
2. **Animal** is to **zoologist** as **rock** is to ____.
3. **Letter** is to **word** as **sentence** is to ____.
4. **Time** is to **watch** as **speed** is to ____.
5. **Around** is to **circumference** as **through** is to ____.
6. **Picture** is to **photograph** as **signature** is to ____.
7. **Stove** is to **cookery** as **camera** is to ____.

Complete the Sentences Write a spelling word to complete each sentence.

8. The company hired a ____ design artist to illustrate the book.
9. The ____ wrote Martin Luther King, Jr.'s life story.
10. The scientists studied the ____ of the earthquake site.
11. You can use ____ to determine the area of that field.
12. The ____ dropped rapidly, indicating an approaching storm.
13. In 1866, the first successful ____ cable was laid.
14. Frederick Douglass, an ____, wrote about his own life.
15. They are studying the ____ of pond life.

Complete the Paragraph Write spelling words from the box to complete the paragraph.

To explore the ocean, an __16.__ must wear a __17.__ suit for protection from the cold. The diver uses a special __18.__ to record water temperature. The diver explores the __19.__ of the ocean floor. A __20.__ uses this information to learn about the earth.

> thermometer
> thermal
> oceanographer
> geographer
> geography

208

Spelling and Writing

Proofread a Paragraph

Six words are not spelled correctly in this paragraph. Write the words correctly.

Jacques Cousteau was an oceanagrapher who studied the biolagy of the ocean's animals and plants. Cousteau, also an autobiografer, wrote in graphick detail about his own life experiences. Each paragraf in his books is filled with interesting details. His photography of the undersea world is breathtaking. More than one biographor has written about Cousteau's life.

Write a Paragraph

Expository Writing

Scientific discoveries are made by men and women who are curious to find out why and how things work. Write a paragraph about a scientist who interests you.

- Describe the scientist.
- What did he or she learn?
- Explain the significance of the discovery.
- Follow the form used in the proofreading sample.

Use as many spelling words as you can.

Writing Process

Prewriting

⇩

Drafting

⇩

Revising

⇩

Editing

⇩

Publishing

Proofread Your Writing During ➤

Proofread your writing for spelling errors as part of the editing stage in the writing process. Be sure to check each word carefully. Use a dictionary to check spelling if you are not sure.

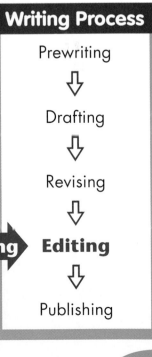

Vocabulary

Strategy Words

Review Words: Greek Roots

Write a word from the box that matches each clue.

biography	homograph	kilowatt
perimeter	telecast	

1. the measurement of distance around an area
2. a television broadcast
3. a word that has the same spelling as another word but differs in meaning, origin, and sometimes pronunciation
4. a written account of a person's life
5. a unit of electric power

Preview Words: Greek Roots

Write a word from the box to complete each sentence.

autobiographical	diagram	physiology
telephone	topography	

6. The hikers used a map to study the _____ of the region.
7. He drew a _____ showing how bicycle gears work.
8. *Anne Frank: The Diary of a Young Girl* is an _____ book.
9. Joan went to South America to study the _____ of rain forest plants.
10. Alexander Graham Bell patented the first successful _____ in 1876.

Connections

Content Words

Science: Matter

Write words from the box to complete the paragraph.

atom	nucleus	electron	proton	neutron

An __1.__ is the building block of matter. As tiny as it is, it is made up of even tinier parts. At the center is a core called a __2.__. A __3.__ carries one unit of positive electricity. An atomic particle that carries no electric charge is a __4.__. A tiny particle carrying one unit of negative electricity is an __5.__. Together these particles make up atomic matter.

Science: Weather

Write a word from the box to match each definition.

cirrus	stratus	cumulus
nimbostratus	cumulonimbus	

6. a low-altitude cloud, often resembling fog
7. a high-altitude cloud composed of narrow bands
8. a dense, white, fluffy cloud
9. an extremely dense, vertical cloud with a hazy outline
10. a low gray cloud that may cause snow or sleet

Apply the Spelling Strategy

These words are all from Greek roots and may be hard to pronounce. Listening for syllables can help. Circle the content words you wrote that have two syllables.

Spelling and Thinking

READ THE SPELLING WORDS

1.	rpm	*rpm*	The car shifted gears at 40,000 **rpm**.
2.	laser	*laser*	A powerful **laser** beam cut the steel.
3.	scuba	*scuba*	The **scuba** divers took pictures of the fish.
4.	P.M.	*P.M.*	Herb's play will begin at 7 **P.M.** sharp.
5.	PBS	*PBS*	We watched a science special on **PBS**.
6.	OPEC	*OPEC*	Many **OPEC** nations are in the Middle East.
7.	POW	*POW*	The **POW** spent a year in prison.
8.	DOB	*DOB*	The form asks for **DOB** and place of birth.
9.	IRA	*IRA*	He adds some money every year to his **IRA**.
10.	IRS	*IRS*	The **IRS** collects federal taxes.
11.	CPU	*CPU*	Every digital machine contains a **CPU**.
12.	CEO	*CEO*	The bank **CEO** approved the new plan.
13.	COD	*COD*	Pay for the package when it arrives **COD**.
14.	SALT	*SALT*	The **SALT** meetings started in 1969.
15.	BASIC	*BASIC*	She knows how to program in **BASIC**.
16.	VCR	*VCR*	We taped the TV special on the **VCR**.
17.	A.M.	*A.M.*	His alarm went off at 7 **A.M.**
18.	sonar	*sonar*	Submarines rely on their **sonar** devices.
19.	bit	*bit*	A **bit** is information stored on a computer.
20.	mph	*mph*	The speed limit in this area is 30 **mph**.

SORT THE SPELLING WORDS

1.–6. Write the spelling words that are written with all lowercase letters.

7.–20. Write the spelling words that are written with all uppercase letters.

REMEMBER THE SPELLING STRATEGY

Remember that an **abbreviation** is a shortened form of a word or phrase. For example, **mph** is the abbreviation for "miles per hour." An **acronym** is a word formed by combining the first letters or parts of a series of words. The acronym **bit** stands for "<u>bi</u>nary dig<u>it</u>."

Spelling ^{and} Vocabulary

Word Meanings

Write the spelling word that is an abbreviation or acronym for each phrase.

1. self-contained underwater breathing apparatus
2. in the afternoon or evening
3. Organization of Petroleum Exporting Countries
4. cash on delivery
5. sound navigation ranging

Word Replacements

Write the spelling words that are abbreviations or acronyms for the underlined phrases.

6.–10. Computer technology has added its own vocabulary to the American language. Shortened forms of computer terms make them easier to say and remember. The smallest unit that a central processing unit can store is a binary digit. Using Beginner's All-purpose Symbolic Instruction Code, a programmer can record information in the computer. You probably know that light amplification by stimulated emission of radiation printing is one means of getting computer information on paper. One byproduct of the computer age is the videocassette recorder.

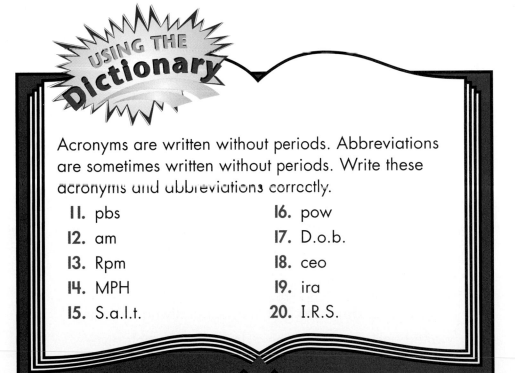

USING THE Dictionary

Acronyms are written without periods. Abbreviations are sometimes written without periods. Write these acronyms and abbreviations correctly.

11. pbs
12. am
13. Rpm
14. MPH
15. S.a.l.t.
16. pow
17. D.o.b.
18. ceo
19. ira
20. I.R.S.

Spelling and Reading

rpm	laser	scuba	P.M.	PBS
OPEC	POW	DOB	IRA	IRS
CPU	CEO	COD	SALT	BASIC
VCR	A.M.	sonar	bit	mph

Answer the Questions Write spelling words to answer these questions.

1. What piece of information is on a driver's license?

2. What is someone held captive during a war called?

3. Who is at the head of a company?

4. What helps people save for their retirement?

5. What meetings were held to limit nuclear weapons?

6. What organization was formed by nations dependent on oil exports for their income?

7. What is the smallest unit of storage in a computer?

Complete the Sentences Write a spelling word to complete each sentence.

8. There are many versions of the _____ programming language.

9. A _____ frequently scans the computer for new instructions from the keyboard or from a program.

10. _____ is a network of public television stations.

11. He filed his income tax form with the _____ late this year.

12. The radar detector shows he is driving 60 _____.

13. They rented a video to play on their new _____.

14. The doctor used a _____ to perform the delicate surgery.

15. The new engine gives off less heat at a high _____.

Complete the Paragraph Write spelling words from the box to complete the paragraph.

A package arrived __16.__, so Erin paid the mail carrier. The package contained her new __17.__ gear. When the sun set at 8 __18.__, she and a friend boarded the research vessel. At sea, they used a __19.__ device to find their exact diving location. They waited until 7 __20.__ the next day to begin their dive.

P.M.
COD
sonar
A.M.
scuba

214

Spelling ᴬⁿᵈ Writing

Proofread a Paragraph

Six words are not spelled correctly in this paragraph. Write the words correctly.

Gus's alarm woke him at 7 Am for his first day of work. Before he left, he set his vcr for 8 pM to record a pbs program about scuba diving. Gus was starting as a cashier at the supermarket. During his training, he learned that his check-out computer is part of a network of computers that lead to the cPu at the main office. Gus learned all about the bar-code reader, the swipe-card reader, and the lasor scanner.

Proofreading Marks

☰   Make a capital.

/   Make a small letter.

∧   Add something.

ℓ   Take out something.

⊙   Add a period.

#⃒   New paragraph

SP   Spelling error

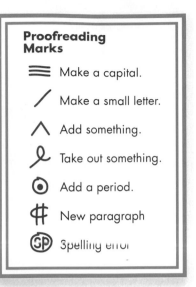

Write a Paragraph

Descriptive Writing

Modern technology is rapidly changing our world. Many modern conveniences have made our lives easier. Write a paragraph about a modern invention that has affected your life in some way.

- Describe how the invention has made your life easier or more pleasurable.
- How was the same chore or activity performed before the invention?

Use as many spelling words as you can.

Writing Process

Prewriting
⇩
Drafting
⇩
Revising
⇩
Editing
⇩
Publishing

Proofread Your Writing During ➤ **Editing**

Proofread your writing for spelling errors as part of the editing stage in the writing process. Be sure to check each word carefully. Use a dictionary to check spelling if you are not sure.

Vocabulary

Strategy Words

Review Words: Abbreviations and Acronyms

Write the word from the box that fits each clue.

etc.	modem	TX	wt.	yd.

1. a device that converts data from one form to another; acronym from **modulator** and **demodulator**
2. abbreviation for **et cetera,** meaning "and other things"
3. abbreviation for **weight**
4. abbreviation for **yard**
5. abbreviation for **Texas**; used in addresses

Preview Words: Abbreviations and Acronyms

Each sentence can be completed by a word in the box.
Write the abbreviation or shortened version of the word.
Consult a dictionary if you are not sure.

acre	edition	facsimile	laboratory	organization

6. The farmer agreed to sell one _____ of his land.
7. The biologist went to the _____ to study the cells.
8. She sent me a _____ about the construction of the new library.
9. The _____ is working to protect civil rights.
10. This is only the second _____ of the dictionary.

Connections

Health: Nutrition

Write words from the box to complete the paragraph.

calorie	nourish	dietitian	nutrition	metabolism

A __1.__ studies foods to learn what will best __2.__ the human body. He or she determines an individual's rate of __3.__ to see how fast the energy from one __4.__ is burned. Then, he or she can provide patients with a plan for good __5.__ .

Science: Experiments

Write words from the box to complete these sentences.

Celsius	Fahrenheit	exponent
squared	scientific notation	

6.–7. The temperature scale that registers the freezing point of water at 0° is called _____; the one that registers freezing at 32° is called _____.

8. The _____ of a number shows how many times the base number is to be multiplied by itself.

9. Writing numbers in powers of ten is called _____.

10. When a number is _____, it is multiplied by itself.

Apply the Spelling Strategy

Circle the content words you wrote that have the following abbreviations: **cal., C, F**.

Assessment and Review

Assessment — Units 31–35

Each Assessment Word in the box fits one of the spelling strategies you have studied over the past five weeks. Read the spelling strategies. Then write each Assessment Word under the unit number it fits.

Unit 31

1.–5. The suffixes **-eer, -ian, -ant,** and **-ent** can be used to form nouns. These nouns often name people: **engineer, librarian, assistant,** and **resident**.

Unit 32

6.–10. The suffixes **-ance** and **-ence** can be used to form nouns: **clearance, experience**.

Unit 33

11. Homographs are words that are spelled the same but have different meanings, origins, or pronunciations.

Unit 34

12.–16. Many English words have Greek roots. For example, the words **thermometer, barometer,** and **speedometer** all share the root **meter,** meaning "measure."

Unit 35

17.–20. An **abbreviation** is a shortened form of a word or phrase. For example, **mph** is the abbreviation for "miles per hour." An **acronym** is a word formed by combining the first letters or parts of a series of words. The acronym **bit** stands for "binary dig<u>it</u>."

beautician
interference
autopilot
PTA
odometer
presence
mountaineer
EPA
magician
conference
telemeter
photographer
radiance
migrant
Y2K
accountant
sow
resistance
photosynthesis
P.S.

Unit 31: Suffixes -eer, -ian, -ant, -ent

| volunteer | librarian | applicant | lieutenant | engineer |
| musician | merchant | servant | assistant | opponent |

Write the spelling word that names these people.

1. a person who helps you find books
2. someone who applies for a job
3. an officer in the armed forces
4. one who designs the construction of buildings
5. the team on the opposite side
6. one who assists the director
7. a person who serves an employer
8. someone who plays violin in an orchestra
9. one who helps free of cost
10. the owner of a store

Review Unit 32: Suffixes -ance, -ence

| attendance | performance | patience | experience | appearance |
| silence | importance | balance | instance | distance |

Find the misspelled words. Write each word correctly.

11. We have learned much by experence.
12. Please maintain silance when you enter.
13. You need to have more pashunse with the new players.
14. How much distunce have the runners covered?
15. There is a balence of $3.50 in the treasury.
16. This is a matter of great importence.
17. The rule is just for this instanse.
18. She gives the apearance of being calm.
19.–20. The attendce at last night's performance was small.

Review | Unit 33: Homographs

conduct	present	minute	object	aged
wound	compound	content	refuse	progress

Write the spelling word that fits both places in each sentence.

1. She _____ the bandage around the _____ on her knee.
2. I'd like to _____ you this _____ for your birthday.
3. One _____ will make only a _____ difference.
4. Do you _____ to looking for the lost _____?
5. Her _____ grandparents are _____ 88 and 90.
6. We're quite _____ with the _____ of the lecture.
7. Be careful not to _____ the problem by adding the wrong chemical _____.
8. I _____ to take out smelly _____ I didn't create.
9. At last, we _____ slowly toward making successful _____.
10. The judge will _____ an investigation into the _____ of the group.

Review | Unit 34: Greek Roots

biographer	geography	geometry	thermometer	photography
telegraph	paragraph	biology	diameter	geologist

Write a spelling word by combining a word part from each column.

11. bio   metry
12. geo   mometer
13. geo   graph
14. ther   grapher
15. tele   graphy

16. photo   logist
17. dia   graphy
18. bio   logy
19. para   graph
20. geo   meter

220

rpm	laser	scuba	BASIC	A.M.
P.M.	VCR	PBS	DOB	IRS

Write the abbreviation or acronym that fits the clue.

1. hours of the morning
2. hours of the evening
3. public television
4. needed for many applications
5. the place taxes are sent
6. referring to underwater diving
7. for showing movies on television sets
8. is used in some surgeries
9. refers to how fast something goes around
10. a computer programming language

WORD SORT **Spelling Study Strategy**

Sorting by Endings

One good way to practice spelling words is to place words into groups according to some spelling pattern. Here is a way to practice some of the spelling words you have been studying in the past few weeks.

1. Make six columns across a large piece of paper or on the chalkboard.

2. Write one of these words at the top of each column: **volunteer, librarian, assistant, opponent, attendance,** and **experience**. Include the underlines.

3. Have a partner choose a spelling word from Units 31 and 32 and say it aloud.

4. Write the spelling word in the column under the word with the same ending.

WRITER'S

Grammar, Usage, and Mechanics

Sentences and Their Parts

An interjection expresses emotion. **Oh, ouch, hey, hurray,** and **wow** are common interjections.

Wow, that is a big dog!

Practice Activity

A. Write the interjection in each sentence below.

1. Hey, we're going to be late if you don't hurry.
2. Paula said, "Gee, I'd like to see that movie, too."
3. When I showed Dad my report, he said, "Wow! That's good!"
4. Ouch, that railing gave me a splinter.
5. Take your lunch; oh, don't forget your thermos.
6. Hurray, your poster won first prize!
7. Gee, I really liked that show.

B. Complete each sentence with a word from the spelling lists in Units 31–35.

8. Oh, can we attend the next _____?
9. Well, a _____ will show you the temperature.
10. Hey, I'm better at _____ than I was at algebra.
11. Gee, you are the first _____ for this job.
12. Wow, that portrait shows you have a future in _____.
13. The _____ began, "Hurray, you're now a cousin!"
14. Ouch, I just learned the _____ of well-fitting shoes.

WORKSHOP

Pair Up With a Partner!

Good writers always proofread their papers for spelling errors. Here's a strategy that you can use to proofread your writing.

Instead of proofreading all by yourself, pair up with a partner. Ask your partner to read your work aloud slowly. While your partner reads, you look at each word. Is it spelled correctly?

Hearing each word read aloud helps you focus on the word and its spelling instead of on the sentence. A second benefit is that a partner can help you fix misspellings. This strategy works. Try it!

Electronic Spelling

Computer Language

Technology is changing language and bringing new words into common use. Some of these words are so new that they may not appear in older dictionaries or spell checkers.

A knowledge of prefixes and suffixes can help you spell such words. Several, for instance, begin with the prefix **multi-** or end with the suffix **-tion**. Knowing these word parts can help you spell words correctly.

Look at these words. Which are misspelled? Write those words correctly. Write **OK** if a word is correct.

1. multemedia
2. resolutoin
3. mutitask
4. protection
5. introduction
6. multilevel

Challenge Activities

adequate	elastic	container
ancestor	exclaim	complaint

A. Write the challenge word that fits each "Who or What Am I" statement.

  1. I return to my normal shape after I'm stretched.

  2. I may be enough or suitable, but I'm not of the best quality.

  3. I am a statement expressing annoyance or unhappiness. Sign me "Gripe."

  4. I am family. I was born before your grandparents.

  5. I am used to hold something. Call me a box or a barrel.

  6. I am a verb that tells how you might speak.

B. Write challenge words to complete this "vacation album" story.

  A great-grandfather, one __1.__ of mine, enjoyed spending his summer vacation at home. But he hated to live in his home in the winter. His landlord never provided __2.__ heat for the house. He said it was cold enough to freeze __3.__ ! My great-grandfather did not write the landlord a letter of __4.__ . He did not knock on the landlord's door to __5.__ about how cold it was. He put one piece of coal into a __6.__ and sent it to the landlord as a hint!

C. Pretend that you are the landlord mentioned in Activity B. Write a letter in response to the man who sent you a piece of coal. Tell what you think he should have done. Tell him how you plan to correct the situation. Use as many challenge words as possible.

definite	velvet	appeal
prevent	cheetah	charity

A. Write the challenge word that completes each analogy.

1. **Unclear** is to **exact** as **uncertain** is to _____.
2. **Wild pig** is to **boar** as **wild cat** is to _____.
3. **Stingy** is to **selfishness** as **generous** is to _____.
4. **Metal** is to **steel** as **fabric** is to _____.
5. **Answer** is to **ask** as **help** is to _____.
6. **Work for** is to **encourage** as **hold off** is to _____.

B. Write the challenge word that belongs in each group.

1. stop, halt, check
2. ask, request, plea
3. good will, sympathy, brotherly love
4. precise, exact, certain
5. tiger, leopard, lion
6. cotton, silk, corduroy

C. Write a story about a musical event given at a zoo to raise money for your favorite charity. Use some of the challenge words in your story.

Challenge Activities

categorize	hibernate	logic
glimpse	citrus	inhabit

A. Write the challenge word that would be part of the answer to each question. Tell what you could do in the situation given.

1. You see a stack of books that is not arranged in any kind of order. What could you do with these books?

2. You are Sherlock Holmes explaining how you solved a mystery. What do you claim helped you to solve the mystery?

3. You are a bear who doesn't want to be active in the winter. What could you do?

4. You are in a crowded store. You think you see a friend of yours walk by, but you do not get a good look. What kind of a look were you able to get?

5. Your family has bought a new house. What will you do there?

B. Write the challenge word that would be found on a dictionary page with each pair of guide words below.

1. cause | city
2. catchy | citizen
3. log | logrolling
4. glisten | hiccup
5. hibiscus | inhale
6. glimmer | hibachi

C. Write what the main character, Blob, might do in a science fiction story that takes place on a strange planet covered with fruit trees. Use as many challenge words as possible.

Challenge Activities

focus	melodious	devote
commotion	Congress	monument

A. Write challenge words to complete the news story. One of these words should be capitalized.

A concert was held on the steps of the Lincoln Memorial. It was in honor of the brave men and women who __1.__ their lives in service to their country. People from across the country, as well as members of __2.__, crowded around this historic __3.__. Police were standing by in case there was any __4.__, but the crowd was orderly. The band struck up a __5.__ tune. Then the speeches began. The __6.__ of the speeches was on national pride.

B. Write a challenge word that relates to each group.

1. Statue of Liberty, Jefferson Memorial, Mount Rushmore
2. camera, eye, attention
3. lawmakers, legislators, representatives
4. voice, violin, bird
5. pledge, vow, dedicate
6. riot, mutiny, disorder

C. Write a short report telling about an event that you would organize if you were the President of the United States. What would be the focus of the event? Who would be invited? Where would the event be held? Use some of the challenge words in your report.

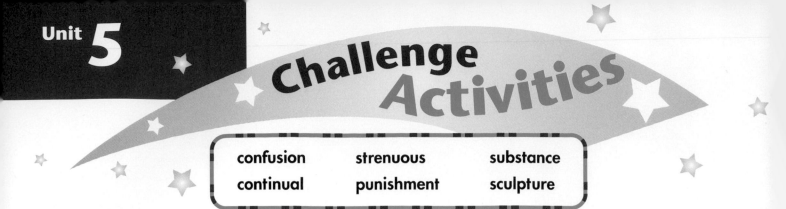

| confusion | strenuous | substance |
| continual | punishment | sculpture |

A. Complete this short story about a tour guide's first day on the job at the Statue of Liberty.

"This is __1.__ work!" I thought to myself. All day long there is a __2.__ flow of sightseers. Surprisingly, things run quite smoothly. There is very little __3.__. But standing on my feet all day is torture. My shoes take a lot of __4.__. It's all worth it, however. The Lady is a marvelous piece of __5.__, and she stands for important ideas with great __6.__.

B. Look at each base word in parentheses. To complete each sentence, write a challenge word that is the same part of speech as the abbreviation shown beside the base word. Then underline the suffix in each challenge word.

  1. Should the (punish, *n.*) fit the crime?
  2. What is the name of this huge (sculpt, *n.*)?
  3. I lost my keys in all this (confuse, *n.*).
  4. This month, it seemed as though I was on a (continue, *adj.*) diet of fresh fruit.

C. Write the challenge word that is related to each word.

  1. strain   **2.** substantial

D. Write two tongue twisters. In the first, use words beginning with the letter **c,** and include two challenge words. Your tongue twister could be, for example, "Cam's cousin created continual confusion." In the second, use words beginning with the letter **s**. Include three challenge words.

228

Challenge Activities

renewal	juvenile	supermarket
distribute	supreme	bulldozer

A. Write an antonym for each word in Column A. Write a synonym for each word in Column B. Use challenge words.

Column A

1. adult
2. collect
3. cancellation

Column B

4. highest
5. tractor
6. self-service store

B. Read the sentences. Write a challenge word to replace the underlined word(s) in each sentence.

1. Mr. Moyer's lease was up last year. He went to the landlord to ask for <u>an extension</u>.

2. Miss Andrews was new in the neighborhood. She was looking for a <u>store where she could buy groceries</u>.

3. Steve loved his younger brother Eddie, but sometimes Eddie was too <u>young</u> to be included in Steve's activities.

4. There was a farm auction last week. The best <u>tractor for moving earth</u> was sold right away.

5. Divide the stacks of newspapers and <u>give</u> them <u>out</u>.

6. The case went before the <u>highest Court in the country</u>.

C. What could you say or do to show good manners in each of the following situations?

1. You accidentally bump your shopping cart into someone at the store.

2. You are walking past a construction site. You recognize one of the workers.

3. You forgot to renew your library card.

4. A neighbor asks you to watch her child for an hour.

229

Challenge Activities

overview	fiendish	chiefly
surveillance	deceit	piercing

A. Write the challenge word that would be part of the answer to each question.

   1. What kind of noise or cry could penetrate the air?

   2. What kind of wicked act could you expect in a mystery movie?

   3. What do you call the practice of telling a falsehood in order to trick someone?

   4. What might a speaker give in his or her speech to let the audience know the broad picture of a topic?

   5. What do you call the close observation of a person under suspicion by the police?

   6. Which challenge word is an adverb?

B. Use challenge words to complete this list started by Detective R3.

   ___1.___ **of Contents of Detective Kit**

   • One whistle with ___2.___ tone to use ___3.___ in emergencies

   • A pair of binoculars to use for ___4.___

   • A scary face disguise with ___5.___ grin

   • A shiny badge that is for show, not ___6.___

C. Complete this science fiction story. Include as many challenge words as you can.

   Detective R3 heard a chilling sound near the secret lab station. He quickly boarded his rocket car that had special equipment.

Challenge Activities

nursery	garment	dormitory
departure	porcelain	formation

A. Write the challenge word that relates to each group.

   1. room, babies, cribs

   2. rooms, school, beds

   3. dress, shirt, sweater

   4. good-bye, takeoff, liftoff

   5. china, earthenware, teacups

   6. arrangement, order, organization

B. Read each job description. Then write the challenge word that would be in the answer to each question.

   1. I work in a college. My job is to supply fresh laundry to the rooms where the students sleep. Where do I spend my working hours?

   2. I work in a factory. My job is to sew clothes that will be sold in stores. In which type of industry do I work?

   3. I work outdoors where young trees and plants are raised for transplanting. Where do I work?

   4. I work in a studio. I make fine cups and dishes out of clay. What is the material I often use in my work?

C. Write the challenge word that is formed from each of these base words.

   1. depart   **2.** form

D. Write a job description of a job you would like to have. Use challenge words when you can.

Challenge Activities

| hysterical | interval | jovial |
| cordial | frequent | inhabitant |

A. Answer each "What would you be?" question with a challenge word.

   1. What would you be if you were good-hearted and full of fun?
   2. What would you be if you were unusually emotional or showing a lack of self-control?
   3. What would you be if you lived in a certain town?
   4. What would you be if you had a warm and friendly nature?
   5. What would you be if you were a period of time between now and then?
   6. What would you be if you were something that happened often?

B. Write challenge words to complete each sentence. After each word, write **N** if it was used as a noun and **A** if it was used as an adjective.

   At each ___1.___ in the road was an ___2.___ of the town who was helping people evacuate the area during the emergency. This police officer tried to be ___3.___, even ___4.___, to drivers who became ___5.___ when they got stuck in ___6.___ traffic jams in the Midtown Tunnel.

C. Imagine that you are a smart and friendly mole. You like to have many guests over to your tunnel home. Write a fanciful story about one of the "down-to-earth" parties you gave. Use some of the challenge words in your story. If you'd prefer to be a rat or a chipmunk or some other animal, go right ahead and change the main character.

Challenge Activities

frontward	politely	actively
practically	perfectly	vigorously

A. Write a challenge word to complete each analogy.

1. **Back** is to **front** as **backward** is to _____.
2. **Nearly** is to **closely** as **almost** is to _____.
3. **Faultily** is to **imperfectly** as **ideally** is to _____.
4. **Noisily** is to **quietly** as **rudely** is to _____.
5. **Powerfully** is to **forcefully** as **strenuously** is to _____.
6. **Tamely** is to **wildly** as **passively** is to _____.

B. Write a challenge word to complete each sentence.

1. Shake the bottle _____ so the two liquids blend.
2. Move the chess piece _____ to advance two spaces.
3. Ask the operator _____ for the phone number of the nearest library.
4. Check the content, grammar, and punctuation to make sure you wrote your report _____.
5. Your heart rate increases when you _____ play sports.
6. When you turn left at the barn, you'll know you are _____ at the farmhouse.

C. Answer each question with a complete sentence that includes a challenge word.

1. If you wanted a favor from your parents, how would you ask them?
2. If you went to a parade and you wanted to get a good view, which way would you move?
3. If someone offered you a free ticket to see a famous rock star, how would you answer?

| finalist | tariff | offense |
| fantastic | sheriff | phobia |

A. Write the challenge word that fits each definition.

1. a breaking of the law
2. a system of taxes on imports or exports
3. a person who takes part in a final competition
4. a deep, unreasonable fear of something
5. the chief law-enforcement official of a county
6. fanciful or imaginary

B. Write a challenge word to complete each sentence.

1. If you get into trouble in this county, call the _____.
2. Jay took part in the event as a _____.
3. You can be fined or imprisoned for an _____.
4. Their fear of riding on escalators may be a _____.
5. Sandy's dream was strange and _____.
6. On imported cars there is a high _____.

C. A person could have several different feelings about a dream, a fear, or an incident. Write a sentence about more than one feeling someone might have in each situation below. Use the underlined challenge word in the sentence.

1. Someone becomes a <u>finalist</u> in a talent contest for the very first time.
2. The <u>sheriff</u> gives someone a ticket for a speeding <u>offense</u>.
3. Someone dreams that he or she has to pay a high <u>tariff</u> for the imported watch he or she bought.
4. The shapes someone sees in clouds are <u>fantastic</u>.
5. Someone has a <u>phobia</u> of heights but had to climb a ladder one day.

| drizzle | disaster | excursion |
| amusing | mayonnaise | pleasurable |

A. Complete this silly poem with a challenge word that rhymes with the underlined word above it.

Yesterday was quite <u>confusing</u>,
Though I found it rather ___1.___.
The sun was so hot, it began to <u>sizzle</u>.
Then from the clouds it began to ___2.___.
It poured and poured, faster and <u>faster</u>
Until there was almost a major ___3.___ !
Then it happened. What a sight!
Everyone running to get a bite.
They ran for the jar they all thought so <u>treasurable</u>.
In it was something smooth and ___4.___.
Could it be? Could that explain their <u>ways</u>?
Surely they weren't eating all the ___5.___ !
No, it was just a <u>diversion</u>,
Surely it was a very strange ___6.___ !

B. Write the challenge word associated with each set of words.

   1. joke, silly song, comics
   2. salad dressing, sandwich spread, egg salad
   3. ferryboat ride, field day, family hike
   4. earthquake, forest fire, plane crash
   5. cloud, sleet, light rain
   6. fun, enjoyable, pleasing

Challenge Activities

discovered	satisfied	overlapped
discovering	satisfying	overlapping

A. Write the challenge word or words that were formed by following these rules.

    1. + **ed** only

    2. change **y** to **i** + **ed**

    3. double final consonant + **ed**

  4.–5. + **ing** only

    6. double final consonant + **ing**

B. Write the challenge word that can be used as a synonym for the group of words given below.

    1. fulfilling, convincing, gratifying

    2. found, came upon, learned

    3. coincided partly, extended over, shingled

C. Use the correct ending for each word in parentheses to complete the sentences. Write the challenge words.

    1. He is (overlap) the wallpaper as he hangs it.

    2. The teacher is not (satisfy) with our test results.

    3. Scientists are (discover) new things every day.

D. Write a short report about the things a group of friends can do or share together. Mention the satisfactions or rewards that come from sharing experiences as a group. Use some of the challenge words.

Challenge Activities

rhinoceros	**symptom**	**naphtha**
rhubarb	**subpoena**	**condemn**

A. What do you associate with certain occupations? Answer each question below with a challenge word.

    1. What might a pie baker use?

    2. What might a lawyer send someone?

    3. What might a dry cleaner use to get out stains?

    4. What might a doctor check a patient for?

    5. What might a zookeeper show off?

    6. What might a building inspector do to a dilapidated building?

B. Decide what the challenge word is for each clue. Write the challenge word.

    1. I am a liquid made from coal. I am used as fuel or as a spot remover.

    2. I am a written summons to appear in a court of law.

    3. I am a plant used for making sauces or pies.

    4. I am what you do to someone or something you disapprove of strongly.

    5. I am a change in the normal working of the body that shows sickness.

    6. I am a large thick-skinned mammal with horns.

C. You are a newspaper reporter who wants to know everything and find out who is the busiest person in town. Use the cast of characters given in Activity A. Write your findings and your final decision. Give reasons for your decision. Use challenge words where you can.

Challenge Activities

quizzical	irritate	plummeted
rapport	possession	propeller

A. Choose a challenge word that is more descriptive than the underlined word in each sentence. Write the word.

1. The two kites collided and <u>fell</u> to the ground.
2. A mechanic repaired the <u>fanlike device</u> on the boat.
3. The student had a <u>perplexed</u> expression on his face because he didn't understand the question.
4. Some soaps <u>bother</u> my skin.
5. My friend and I have a good <u>relationship</u> because we agree on many things.
6. Ellen has many books in her <u>holding</u>.

B. Write the challenge word that is suggested by each situation. Look for hidden clues in each statement.

1. "You and I get along," said one musician to another.
2. "You rub me the wrong way," said the dog to the flea.
3. "You can't move without oars," said the plane forcefully to the boat.
4. "How does this thing work?" the customer asked the salesperson.
5. "I hope this parachute opens!" said the skydiver.
6. "Everything here is mine!" said the spoiled child.

C. Choose a living being from the animal kingdom that you might like to be for a day. Then write a short story as if you were that animal. Mention the things you might value. For example, if you were a bird you might value nature, freedom, and communicating with other birds. Use some of the challenge words in your story.

Challenge Activities

breakable	perceptible	amiable
deductible	understandable	digestible

A. Think of a synonym for each verb below. Then add the suffix **-able** or **-ible** to the base of each synonym. Write the new adjective. Each answer should be a challenge word.

1. smash
2. comprehend

3. subtract
4. consume

B. Write the challenge word that relates to each pair of words.

1. visible, discernible
2. pleasant, agreeable
3. satisfying, nourishing

C. Write challenge words to complete the paragraph.

Amy wants to open her own savings account at a bank. She knows how to manage her money. The application form is easy to fill out. It is __1.__. The bank clerks are very helpful and __2.__. They'll explain to Amy that a service charge is added to her monthly statement. This charge is automatically __3.__ and will be subtracted from her savings each month. If there is any problem with Amy's account, the clerks will observe it quickly. Problems are very __4.__. The only thing they'll warn Amy about is not to bring her piggy bank with her. It is __5.__!

D. It's tax time! Imagine that you are an IRS official collecting taxes from people. How will you act with these people when they come to your office? What will you tell them? Write your answers using challenge words or forms of them. For example, you might use **digest** to mean **comprehend** rather than use the word **digestible**.

239

Challenge Activities

mispronounce	antidote	nondescript
misunderstand	nonchalant	nonproductive

A. Write a challenge word to complete each analogy.

1. **Warm** is to **enthusiastic** as **cool** is to _____.

2. **Particular** is to **distinctive** as **common** is to _____.

3. **Grasp** is to **comprehend** as **confuse** is to _____.

4. **Distinct** is to **enunciate** as **mumbled** is to _____.

5. **Idle** is to **profitless** as **useless** is to _____.

6. **Infection** is to **poison** as **healing** is to _____.

B. Read the first sentence. Complete the second sentence with a challenge word.

1. People take your meaning the wrong way. They _____.

2. The houses had no particular style. They were _____.

3. What the patient needs is something that will counteract the poison. The patient needs an _____.

4. She was so casual that she didn't seem to have a care in the world. She was _____.

5. This factory must be shut down because it hasn't yielded much in years. It is _____.

6. I thought your name rhymed with **cane**. Did I _____ it?

C. You collect strange and funny mistakes in news stories. Give examples from your own "collection." Be as creative as you like. You could record an example of a word that a famous politician might have mispronounced. You could also tell about the time when a reporter, who was sent to cover a famous, colorful wedding, wrote that the guests and the wedding decorations were nondescript! Use challenge words or forms of them in your examples.

Challenge Activities

leverage	puzzlement	enrichment
breakage	detriment	compartment

A. Write a challenge word to complete each analogy.

  1. **Handicap** is to **disadvantage** as **benefit** is to _____.

  2. **Content** is to **contentment** as **enrich** is to _____.

  3. **Bewilder** is to **problem** as **confuse** is to _____.

  4. **Building** is to **construction** as **smashing** is to _____.

  5. **House** is to **room** as **toolbox** is to _____.

  6. **Help** is to **harm** as **well-being** is to _____.

B. Write a challenge word to complete each sentence.

  1. Each small _____ in a stable is called a **stall**.

  2. The boy did not understand the question, and his _____ showed on his face.

  3. Falling into the cold water could be a _____ to her health.

  4. They put a wedge under the crowbar to get _____.

  5. Music and art provided _____ for the students.

  6. Insurance covered any _____ during the shipment of the crystal dishes.

C. Imagine that you are a riding instructor. You love horses, and you want people to learn how to ride them correctly. Your greatest concern is that nobody gets hurt. Write an ad for horseback riding lessons. Use the challenge words.

Challenge Activities

faithful	forceful	troublesome
blameless	countless	speechless

A. Write a challenge word to describe each pet.

I. Rex always waits at the door for me to come home, and then he brings me the newspaper. Rex is _____.

2. Fluffy wasn't the cat who broke the dish. She is innocent. Fluffy is _____.

3. Lora, the parrot, was surprised when the cat jumped on her birdcage. For once, she couldn't talk! Lora was _____.

4. Duke is always up to some kind of mischief. This dog gives me more to worry about than all the others. Duke is _____.

5. Twinkle is strong and full of drive. She protects her food from the other cats. Twinkle is _____.

6. Silver is a guppy. She and Pewter, my other fish, have had lots of baby guppies. Their offspring are _____.

B. Write a synonym for each word in Column A. Write an antonym for each word in Column B. Use challenge words.

Column A	Column B
I. loyal	**4.** limited
2. powerful	**5.** talkative
3. difficult	**6.** guilty

C. Write five different descriptions of a dog or a cat whose behavior could be associated with challenge words. Give clues. You may use Activity A as a guide. Then exchange papers with a partner to identify each other's descriptions.

videotape	volleyball	hindsight
bookmobile	public school	weather-beaten

A. Make each challenge word by matching a word in Column A with a word in Column B. Write the challenge word.

Column A	Column B
1. weather	school
2. hind	ball
3. book	sight
4. volley	tape
5. public	beaten
6. video	mobile

B. Write a challenge word to answer each question.

1. What would you be watching if you were looking at a prerecorded TV show?

2. What would you be using to figure out past events that you didn't fully understand at the time?

3. What would you call wood or a house that is worn by exposure to the weather?

4. What would you be looking at if you saw a truck with book-lined shelves that is used as a traveling library?

5. What game would you be playing if you hit a ball back and forth across a net with your hands?

6. What place is supported by taxes and provides free education to children in a community?

C. Think of an ideal campsite. What would it look like? What things could you do there? Write your description using challenge words. Then interview someone who has gone to camp. Review your paper. What things would you change?

243

extemporary	dietary	immaculate
culinary	intricate	considerate

A. Write the challenge word that completes each description.

1. I am not simple. I have a complicated pattern. I am an _____ design.

2. I don't like to plan things. I like to do and say _____ things.

3. I am thoughtful and _____ about other people's feelings.

4. I am a list of _____ rules that tell what foods to eat and how to prepare them for healthful living.

5. I always make sure that my clothes are clean, in good repair, and without wrinkles. My clothes are _____.

6. I have studied many cookbooks and produced extraordinary meals. I possess _____ skills.

B. Write a challenge word to describe the opposite kind of person or thing described below.

1. A person who does not take into account other people's feelings.

2. A room that is quite messy and dirty.

3. An uncomplicated story with no plot twists.

4. Dialogue in a play that is written and rehearsed.

C. 1.–2. Write the two challenge words that relate to food.

D. Complete this story about the life of a dancer. Use the challenge words in your story.

I love to dance, but the life of a professional dancer is not easy. For example, I must practice every day. I must watch my weight all the time.

Challenge Activities

midyear	interject	substandard
interfere	superpower	underlying

A. Prefixes and bases are mismatched in the challenge words below. Write these words correctly.

1. midject
2. interpower
3. interyear
4. superfere

B. Write the challenge word that would be found on a dictionary page with each pair of guide words below.

1. Superior, Lake │ supper
2. intention │ interim
3. subset │ suburb
4. interior │ intern
5. undergo │ understand

C. Use a challenge word to replace the underlined combination that matches it in meaning.

1. Shane got an A on his <u>middle-annual</u> exam.
2. In my opinion, this car is <u>below an acceptable level of quality</u>.
3. The <u>beneath-the-surface</u> reason for my lateness is that I overslept.

D. Imagine you are a sports announcer at an imaginary sports game of your choice. The team that all the experts expected would win the game is losing badly. What is going wrong? Write an explanation of why the team is losing so badly. Use challenge words in your explanation.

Challenge Activities

hideous	anxious	harmonious
monstrous	contagious	treacherous

A. Write the challenge word that fits both definitions.

1. **a.** agreeable; **b.** pleasing to the ear
2. **a.** very ugly; **b.** frightful
3. **a.** like a monster; **b.** huge
4. **a.** worried; **b.** eager
5. **a.** tending to spread from person to person, as in yawning; **b.** easily catching, as in a disease
6. **a.** disloyal; **b.** dangerous

B. Write a challenge word to complete each sentence. Next to each challenge word write the letter **a** or **b** for the meaning given in Activity A that matches the use of the word in the sentence.

1. The feeling of excitement and anticipation spread like a ripple of _____ laughter throughout the grandstand.
2. The cheerleaders sang a lovely, _____ cheer.
3. One team mascot was _____ in size.
4. The other team mascot was a person in a _____ disguise.
5. The fans were _____ about the outcome of the game.
6. The mountain road didn't cause the bus driver immediate alarm, but it turned out to be _____.

C. What do you know about ice hockey? How dangerous is it? How exciting is it? Write your own similes, using the challenge words to describe the game. For example, you can use your own version of "as happy as a clam" in this way: The players are as harmonious as clams.

Challenge Activities

sherbet	banquet	luncheon
guidance	naive	jeopardize

A. Write the challenge word that answers each question.

1. Suppose you were invited to eat lunch to celebrate the annual gymnastics contest. Would you go to a lunchon or a luncheon?

2. If you wanted to eat a frozen, fruit-flavored dessert, would you order a sherbet or a shebert?

3. For a special event, would the large meal be a banquet or a banqet?

4. If the star gymnast was an adult but thought like a child, would he or she be niave or naive?

5. Would the coach give the athletes guidance or giudance?

6. Would an accident jeopardize or jepardize an athlete's career?

B. Write the challenge word or words you associate with the following things.

1.–3. three things associated with food
4. something associated with leadership
5. a word associated with risk
6. a word associated with a childlike quality

C. You are invited to a luncheon in honor of your favorite famous athlete. Write a testimonial, or a speech showing admiration, for your favorite athlete. Don't forget to thank the sponsors of the event for the food they have provided! Use challenge words in your testimonial.

Challenge Activities

connection	collection	donation
contribution	recession	explanation

A. Write the challenge words that fit each spelling rule below.

1.–3. Add the suffix **-ion** to the base word with no spelling change.

4.–5. Drop **e** to add **-ion** to the base word.

6. Change the base word before adding the suffix **-ion**.

B. Write the challenge word (a noun) that is made from each verb below.

1. donate
2. connect
3. explain

4. contribute
5. recess
6. collect

C. Suppose you and your classmates wanted to set up a fund to repair the old pool in the school gym so that the swimming team can use it. Make a list of several activities that might be good fund-raisers. Then choose one activity and write a plan for carrying it out. Include challenge words in your written plans.

Challenge Activities

auctioneer	pediatrician	defendant
historian	vice president	contestant

A. Write the challenge word that describes each of the following persons.

1. one who holds the second place in authority
2. one who is an expert in or writes about important past events
3. one who conducts a public sale of things to be sold for the most money offered
4. one who takes part in a game or a race
5. one who specializes in the branch of medicine dealing with children and their diseases
6. one who is accused or sued in a court of law

B. Write the challenge word formed from each base word below.

1. defend
2. auction
3. contest

4. history
5. pediatric
6. preside

C. Make headings for six columns by using the challenge words. List other people that each person listed might encounter in the course of a day. Some of your lists will probably be longer than others. Then select one list. Use some of the people as characters for a short play. What will your setting be? What names will you give your characters? What will they say? What will be the plot and the climax of your play? How will it end? After you have considered answers to these questions, write your play.

Challenge Activities

admittance	annoyance	diligence
reluctance	existence	indifference

A. Write the challenge word that is formed when **-ance** or **-ence** is added to each verb below.

    1. annoy   **3.** admit

    2. exist   **4.** differ

B. Write the challenge word that is an antonym for each of these words.

    1. eagerness   **2.** laziness

C. Write a challenge word for each meaning below.

    1. permission to enter
    2. feeling of irritation or impatience
    3. careful and steady effort
    4. unwillingness
    5. lack of interest or caring
    6. being; life

D. Some of the challenge words on this list have or imply positive meanings. Other words have or imply negative meanings. Choose the words that fall into the first category, and write what they mean to you and what situations they suggest. Then do the same thing with the words that fall into the second category. Add other words and explanations of your own to each category.

250

Challenge Activities

verses	cession	palate
versus	session	pallet

A. Choose the correct homophone in parentheses to answer each question. Write the appropriate challenge word.

1. What might a person sleep on? (palate, pallet)
2. What part of the mouth do you use when you eat? (palate, pallet)
3. What might a poet write? (versus, verses)
4. What is a synonym for **against**? (versus, verses)
5. What might you call a meeting or a period of lessons? (cession, session)
6. What describes the act of giving up territory to another country? (cession, session)

B. Write the homophone that completes each sentence.

1. The biggest game of the school year is almost always the Reds _____ the Blues. (verses, versus)
2. The dentist looked at my mouth, especially the _____. (pallet, palate)
3. We signed up for a _____ of swimming lessons. (cession, session)
4. Do you only like _____ that rhyme? (versus, verses)
5. I'd rather sleep on a fluffy mattress than a _____. (palate, pallet)
6. The victorious nation demanded the conquered country complete a _____ of its lands. (session, cession)

C. Write a mixed-up message for one of the words in each pair of challenge words that are homophones. Then trade messages with a partner and correct the mistakes.

Challenge Activities

bibliography	altimeter	biologist
lexicographer	telephoto	antibiotic

A. Rearrange the word elements to form a word. Write the challenge word.

1. graph y biblio
2. lexico er graph
3. meter alti
4. log ist bio
5. bio tic anti
6. photo tele

B. Write a challenge word to complete each sentence.

1. I put the _____ lens on my camera to get a good shot of some distant birds.
2. Penicillin is an _____ that doctors sometimes prescribe.
3. The pilot studied the measuring device called an _____ while the plane was in flight.
4. **Lexis** means **word**, and the person who writes a dictionary is called a _____.
5. Our social studies books usually have a list of books, or a _____, referring to the topic of the unit.
6. A person who studies living organisms is known as a _____.

C. Use the information in Activity B to write a "Who or what am I" riddle for each challenge word. Add other words from Greek words or forms and write riddles for them, too.

emcee	Fortran	NASA
R.S.V.P.	COBOL	NATO

A. An **acronym** is a word or name that is created by combining the first letters in a group of words. For example, **radar** is an acronym made from "**ra**dio **d**etection **a**nd **r**anging."

Write the acronym for each group of words below. Use challenge words.

   1. North Atlantic Treaty Organization
   2. Common business-oriented language
   3. National Aeronautics and Space Administration
   4. Formula translation
   5. répondez s'il vous plaît
   6. master of ceremonies

B. A challenge word is used incorrectly in each sentence. Write the correct challenge word for each sentence.

   1. The talent show was a huge success, and the NATO did a great job as the announcer.
   2. At the end of the invitation, there was a request for a reply, or a COBOL.
   3. The sign at the space research building read Fortran.
   4. To solve the math problems, use the programming language called NATO.
   5. The member countries of NASA agree to protect one another from attack by outside aggressors.
   6. The scientists used emcee to program their work.

C. Write an invitation for a fund-raising event for a space agency or an international organization. Use as many challenge words as possible in your invitation.

WRITER'S HANDBOOK
Contents

Spelling Strategy
When You Take a Test

1 **Get** ready for the test. Make sure your paper and pencil are ready.

2 **Listen** carefully as your teacher says each word and uses it in a sentence. Don't write before you hear the word **and** the sentence.

3 **Write** the word carefully. Make sure your handwriting is easy to read. If you want to print your words, ask your teacher.

4 **Use** a pen to correct your test. Look at the word as your teacher says it.

5 **Say** the word aloud. Listen carefully as your teacher spells the word. Say each letter aloud. Check the word one letter at a time.

6 **Circle** any misspelled parts of the word.

7 **Look** at the correctly written word. Spell the word again. Say each letter out loud.

8 **Write** any misspelled word correctly.

Spelling Strategy
When You Write a Paper

1 **Think** of the exact word you want to use.

2 **Write** the word, if you know how to spell it.

3 **Say** the word to yourself, if you are not sure how to spell it.

4 **Picture** what the word looks like when you see it written.

5 **Write** the word.

6 **Ask** yourself whether the word looks right.

7 **Check** the word in a dictionary if you are not sure.

SPELLING AND THE Writing Process

Writing anything—a friendly letter, a paper for school—usually follows a process. The writing process has five steps. It might look like this if you tried to draw a picture of it:

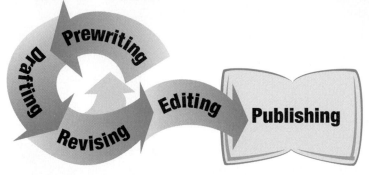

Notice that part of the writing process forms a loop. That is because not every writing task is the same. It is also because writers often jump back and forth between the steps as they change their minds and think of new ideas.

Here is a description of each step:

Prewriting This is thinking and planning ahead to help you write.

Drafting This means writing your paper for the first time. You usually just try to get your ideas down on paper. You can fix them later.

Revising This means fixing your final draft. Here is where you rewrite, change, and add words.

Editing This is where you feel you have said all you want to say. Now you proofread your paper for spelling errors and errors in grammar and punctuation.

Publishing This is making a copy of your writing and sharing it with your readers. Put your writing in a form that your readers will enjoy.

Confident spellers are better writers. Confident writers understand better their own writing process. Know the five steps. Know how they best fit the way you write.

SPELLING AND Writing Ideas

Being a good speller can help make you a more confident writer. Writing more can make you a better writer. Here are some ideas to get you started.

Ideas for Descriptive Writing

You might…

- describe something very, very small and something very, very big.
- describe something from the point of view of an insect.
- describe your most prized possession.

Ideas for Narrative Writing

You might…

- write a story about your first visit to someplace new.
- write a story about an event that helped you "grow up."
- write a story about a bad day or a best day playing your favorite sport.

Ideas for Persuasive Writing

You might…

- try to persuade your classmates to read a book you like.
- try to persuade your parents to let you have a pet.
- try to persuade your teacher to change a class rule.

Ideas for Expository Writing

You might…

- write how to prepare your favorite dish.
- inform your classmates how to create a craft object.
- write instructions on how to care for a lawn mower or carpentry tool.

More Ideas for Expository Writing

You might…

- find out how your local government works and write a report.
- interview an animal caregiver and write a report about the job.
- choose a career you might like and write a report about it.

Manuscript Handwriting Models

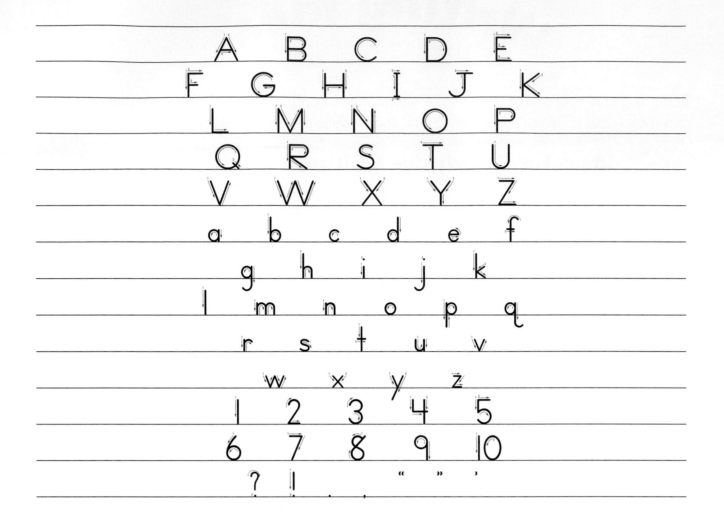

Cursive Handwriting Models

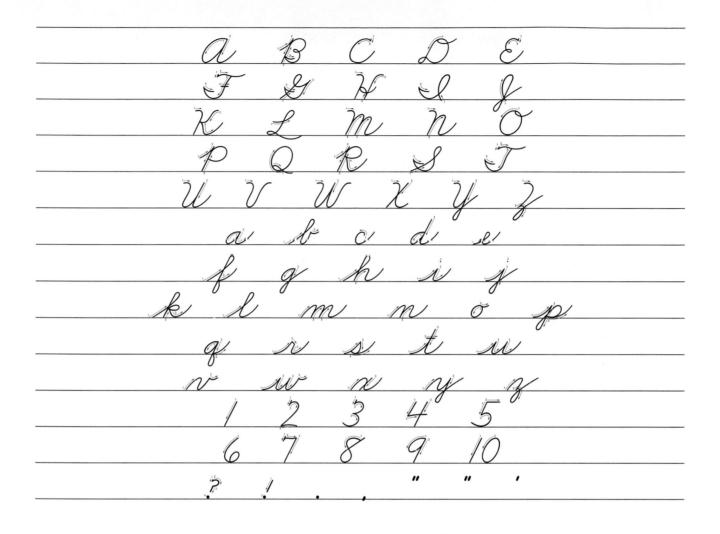

High Frequency Writing Words

A

a
about
afraid
after
again
air
all
almost
also
always
am
America
an
and
animal
animals
another
any
anything
are
around
as
ask
asked
at
ate

away

B

baby
back
bad
ball
balloons
baseball
basketball
be
bear
beautiful
because
become
bed
been
before
being
believe
best
better
big
bike
black
boat
book

books
both
boy
boys
bring
broke
brother
build
bus
but
buy
by

C

call
called
came
can
candy
can't
car
care
cars
cat
catch
caught
change

charge
children
Christmas
circus
city
class
clean
clothes
come
comes
coming
could
couldn't
country
cut

D

Dad
day
days
decided
did
didn't
died
different
dinner
do

does
doesn't
dog
dogs
doing
don't
done
door
down
dream

E

each
earth
eat
eighth
else
end
enough
even
every
everybody
everyone
everything
except
eyes

F

family
fast
father
favorite
feel
feet
fell
few
field
fight
finally
find
fire
first
fish
five
fix
food
football
for
found
four
free
Friday
friend
friends
from

front
fun
funny
future

G

game
games
gas
gave
get
gets
getting
girl
girls
give
go
God
goes
going
good
got
grade
grader
great
ground
grow

H

had
hair
half
happened
happy
hard
has
have
having
he
head
heard
help
her
here
he's
high
hill
him
his
hit
home
homework
hope
horse
horses
hot

hour
house
how
hurt

I

I
I'd
if
I'm
important
in
into
is
it
its
it's

J

job
jump
just

K

keep
kept
kids

killed
kind
knew
know

L

lady
land
last
later
learn
leave
left
let
let's
life
like
liked
likes
little
live
lived
lives
long
look
looked
looking
lost

lot
lots
love
lunch

M

mad
made
make
making
man
many
math
may
maybe
me
mean
men
might
miss
Mom
money
more
morning
most
mother
mouse
move

Mr.
Mrs.
much
music
must
my
myself

N

name
named
need
never
new
next
nice
night
no
not
nothing
now

O

of
off
oh
OK
old

on
once
one
only
or
other
our
out
outside
over
own

P

parents
park
party
people
person
pick
place
planet
play
played
playing
police
president
pretty
probably

problem
put

R

ran
read
ready
real
really
reason
red
responsibilities
rest
ride
riding
right
room
rules
run
running

S

said
same
saw
say
scared
school

schools
sea
second
see
seen
set
seventh
she
ship
shot
should
show
sick
since
sister
sit
sleep
small
snow
so
some
someone
something
sometimes
soon
space
sport
sports

start
started
states
stay
still
stop
stopped
store
story
street
stuff
such
sudden
suddenly
summer
sure
swimming

T

take
talk
talking
teach
teacher
teachers
team
tell
than

Thanksgiving
that
that's
the
their
them
then
there
these
they
they're
thing
things
think
this
thought
three
through
throw
time
times
to
today
together
told
too
took

top
tree
trees
tried
trip
trouble
try
trying
turn
turned
TV
two

U

united
until
up
upon
us
use
used

V

very

W

walk
walked
walking
want
wanted
war
was
wasn't
watch
water
way
we
week
weeks
well
went
were
what
when
where
which
while
white
who
whole
why

will
win
winter
wish
with
without
woke
won
won't
work
world
would
wouldn't

Y

yard
year
years
yes
you
your
you're

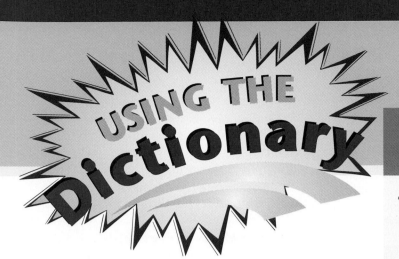

USING THE Dictionary

Guide Words

The **guide words** at the top of each dictionary page can help you find the word you want quickly. The first guide word tells you the first word on that page. The second guide word tells you the last word on that page. The entries on the page fall in alphabetical order between these two guide words.

Entries

Words you want to check in the dictionary are called **entries.** Entries provide a lot of information besides the correct spelling. Look at the sample entry below.

- Practice using guide words in a dictionary. Think of words to spell. Then use the guide words to find each word's entry. Do this again and again until you can use guide words easily.

- Some spellings are listed with the base word. To find **easiest,** you would look up **easy.** To find **remaining,** you would look up **remain.** To find **histories,** you would look up **history.**

- If you do not know how to spell a word, guess the spelling before looking it up. Try to find the first three letters of the word. (If you just use the first letter, you will probably take too long.)

- If you can't find a word, think of how else it might be spelled. For example, if a word starts with the **/k/ sound,** the spelling might begin with **k, c,** or even **ch.**

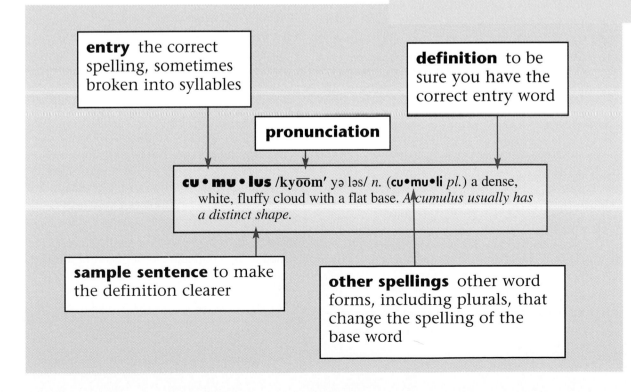

entry the correct spelling, sometimes broken into syllables

pronunciation

definition to be sure you have the correct entry word

cu • mu • lus /kyo͞om′ yə ləs/ *n.* (**cu•mu•li** *pl.*) a dense, white, fluffy cloud with a flat base. *A cumulus usually has a distinct shape.*

sample sentence to make the definition clearer

other spellings other word forms, including plurals, that change the spelling of the base word

267

ab • bre • vi • a • tion /ə brē′ vē ā′ shən/ *n.* a shortened form of a word; a syllable, a letter, or letters standing for a word or words. *"Dr." is an abbreviation for "Doctor."*

-able a suffix, used to form adjectives, that means: **a.** capable of: *understandable.* **b.** worthy of: *lovable.*

ab • sence /ăb′ səns/ *n.* **a.** being away. *Ryan brought a note to excuse his absence.* **b.** not having; a lack: *an absence of interest.*

ab • sent /ăb′ sənt/ *adj.* away; not here. *Kate was absent on Monday but present on Tuesday.*

ac • cent[1] /ăk′ sĕnt/ *n.* **a.** a mark (′) used to show stress. *A syllable with an accent is pronounced more strongly.* **b.** a distinctive way of speaking: *a British accent.*

ac • cent[2] /ăk′ sĕnt/ *v.* **a.** to stress; to emphasize. *Accent the first syllable.* **b.** to add to; to enhance. *Beth's pink scarf accents her white dress.*

ac • cept • a • ble /ăk sĕp′ tə bəl/ *adj.* (**ac•cept•a•bly,** *adv.*) agreeable; satisfactory. *Everyone at the meeting found the plan acceptable.*

ac • ci • dent /ăk′ sǐ dənt/ *n.* **a.** a harmful or unexpected event. *Ali had an accident on his bike.* **b.** something that occurs without being planned for. *The cure for the disease was discovered by accident.*

ac • cord /ə kôrd′/ *n.* agreement; harmony. *The nations were in accord on the issue of world hunger.*

ac • cu • rate /ăk′ yər ǐt/ *adj.* correct; without mistakes. *The witness's testimony was accurate and consistent with the evidence.*

ac • cuse /ə kyo̅o̅z′/ *v.* (**ac•cus•es, ac•cused, ac•cus•ing**) to blame for wrongdoing. *The police accused him of speeding and reckless driving.*

a • chieve /ə chēv′/ *v.* (**a•chieves, a•chieved, a•chiev•ing**) to reach; to accomplish. *If you wish to achieve success you must work hard.*

ac • tion /ăk′ shən/ *n.* **a.** a thing done; a deed. *The firefighter was praised for her brave action.* **b.** motion; movement. *Debbie likes action, but David prefers peace and quiet.*

a • cute /ə kyo̅o̅t′/ *adj.* **a.** severe or sharp; intense: *acute pain.* **b.** having fewer than 90 degrees. *A triangle must have at least two acute angles.*

ad • di • tion • al • ly /ə dǐsh′ ə nə lē/ *adv.* also; moreover; in addition. *Additionally, the movie has won international awards.*

ad • mit /ăd′ mǐt′/ *v.* (**ad•mits, ad•mit•ted, ad•mit•ting**) **a.** to let in. *If you don't have a ticket they can't admit you to the show.* **b.** to acknowledge; to confess. *The mayor admitted that she had not been aware of the problem.* [Latin *admittere,* from *ad-,* to + *mittere,* to send.]

a • dor • a • ble /ə dôr′ ə bəl/ or /ə dōr′-/ *adj.* lovable; charming. *The stuffed animals were cuddly and adorable.*

a • dore /ə dôr′/ or /-dōr′/ *v.* (**a•dores, a•dored, a•dor•ing**) to feel deep love and respect for. *Gandhi was adored by millions of Indians.*

ad • vance[1] /ăd văns′/ *v.* to go forward. *Please advance to the front of the line.*

ad • vance[2] /ăd văns′/ *n.* any forward movement; progress. *Medical research has made great advances.*

ad • vance • ment /ăd văns′ mənt/ *n.* improvement; progress; promotion. *They dedicated their new club to the advancement of poetry.*

ad • van • tage /ăd văn′ tǐj/ *n.* **a.** anything that helps bring about success. *That basketball player has the advantage of being tall.* **b.** help; benefit; gain. *Studying is to your advantage.*

af • ter • ward /ăf′ tər wərd/ *adv.* later. *We'll do some shopping and have lunch afterward.*

-age a suffix, used to form nouns, that means: **a.** a collective or a general group: *baggage.* **b.** a state or condition of: *marriage.* **c.** an act of: *breakage.*

ag•ed /ā′ jĭd/ *adj.* **a.** old; having lived long. *The aged man was having difficulty walking.* **b.** /ājd/ having a certain age: *aged three.*

a•gent /ā′ jənt/ *n.* **a.** a person or company whose business is to represent another: *an insurance agent.* **b.** a substance that causes a certain action to begin. *Yeast is the agent that causes bread to rise.* [Latin *agēns*, doing, from *agere*, to do.]

ag•ri•cul•ture /ăg′ rĭ kŭl′ chər/ *n.* farming; raising food and farm animals. *We all depend on agriculture for food.*

aisle /īl/ *n.* a passage between rows of seats. *The usher stood in the aisle.*

▶ **Aisle** sounds like **isle.**

al•bum /ăl′ bəm/ *n.* **a.** a book with blank pages on which photographs, stamps, etc., may be kept. *Will you sign my autograph album?* **b.** a recording of several different pieces of music. *I like the title song on that album.*

all right¹ /ôl′ rīt′/ *adj.* satisfactory. *Your answer looks all right to me.*

all right² /ôl′ rīt′/ *adv.* **a.** yes; very well. *All right, I'll come home early.* **b.** in a satisfactory way. *Is everything going all right?*

al•ly /ăl′ ī/ *n.* (**al•lies** *pl.*) a person or country united with others for a specific purpose. *During World War II the United States and Great Britain were allies.*

al•ma•nac /ôl′ mə năk′/ *n.* a reference book published yearly. *A farmer may read an almanac to find out when to plant crops.*

al•mond /ä′ mənd/ *n.* the nut of the almond tree. *Toasted almonds make a good snack.*

A.M. or **a.m.** an abbreviation meaning in the morning. *My appointment is Tuesday at 10 A.M.* [Latin *ante meridiem*, before noon.]

am•a•teur /ăm′ ə tûr′ or /-chŏŏr′/ *n.* a person who participates in an activity for fun, not money. *Even an amateur can become skillful with regular practice.*

a•maze /ə māz′/ *v.* (**a•maz•es, a•mazed, a•maz•ing**) to surprise or astonish. *We were amazed at the acrobat's ability to do high jumps.*

Pronunciation Key

ă	pat	ŏ	pot	th	thin
ā	pay	ō	toe	*th*	*th*is
âr	care	ô	paw, for	hw	which
ä	father	oi	noise	zh	vision
ĕ	pet	ou	out	ə	about,
ē	be	ŏŏ	took		item,
ĭ	pit	ōō	boot		pencil,
ī	pie	ŭ	cut		gallop,
îr	pier	ûr	urge		circus

am•bu•lance /ăm′ byə ləns/ *n.* a vehicle for taking people who are hurt or sick to the hospital. *An ambulance is equipped with special lights and a siren.*

ambulance

a•mend•ment /ə měnd′ mənt/ *n.* a formal change in a law or a bill. *An amendment to the Constitution gave women the right to vote.*

am•pli•tude /ăm′ plĭ tōōd′/ or /-tyōōd′/ *n.* the distance between the highest and the lowest point of a wave. *As the amplitude of a sound wave increases, so does the loudness of the sound.*

-ance a suffix, used to form nouns, that means: **a.** state or quality of: *resemblance.* **b.** act of: *resistance.* **c.** thing that: *conveyance.*

an•nounce /ə nouns′/ *v.* (**an•nounc•es, an•nounced, an•nounc•ing**) **a.** to tell; to make known; to give notice. *Would the principal announce that school will be closing early?* **b.** to provide commentary and deliver announcements on radio or TV. *The sportscaster announces the tennis match.*

-ant a suffix used with verbs: **a.** to form adjectives that mean "having the quality of": *resistant.* **b.** to form nouns that mean "person or thing that": *assistant.*

anti- a prefix that means "against": *antiseptic.*

an•ti•freeze /ăn′ tĭ frēz′/ *n.* a liquid mixed with another liquid to keep it from freezing. *Cars need antifreeze during the winter.*

an•ti•so•cial /ăn′ tē sō′ shəl/ *adj.* avoiding the company of others. *It is a mistake to assume that a shy person is deliberately antisocial.*

a•pos•tro•phe /ə pŏs′ trə fē/ *n.* a mark (') used: **a.** to show that a letter or letters have been purposely left out of a word: *it'll, you've.* **b.** to show possession: *Jim's, girls'.*

ap•pear•ance /ə pîr′ əns/ *n.* **a.** being seen by the public. *The TV star made a personal appearance at the shopping mall.* **b.** the looks of a place or person. *New paint really improved the room's appearance.*

ap•pli•cant /ăp′ lĭ kənt/ *n.* a person applying for a job or position. *There were many applicants for the after-school job.*

ap•ply /ə plī′/ *v.* (ap•plies, ap•plied, ap•ply•ing) **a.** to put on: *apply paint.* **b.** to put to use. *We did an experiment to apply what we learned in science.* **c.** to make a request. *She applied to join the Girl Scouts.*

ap•point•ment /ə point′ mənt/ *n.* an arrangement to meet someone at a certain time. *I have a two o'clock appointment.*

ap•pos•i•tive /ə pŏz′ ə tĭv/ *n.* a noun or noun phrase placed next to another noun for further explanation or description. *In the sentence "Brian, Dan's brother, also came," the appositive is "Dan's brother."*

ap•pre•ci•ate /ə prē′ shē āt′/ *v.* (ap•pre•ci•ates, ap•pre•ci•at•ed, ap•pre•ci•at•ing) **a.** to see the value of something. *The recital made us appreciate my brother's hours of piano practice.*

ap•proach /ə prōch′/ *v.* to come near. *The deer ran away as we approached.*

ap•proach•a•ble /ə prō′ chə bəl/ *adj.* friendly; easy to approach. *The librarian's smile made her seem approachable.*

ap•prove /ə prōōv′/ *v.* (ap•proves, ap•proved, ap•prov•ing) **a.** to give official consent to. *The board approved the plans for the new gym.* **b.** to have a good opinion of. *Do you approve of his choice of colors?*

ap•prox•i•mate /ə prŏks′ ə mĭt/ *adj.* nearly right; almost correct. *The architect gave them an approximate cost of the new house.*

ap•ti•tude /ăp′ tĭ tōōd′/ or /-tyōōd′/ *n.* a talent or ability for learning. *She has an aptitude for languages; she speaks French, German, and Italian.*

ar•a•ble /ăr′ ə bəl/ *adj.* able to be farmed or cultivated. *Rocky land is not arable.*

arc /ärk/ *n.* a curved line; a line that is part of a circle. *A famous landmark in St. Louis is an arc.*

arc

a•rise /ə rīz′/ *v.* (a•ris•es, a•rose, a•ris•en, a•ris•ing) **a.** to get up. *On school days we arise early.* **b.** to appear; to begin. *If any problems should arise, phone us at this number.*

ar•ter•y /är′ tə rē/ *n.* (ar•ter•ies *pl.*) any of the body's vessels that carry blood from the heart to all parts of the body. *Which artery carries blood to the brain?*

-ary a suffix that means "of" or "relating to," used to form adjectives: *honorary.*

as•sign /ə sīn′/ *v.* **a.** to give out; to distribute. *Our teacher assigns us homework every evening.* **b.** to appoint to a position. *The teacher assigned him to be hall monitor this month.*

as•sign•ment /ə sīn′ mənt/ *n.* a thing assigned. *It took me three hours to complete my homework assignments.*

as•sist /ə sĭst′/ *v.* to help; to aid. *I assisted Mother in preparing dinner.*

as•sis•tant /ə sĭs′ tənt/ *n.* a person who assists another; a helper. *We need an assistant to help with the project.* [Latin *assistere*, to assist, from *ad-*, near to + *sistere*, to stand.]

as•so•ci•ate¹ /ə sō′ shē āt′/ *v.* **a.** to think of as related. *Most people associate tears with sadness, but many people cry when they are happy.* **b.** to join as a friend. *Joy associates with her softball teammates regularly.*

as•so•ci•ate² /ə sō′ shē ĭt/ *n.* a friend or fellow worker. *Mr. Ortiz is an associate of my father's.*

as•sume /ə sōōm′/ *v.* (as•sumes, as•sumed, as•sum•ing) **a.** to accept as true; to take for granted. *People once assumed the earth was flat.* **b.** to accept; to take upon oneself. *Megan assumed the job of decorating the room.*

as•tron•o•my /ə strŏn′ ə mē/ *n.* the study of planets, stars, and other bodies in outer space. *Telescopes are used in astronomy.*

-ate a suffix used: **a.** to form adjectives that mean "having" or "characterized by": *fortunate.* **b.** to form verbs that mean "to act upon": *renovate.*

ath•lete /ăth′ lēt′/ *n.* a person who performs in competitive sports. *An athlete trains daily.*

athlete

-ation a suffix, used to form nouns, that means: **a.** an action or process: *consideration.* **b.** the result of an action or process: *inflammation.*

at•las /ăt′ ləs/ *n.* (**at•las•es** *pl.*) a book of maps. *Our atlas has maps of all the major highways.*

at•om /ăt′ əm/ *n.* the smallest particle into which a chemical element can be divided. *Everything around us is made up of atoms.*

at•tend /ə tĕnd′/ *v.* to go to; to be present at. *Did you attend the last meeting?*

at•ten•dance /ə tĕn′ dəns/ *n.* **a.** the act of being present. *His attendance at school has been perfect all year.* **b.** the number of persons present. *During a losing streak attendance drops at baseball games.*

at•ten•dant /ə tĕn′ dənt/ *n.* a person who serves or waits on others. *There are always four attendants working at this gas station.*

at•ten•tion /ə tĕn′ shən/ *n.* **a.** staying alert to what is happening. *Always pay attention in class.* **b.** thoughtfulness; consideration. *Rhonda gave a lot of attention to her grandparents during their visit.*

at•tic /ăt′ ĭk/ *n.* a room just below the roof of a house. *We found a big box up in our attic.*

au•thor•i•ty /ə thôr′ ĭ tē/ or /-thŏr′-/ or /ō-/ *n.* (**au•thor•i•ties** *pl.*) **a.** the right or power to control, command, or enforce. *Police officers have the authority to enforce laws.* **b.** any source of correct information. *The encyclopedia is an authority on many different subjects.*

Pronunciation Key

ă	pat	ŏ	pot	th	**th**in
ā	pay	ō	toe	*th*	**th**is
âr	care	ô	p**aw,** f**or**	hw	**wh**ich
ä	father	oi	n**oi**se	zh	vi**s**ion
ĕ	pet	ou	**ou**t	ə	**a**bout,
ē	be	ŏŏ	t**oo**k		it**e**m,
ĭ	pit	ōō	b**oo**t		penc**i**l,
ī	pie	ŭ	c**u**t		gall**o**p,
îr	pier	ûr	**ur**ge		circ**u**s

au•to•bi•og•ra•pher /ô′ tō bī ŏg′ rə fər/ *n.* a person who writes the story of his or her own life. *A good autobiographer is honest and descriptive.*

au•to•bi•og•ra•phy /ô′ tō bī ŏg′ rə fē/ *n.* (**au•to•bi•og•ra•phies** *pl.*) a person's life story told or written by himself or herself. *Helen Keller wrote an autobiography.* [Greek *autos,* self + *bios,* life + *graphein,* to write.]

au•to•graph[1] /ô′ tō grăf′/ *n.* anything written in a person's own handwriting, especially his or her name. *I collected the autographs of all the students in my class.*

au•to•graph[2] /ô′ tō grăf′/ *v.* to sign one's name. *She asked the pitcher to autograph her ball.* [Greek *autos,* self + *graphein,* to write.]

au•to•ma•tion /ô′ tə mā′ shən/ *n.* the automatic operation of a system, a process, or equipment. *Most factories rely heavily on automation.*

au•tumn /ô′ təm/ *n.* the season that comes after summer and before winter; fall. *In autumn, many leaves turn beautiful colors.*

a•vail•a•ble /ə vā′ lə bəl/ *adj.* able to be used or obtained. *The firefighters used all the available equipment.*

av•a•lanche /ăv′ ə lănch′/ *n.* **a.** a large mass of snow sliding swiftly down a mountain. *The avalanche buried several trees.* **b.** anything that comes on suddenly: *an avalanche of orders.*

Spelling Dictionary

back•ground /bǎk′ ground′/ *n.* the distant part of a picture or scene. *Mountains are painted in the background.*

baf•fle /bǎf′ əl/ *v.* (**baf•fles, baf•fled, baf•fling**) to puzzle; to bewilder. *The riddles baffled the students.*

bal•ance¹ /bǎl′ əns/ *n.* **a.** equality in weight or number. *Our teacher keeps a good balance between praise and criticism.* **b.** a steady position. *I tripped and lost my balance.*

bal•ance² /bǎl′ əns/ *v.* **a.** to weigh or measure in or as in a balance. *Amy added one more weight to balance the scales.* **b.** to bring into a condition of balance. *Antoine balanced the basketball on his fingertip.*

bal•lad /bǎl′ əd/ *n.* a poem, often sung, that tells a simple story. *Many country and western songs are ballads.*

ban•dage /bǎn′ dĭj/ *n.* a strip of cloth used to cover a wound. *He put a bandage over the cut.* [French *bande*, band, strip.]

ban•ner¹ /bǎn′ ər/ *n.* **a.** a flag. *"The Star-Spangled Banner" is a song about the American flag.*
b. a piece of cloth with a picture, design, or writing on it. *The owners hung a banner for the grand opening.*

banner

ban•ner² /bǎn′ ər/ *adj.* very good: *a banner season.*

bar•be•cue /bär′ bĭ kyōō′/ *n.* a meal cooked over an open fire, especially outdoors. *They served hamburgers at the barbecue.*

bare•ly /bâr′ lē/ *adv.* hardly; scarcely. *We could barely see the cars because of the fog.*

bar•gain¹ /bär′ gĭn/ *n.* **a.** an agreement. *I made a bargain with Molly to rake the leaves if she would bag them.* **b.** something with a low price. *He found a bargain at the sale.*

bar•gain² /bär′ gĭn/ *v.* to try to agree on the terms of a deal. *The employer and employees bargained over the new labor contract.*

ba•rom•e•ter /bə rŏm′ ĭ tər/ *n.* an instrument that measures air pressure. *A falling reading on a barometer can indicate worse weather to come.* [Greek *baros*, weight + *metron*, measure.]

BA•SIC /bā′ sĭk/ *n.* an acronym for a common computer programming language. *We wrote a math program in BASIC.* [**B**eginner's **A**ll-purpose **S**ymbolic **I**nstruction **C**ode.]

be•have /bĭ hāv′/ *v.* (**be•haves, be•haved, be•hav•ing**) **a.** to act properly; to do the right things. *If you don't behave, you won't be invited again.* **b.** to act; to conduct oneself. *How did the toddler behave at the movies?*

be•yond /bē ŏnd′/ or /bĭ ŏnd′/ *prep.* in a place farther away than; past. *The grocery store is just beyond the park.*

bi•lin•gual /bī lĭng′ gwəl/ *adj.* able to speak two languages equally well. *Manuel is bilingual; he speaks Spanish and English.*

bill of sale /bĭl′ əv sāl′/ *n.* a document stating that personal property has been transferred to a new owner. *The lawyers drew up a bill of sale for our old house.*

bi•og•ra•pher /bī ŏg′ rə fər/ *n.* a person who writes a life history of another person. *A good biographer does careful research.* [Greek *bios*, life + *graphein*, to write.]

bi•ol•o•gy /bī ŏl′ ə jē/ *n.* the scientific study of living things. *Botany and zoology are two branches of biology.* [Greek *bios*, life + *logos*, word, speech.]

bit /bĭt/ *n.* an acronym for the smallest unit of storage in a computer; a tiny memory space that can contain one of two choices. *A byte is made up of eight bits.* [**B**inary dig**it**.]

bleed /blēd/ *v.* (**bleeds, bled, bleed•ing**) to lose blood. *Her knee began to bleed when she scraped it.*

block • ade /blŏ kād′/ *n.* the closing off of an area. *During the Civil War, blockades were formed to prevent supplies from reaching the other army.*

book • store /bŏŏk′ stôr′/ or /-stōr′/ *n.* a store where books are sold. *That bookstore has a good selection of books for children.*

bound • a • ry /boun′ də rē/ or /-drē/ *n.* (**bound•a•ries** *pl.*) the ending line or edge of one thing and the beginning edge or line of another. *The fence marks the boundary of our property.*

broad • cast[1] /brŏd′ kăst′/ *v.* (**broad•cast** or **broad•cast•ed, broad•cast•ing**) to send through the air by radio or TV. *The President's speech was broadcast last evening.*

broad • cast[2] /brŏd′ kăst′/ *n.* a radio or television program. *Many viewers watch the six o'clock news broadcast.*

bro • chure /brō shŏŏr′/ *n.* a small booklet or pamphlet. *Zachary sent for a brochure on soccer camps.*

bronze /brŏnz/ *n.* an alloy of copper and tin or certain other metals. *The Olympic teams may win medals of gold, silver, or bronze.*

browse /brouz/ *v.* (**brows•es, browsed, brows•ing**) **a.** to look at in a leisurely way; to skim through. *Sam browsed through the magazines in the dentist's office.* **b.** to feed on leaves. *Giraffes browse on tall trees.*

budge /bŭj/ *v.* (**budg•es, budged, budg•ing**) to move slightly. *The car wheels were stuck in the mud and did not budge.*

buf • fet[1] /bə fā′/ or /bŏŏ-/ *n.* a meal at which guests may serve themselves from food laid out on a table or sideboard. *After the meeting, we served a salad buffet.*

buf • fet[2] /bŭf′ ĭt/ *v.* to strike; to knock about with force. *The wind buffeted the fragile flowers.*

bu • gle /byŏŏ′ gəl/ *n.* a brass instrument similar to a trumpet, used for military signals. *The soldiers woke up to a bugle call.*

bugle

Pronunciation Key

ă	pat	ŏ	pot	th	thin
ā	pay	ō	toe	th	this
âr	care	ô	paw, for	hw	which
ä	father	oi	noise	zh	vision
ĕ	pet	ou	out	ə	about,
ē	be	ŏŏ	took		item,
ĭ	pit	ōō	boot		pencil,
ī	pie	ŭ	cut		gallop,
îr	pier	ûr	urge		circus

bul • le • tin /bŏŏl′ ĭ tn/ *n.* **a.** a short news report. *The television program was interrupted for a bulletin about the storm.* **b.** a small magazine or newspaper. *The club puts out a bulletin twice a month.*

bu • reau /byŏŏr′ ō/ *n.* **a.** a chest of drawers for holding clothing. *My socks are in the top drawer of the bureau.* **b.** an office for a special kind of business. *We visited the passport bureau.*

cab • i • net /kăb′ ə nĭt/ *n.* **a.** a piece of furniture in which things are stored on shelves: *a medicine cabinet.* **b.** a group of persons chosen by the head of state to help run the government. *Members of the cabinet are often heads of government departments.*

cal • o • rie /kăl′ ə rē/ *n.* a unit of heat used to measure the energy-producing value of food. *Exercise burns up calories.*

camp • fire /kămp′ fīr′/ *n.* a fire in a camp, for keeping warm or for cooking. *It is fun to sit around a campfire at night and sing songs.*

camp • site /kămp′ sīt′/ *n.* a place to camp. *We chose a beautiful campsite near a waterfall.*

can • cel /kăn′ səl/ *v.* **a.** to cross out; to mark with lines. *The post office cancels stamps.* **b.** to do away with; to call off. *The game was canceled due to rain.*

can•di•date /kăn′ dĭ dāt′/ or /-dĭt/ *n.* a person seeking an office or an honor. *She is a candidate for governor.*

ca•pa•ble /kā′ pə bəl/ *adj.* (**ca•pa•bly,** *adv.*) having the skill to; able to. *She is capable of fixing almost any machine.*

ca•pac•i•ty /kə păs′ ĭ tē/ *n.* **a.** the amount that can be held. *The capacity of that bottle is one quart.* **b.** ability; capability. *Sarah has a capacity for solving math problems quickly.*

cap•i•tal•i•za•tion /kăp′ ĭ tl ĭ zā′ shən/ *n.* the process of writing or printing in capital letters. *Do you know the rules of punctuation and capitalization?*

cap•tain /kăp′ tən/ *n.* a person who commands, as a ship, army, or team. *The captain is responsible for the safety of all those on board the ship.*

car•a•van /kăr′ ə văn′/ *n.* a band of people, pack animals, or vehicles traveling together. *The caravan of merchants and camels stretched across the Sahara.*

car•bon /kär′ bən/ *n.* a common chemical element found in all organic substances. *Diamonds are pure carbon, but carbon is also present in coal, graphite, and charcoal.*

car•bon di•ox•ide /kär′ bən dī ŏk′ sīd′/ *n.* a colorless, odorless gas composed of carbon and oxygen and present in Earth's atmosphere. *The carbon dioxide exhaled by animals is absorbed by green plants.*

care•ful•ly /kâr′ fə lē/ *adv.* with care; cautiously or thoroughly. *Peter dusted the tiny figurines carefully.*

Car•ib•be•an /kăr′ ə bē′ ən/ or /kə rĭb′ ē ən/ *adj.* relating to the Caribbean Sea and its islands. *The Caribbean islands attract tourists from all over the world.*

car•pen•ter /kär′ pən tər/ *n.* a person who can make things from wood or repair them. *We hired a carpenter to make the new cabinets.*

car•riage /kăr′ ĭj/ *n.* a four-wheeled vehicle pulled by horses and used for carrying people. *Carriages were popular until the car was invented.* [Norman French *carier,* to carry.]

car•ti•lage /kär′ tl ĭj/ *n.* the tough white connective tissue that is attached to the surfaces of bones near joints. *Cartilage helps protect the bones from injury.*

car•ton /kär′ tn/ *n.* a container made of cardboard or plastic. *We looked for a big enough carton to hold all the gifts.*

carton

cas•ta•nets /kăs′ tə nĕts′/ *n. pl.* a rhythm instrument consisting of hollow shells of wood or ivory that are clicked together with the fingers. *Spanish flamenco dancers often perform with castanets.*

ca•su•al /kăzh′ ōō əl/ *adj.* **a.** without plan; happening by chance. *He paid a casual visit to his old friends.* **b.** everyday; informal. *We wore casual clothes to the party.*

cat•a•log or **cat•a•logue** /kăt′ l ôg′/ or /-ŏg′/ *n.* a list of things arranged in alphabetical order with descriptions. *A library has a catalog of all the books in it.*

cau•tious /kô′ shəs/ *adj.* careful; keeping away from danger. *The bus driver was cautious in the storm.* [Latin *cautiō,* from *cavēre,* to take care.]

ceil•ing /sē′ lĭng/ *n.* the top of a room. *In most rooms there is a light attached to the ceiling.*

cel•list /chĕl′ ĭst/ *n.* a person who plays the stringed instrument called the cello. *Cellists sit on chairs and hold their cellos between their knees.*

Cel•si•us /sĕl′ sē əs/ or /-shəs/ *adj.* relating to the Celsius temperature scale, which registers the freezing point of water as 0° and the boiling point as 100°. *Normal body temperature is about 37° Celsius.*

cen•tral /sĕn′ trəl/ *adj.* **a.** in or at the middle; near the center. *The biggest stores are in the central part of the city.* **b.** main; leading; chief. *What is the central idea that the author wants us to understand?*

CEO an abbreviation for "chief executive officer." *The CEO of the bank approves all loans.*

ce•ram•ics /sə răm′ ĭks/ *n.* the art or technique of making objects from clay and firing them at high temperatures. *In our class in ceramics, we made both soup mugs and figurines.*

cer•e•mo•ny /sĕr′ ə mō′ nē/ *n.* (**cer•e•mon•ies** *pl.*) a special set of acts done in a certain way. *The wedding ceremony was held outdoors.*

cer•tain•ly /sûr′ tn lē/ *adv.* definitely; surely. *Your grades will certainly improve if you study hard.*

change•a•ble /chān′ jə bəl/ *adj.* subject to change; variable: *changeable weather.*

chan•nel /chăn′ əl/ *n.* **a.** a body of water connecting two larger bodies of water. *The English Channel lies between the Atlantic Ocean and the North Sea.* **b.** any passage through which a liquid can flow. *The workers dug a channel to remove water.* **c.** a frequency used for radio or TV. *The community channel is asking viewers for money.*

chap•ter /chăp′ tər/ *n.* a part or main section of a book. *Each chapter is narrated by a different character.*

char•coal /chär′ kōl′/ *n.* a black substance made by partly burning wood in a closed container. *Many people cook outdoors in the summer using charcoal as fuel.*

check•book /chĕk′ boŏk′/ *n.* a book of blank bank checks. *The monthly bank statement also tells how to balance a checkbook.*

chimes /chīmz/ *n. pl.* an instrument used to make bell-like sounds. *One of the percussionists in an orchestra plays the chimes.*

chis•el[1] /chĭz′ əl/ *n.* a tool with a strong, sharp blade. *A chisel is used for carving wood or stone.*

chis•el[2] /chĭz′ əl/ *v.* to cut or shape with a chisel. *The sculptor chiseled a statue out of marble.*

chisel

chord /kôrd/ *n.* three or more musical tones sounding together to produce harmony. *At our first lesson, the guitar instructor went over some basic chords.*

cir•cu•lar /sûr′ kyə lər/ *adj.* round; having the shape of a circle. *A lighthouse is usually a circular building.*

cir•cum•fer•ence /sər kŭm′ fər əns/ *n.* the distance around a circle. *You can measure the circumference of a tree trunk by putting a tape measure around it.*

cir•rus /sîr′ əs/ *n.* a high-altitude cloud consisting of narrow bands or white, fleecy patches. *A cirrus indicates fair weather, not rainfall.*

cit•i•zen•ship /sĭt′ ĭ zən shĭp′/ *n.* the rights, duties, and privileges that come with being a citizen. *Immigrants who apply for United States citizenship promise to uphold the principles of the Constitution.*

ci•vil•ian /sĭ vĭl′ yən/ *n.* a person not serving in the military. *Most civilians do not wear uniforms.*

clas•si•fy /klăs′ ə fī′/ *v.* to sort; to arrange according to category or class. *Librarians do not classify fairy tales with other fiction.*

cleanse /klĕnz/ *v.* to make clean; to remove dirt from. *Always cleanse a cut or scrape before bandaging it.*

clear•ance /klîr′ əns/ *n.* **a.** space; clearing. *There was only a foot of clearance between the branch and the roof.* **b.** a sale at which items are reduced in price for quick sale. *After a clearance, a store has room to display new merchandise.*

COD an abbreviation for "cash on delivery." *Catalog orders can sometimes be sent COD.*

col • lect /kə lĕkt'/ *v.* **a.** to gather; to bring or come together. *Jane collected the test papers.* **b.** to gather and keep as a hobby. *Bob collects stamps.* **c.** to get money that is owed. *The landlord collected the rent.*

col • lec • tive /kə lĕk' tĭv/ *adj.* **a.** of a number of persons acting as one: *the collective decision of the community.* **b.** having a singular form but a plural meaning. *The word "committee" is a collective noun.*

col • umn /kŏl' əm/ *n.* **a.** a support or pillar for a building. *The ivy twines around the porch columns.* **b.** a straight row that goes up and down. *Many books have two columns of print on each page.* **c.** articles appearing regularly and written by one author. *Mr. Vronski writes a column for the paper.*

col • um • nist /kŏl' əm nĭst/ *n.* a person who writes a regular series of articles for a newspaper or magazine. *Teresa is the advice columnist for the school newspaper.*

co • me • di • an /kə mē' dē ən/ *n.* a professional entertainer who tells jokes and does things to make people laugh. *Some comedians have become stars of situation comedies.*

com • mu • ni • ty /kə myōō' nĭ tē/ *n.* (**com•mu•ni•ties** *pl.*) all the people who live in one area; the residents of a town. *The park is for the entire community.* [Latin *commūnis*, common.]

com • pact¹ /kəm păkt'/ or /kŏm' păkt'/ *adj.* arranged within a small space. *Most portable appliances are compact.*

com • pact² /kəm păkt'/ *v.* to pack together tightly. *That machine compacts garbage.*

com • pact³ /kŏm' păkt'/ *n.* a small cosmetic case. *May I borrow the mirror in your compact?*

com • plain /kəm plān'/ *v.* **a.** to find fault. *Don't complain about a problem unless you're willing to help remedy it.* **b.** to report something bad. *The neighbors complained to the police about the noisy motocycle.* [Latin *com-* (intensive) + *plangere*, to lament.]

com • plete • ly /kəm plēt' lē/ *adv.* entirely; totally. *By the end of the party, the food was completely gone.*

com • ple • tion /kəm plē' shən/ *n.* a making or being completed; finishing. *The completion of a job gives one a feeling of accomplishment.* [Latin *complet-*, perfect stem of *complēre*, to fill out, from *com-* (intensive) + *plēre*, to fill.]

com • plex • ion /kəm plĕks' shən/ *n.* the appearance of the face with regard to color and texture. *Limiting your exposure to the sun will keep your complexion healthier.*

com • pos • er /kəm pō' zər/ *n.* a person who composes or creates music. *Leonard Bernstein, who wrote the music for* West Side Story, *earned fame as both conductor and composer.*

com • pound¹ /kŏm' pound'/ *n.* a chemical substance formed of two or more elements. *Water is a compound of hydrogen and oxygen.*

com • pound² /kŏm' pound'/ *adj.* formed of two or more parts: *a compound sentence.*

com • pound³ /kŏm' pound'/ *v.* to add to. *The sunshine compounded our happiness.*

com • pound⁴ /kŏm' pound'/ *n.* a group of buildings enclosed by barriers. *The security was tight around the compound.*

com • pu • ta • tion /kŏm' pyōō tā' shən/ *n.* the process of computing; a mathematical calculation. *The accountant used a calculator to make tax computations.*

com • pu • ter /kəm pyōō' tər/ *n.* an electronic device that stores and analyzes data or performs calculations at high speeds. *Some schools have computers in every classroom.*

computer

con • ceit /kən sēt'/ *n.* an exaggerated opinion of one's worth; vanity. *Conceit is an unattractive quality.*

con • cern /kən sûrn'/ *v.* **a.** to relate to; to have an effect on. *The problem of pollution concerns all of us.* **b.** to make anxious; to worry. *His illness concerned his parents.*

con • clude /kən klōōd'/ *v.* (**con•cludes, con•clud•ed, con•clud•ing**) to end; to finish. *She concluded her speech and sat down.*

con•clu•sion /kən kloo′ zhən/ *n.* **a.** the end. *We left in a hurry at the conclusion of the dinner.* **b.** an opinion arrived at by thinking carefully. *The judge's conclusion was that Mr. Benson was innocent.* [Latin *conclūsiō*, from *conclūdere*, to end, from *com-* (intensive) + *claudere*, to close.]

con•di•tion /kən dĭsh′ ən/ *n.* **a.** something that is needed before something else can be obtained. *Hard work is a condition of success.* **b.** the state in which a person or thing is. *The weather conditions were good.*

con•duct¹ /kŏn′ dŭkt′/ *n.* behavior; way of acting. *Nancy's conduct in class was good.*

con•duct² /kən dŭkt′/ *v.* **a.** to guide; to lead. *The student conducted the visitor through the new building.* **b.** to carry; to be a path for. *Copper conducts electricity.*

con•fide /kən fīd′/ *v.* (**con•fides, con•fid•ed, con•fid•ing**) to trust one's secrets to another. *Pedro confided his plan to his friend.*

con•firm /kən fûrm′/ *v.* to make certain or sure. *The experiment confirmed her theory.*

con•fuse /kən fyooz′/ *v.* (**con•fus•es, con•fused, con•fus•ing**) to mix up in the mind; to throw into disorder. *The loud noises confused the wild animals.*

con•gru•ent /kŏng′ groo ənt/ or /kən groo′-/ *adj.* having exactly the same size and shape as another figure. *Two polygons are congruent if they match exactly.*

con•nect /kə nĕkt′/ *v.* **a.** to join; to link. *Before you turn on the water, connect the hose to the faucet.* **b.** to join two ideas, events, etc., in the mind. *I connect clowns with the circus.* [Latin *com-*, together + *nectere*, to bind.]

con•ser•va•tion /kŏn′ sûr vā′ shən/ *n.* the protection of natural resources from loss, harm, or waste. *The community's efforts toward conservation resulted in a wildlife sanctuary to protect animals.*

con•sid•er /kən sĭd′ ər/ *v.* **a.** to think carefully before doing something. *Have you considered the pros and cons?* **b.** to think of someone or something as; to regard as. *I consider that a compliment.*

Pronunciation Key

ă	pat	ŏ	pot	th	thin
ā	pay	ō	toe	th	this
âr	care	ô	paw, for	hw	which
ä	father	oi	noise	zh	vision
ĕ	pet	ou	out	ə	about,
ē	be	ŏŏ	took		item,
ĭ	pit	ōō	boot		pencil,
ī	pie	ŭ	cut		gallop,
îr	pier	ûr	urge		circus

con•sid•er•a•tion /kən sĭd′ ə rā′ shən/ *n.* **a.** careful thinking. *They gave our plan serious consideration.* **b.** regard for the feelings of others; thoughtfulness. *Selfish people have little consideration for others.*

con•sole¹ /kən sōl′/ *v.* to comfort in time of trouble or sorrow. *The mother tried to console the screaming toddler.*

con•sole² /kŏn′ sōl/ *n.* a cabinet or panel that houses the controls for mechanical or electrical equipment such as a TV, stereo, or computer. *Technicians operate all the theater lights from a central console.*

con•so•nant /kŏn′ sə nənt/ *n.* a speech sound made by partially or completely stopping the flow of air through the mouth; the letter or letters that stand for such a sound. *A is a vowel, but B and C are consonants.*

con•stant /kŏn′ stənt/ *adj.* never changing or stopping; happening again and again. *The constant beat of the rain put us to sleep.*

con•stel•la•tion /kŏn′ stə lā′ shən/ *n.* a group of stars with a name. *Many constellations were named after the animals they seemed to form in the sky.*

constellation

con•tact¹ /kŏn′ tăkt/ *n.* **a.** a coming together of objects; a touching. *My fingers came into contact with a cold, soft material.* **b.** a connection, especially of people: *a business contact.*

con • tact² /kŏn′ tăkt/ *v.* to communicate with. *The pilot contacted the control tower for landing instructions.*

con • tent¹ /kŏn′ tĕnt/ *n.* **a.** often **contents**, what is contained; what a thing holds or encloses. *The contents of the package are listed on the label.* **b.** the ideas expressed; the topic; the substance. *The teacher liked the content of my essay but said its grammar and punctuation needed work.*

con • tent² /kən tĕnt′/ *adj.* satisfied; pleased. *We were content with our one-point victory.*

con • tin • u • ous /kən tĭn′ yoo əs/ *adj.* going on without stopping; unbroken; connected. *A continuous line of people passed the window.*

con • tract¹ /kŏn′ trăkt′/ *n.* a legal agreement. *The striking workers finally accepted the new contract.*

con • tract² /kon′ trăkt′/ or /kən trăkt′/ *v.* **a.** to make a legal agreement. *We contracted to mow their lawn every two weeks.* **b.** to become smaller by shrinking. *Most things expand in warm weather and contract in cold weather.*

con • trib • ute /kən trĭb′ yoot/ *v.* (con•trib•utes, con•trib•ut•ed, con•trib•ut•ing) to give; to donate. *Each student contributed two hours of work for the bake sale.*

con • vert¹ /kən vûrt/ *v.* to change into another form, substance, or condition. *Jim's dad converted their unfinished basement into a playroom.*

con • vert² /kŏn′ vûrt/ *n.* a person who has accepted a new belief. *There are few converts to the new tax proposal.*

con • vict¹ /kən vĭkt′/ *v.* to find guilty. *The defendant was convicted of a felony.*

con • vict² /kŏn′ vĭkt′/ *n.* **a.** a person found guilty of a crime. *The convict was led from the court.* **b.** a person serving a prison sentence. *Some convicts work in the prison garden.*

cor • al¹ /kôr′ əl/ or /kŏr′-/ *n.* a hard substance formed from the skeletons of tiny sea animals. *The island's gleaming beach consists of grains of coral.*

cor • al² /kôr′ əl/ or /kŏr′-/ *adj.* made of coral: *coral reefs.*

cor • rupt /kə rŭpt′/ *adj.* dishonest; influenced by bribery. *There was a citizens' campaign to remove corrupt officials from public office.*

could • 've could have.

cour • age /kûr′ ĭj/ or /kŭr′-/ *n.* the quality of facing danger or a difficult task without giving in to fear. *It takes courage to admit your mistakes.* [French *corage,* from Latin *cor,* heart.]

cou • ra • geous /kə rā′ jəs/ *adj.* being brave; having courage. *The courageous skater attempted a triple jump.*

CPU an abbreviation for "central processing unit," the part of every computer that controls the most basic operations. *The CPU of older computers was found in the main frame.*

cra • ter /krā′ tər/ *n.* a hollow, bowl-shaped surface, such as that formed by a volcano or caused by the impact of a meteorite. *The astronauts photographed the moon's craters.*

crater

crease¹ /krēs/ *v.* (creas•es, creased, creas•ing) to fold, pleat, or wrinkle. *How do you crease paper to make an airplane?*

crease² /krēs/ *n.* a line made by pressing, folding, or wrinkling. *Jan ironed out the creases in her skirt.*

cross-coun • try /krôs′ kŭn′ trē/ or /krŏs′-/ *adj.* **a.** moving across open country instead of following paths or roads: *cross-country skiing.* **b.** from one side of the country to the other: *a cross-country trip.*

cru • el /kroo′ əl/ *adj.* wanting to make others suffer or causing them pain. *The cruel children threw stones at the birds.*

cruise¹ /krōōz/ *v.* (**cruis•es, cruised, cruis•ing**) **a.** to travel leisurely or aimlessly about. *The pleasure boat cruised the bay.* **b.** to travel at a constant, efficient speed. *The jet cruised high above the clouds.*

cruise² /krōōz/ *n.* a sea voyage taken for pleasure: *a Caribbean cruise.*

crumb /krŭm/ *n.* a small piece or fragment, especially of bread or cake. *We fed crumbs to the birds during the winter.*

cu•mu•lo•nim•bus /kyōōm′ yə lō nĭm′ bəs/ *n.* a very dense, vertically shaped cloud that may cause heavy rain or thunderstorms. *A cumulonimbus may bring hail.*

cu•mu•lus /kyōōm′ yə ləs/ *n.* (**cu•mu•li** *pl.*) a dense, white, fluffy cloud with a flat base. *A cumulus usually has a distinct shape.*

cumulus

cup•board /kŭb′ ərd/ *n.* a cabinet with shelves, used for storing food, dishes, etc. *We keep spices in the corner cupboard.*

cur•few /kûr′ fyōō/ *n.* an order requiring persons to remain indoors during set hours, especially at night. *The soldiers had a midnight curfew.*

cu•ri•ous /kyōōr′ ē əs/ *adj.* eager to learn or find out; interested. *I was curious about how the computer program worked.*

cur•tain /kûr′ tn/ *n.* a hanging piece of cloth used to decorate a door or window or to separate the audience from the stage in a theater. *We closed the curtains to darken the room.*

cush•ion /kŏŏsh′ ən/ *n.* a soft pad or a pillow. *Their poodle sleeps on a cushion in a basket.*

cus•to•di•an /kŭs stō′ dē ən/ *n.* a caretaker; a janitor. *The custodian of the building keeps the sidewalks free of snow during the winter.*

cus•to•dy /kŭs′ tə dē/ *n.* **a.** care; safekeeping; guardianship. *The judge granted the parents joint custody of the children.* **b.** detention. *The police have a suspect in custody.*

cus•tom•ar•y /kŭs′ tə měr′ ē/ *adj.* based on custom; usual; routine. *A tuna sandwich and an apple are my customary lunch.*

Pronunciation Key

ă	pat	ŏ	pot	th	thin
ā	pay	ō	toe	th	this
âr	care	ô	paw, for	hw	which
ä	father	oi	noise	zh	vision
ĕ	pet	ou	out	ə	about,
ē	be	ŏŏ	took		item,
ĭ	pit	ōō	boot		pencil,
ī	pie	ŭ	cut		gallop,
îr	pier	ûr	urge		circus

cus•tom•er /kŭs′ tə mər/ *n.* any person who buys something. *The store held a sale to attract new customers.*

czar /zär/ *n.* an emperor of Russia. *Czars had absolute power over their subjects.*

day•dream¹ /dā′ drēm′/ *n.* a pleasant, dreamy thought. *She has daydreams about being a famous poet.*

day•dream² /dā′ drēm′/ *v.* to have pleasant, dreamy thoughts. *Try not to daydream in class.*

deal /dēl/ *v.* (**deals, dealt, deal•ing**) **a.** to have to do with; to be concerned with. *The book deals with the history of America.* **b.** to hand out; to distribute. *Whose turn is it to deal the cards?*

dealt /dĕlt/ *v.* past tense and past participle of **deal**.

de•bate¹ /dĭ bāt′/ *n.* a discussion or argument on a particular subject. *We heard a debate on methods of teaching last night.*

de•bate² /dĭ bāt′/ *v.* to discuss or consider the pros and cons of a subject. *The students debated whether to have a dance or a field trip.*

de•bris /də brē′/ or /dā-/ *n.* remains of something broken, destroyed, or discarded. *The hurricane left much debris on the beach.*

debt /dĕt/ *n.* something owed to another person, usually money. *It is polite to repay a debt as soon as possible.*

279

de•bug /dē bŭg′/ v. (de•bugs, de•bugged, de•bug•ging) to locate and correct errors in a computer program. *If your procedure doesn't work, you'll have to debug it.*

dec•a•gon /dĕk′ ə gŏn′/ n. a geometric figure having ten sides and ten angles. *The sides of a regular decagon are all equal.*

decagon

dec•i•bel /dĕs′ ə bəl/ or /-bĕl′/ n. a unit used for measuring the relative intensity of sounds. *Ordinary conversation reaches a level of about 60 decibels.*

de•ci•sion /dĭ sĭzh′ ən/ n. **a.** a conclusion; a verdict. *Has the committee reached a decision?* **b.** firmness; decisiveness. *The defense lawyer is noted for her courage and decision.*

de•clar•a•tive /dĭ klâr′ ə tĭv/ adj. that which announces or states: *a declarative sentence.*

de•clare /dĭ klâr′/ v. (de•clares, de•clared, de•clar•ing) **a.** to announce publicly and formally; to make known. *The governor declared his opposition to the new bill.* **b.** to say positively and surely. *"I don't believe a word of it," she declared.*

de•fend /dĭ fĕnd′/ v. **a.** to protect from harm or attack; to guard. *The soldiers continued to defend the fort.* **b.** to act or speak in defense of something; to justify: *defend a decision.* **c.** to represent the defendant in court. *The judge assigned a lawyer to defend him.*

de•fense /dĭ fĕns′/ n. **a.** something that defends. *Washing your hands frequently is a good defense against colds.* **b.** the defending team or side. *Our team's defense was outstanding.*

del•i•cate /dĕl′ ĭ kĭt/ adj. **a.** light and pleasing to the senses: *a delicate perfume.* **b.** carefully and expertly done; requiring careful workmanship: *delicate repairs.* **c.** fragile; easily broken or hurt: *a delicate vase.*

de•light•ful /dĭ līt′ fəl/ adj. greatly pleasing; causing joy or delight. *We saw a delightful movie last night.*

del•ta /dĕl′ tə/ n. a deposit of mud and sand at the mouth of a river. *Deltas are formed when a river slows down and drops the materials that are carried by the current.*

dem•on•strate /dĕm′ ən strāt′/ v. **a.** to show; to make clear. *You must demonstrate a willingness to learn in school.* **b.** to prove through an experiment or by using logical thinking. *The teacher demonstrated the force of gravity by dropping objects to the floor.*

de•ple•tion /dĭ plē′ shən/ n. exhaustion; a state of being used up. *Many dry areas of Africa have experienced erosion and depletion of soil.*

der•ma•tol•o•gist /dûr′ mə tŏl′ ə jĭst/ n. a doctor who specializes in skin problems. *A dermatologist can tell you about the best treatments for your complexion.*

der•mis /dûr′ mĭs/ n. the layer of skin beneath the surface layer. *The dermis lies beneath the epidermis.*

der•rick /dĕr′ ĭk/ n. the structure above an oil well to which drilling and pumping equipment is attached. *When the gusher was drilled, the entire derrick was hidden by a spouting stream of oil.*

des•o•late /dĕs′ ə lĭt/ or /dĕz′-/ adj. **a.** barren; without vegetation: *desolate terrain.* **b.** uninhabited; deserted: *a desolate island.* **c.** lonely; dejected. *Julie was desolate when her best friend moved away.*

des•per•ate /dĕs′ pər ĭt/ adj. **a.** almost despairing; frantic. *I made a desperate attempt to catch the teetering vase.* **b.** very bad; critical; extreme. *The driver was in a desperate situation when the brakes failed.*

de•tain /dĭ tān′/ v. **a.** to delay; to hold back. *The flight was detained two hours due to heavy fog.* **b.** to keep in custody. *A suspect was detained for questioning.*

de•vel•op /dĭ vĕl′ əp/ v. **a.** to grow; to come into being. *The bud developed into a blossom.* **b.** to build up; to put to use. *Reading helps develop your mind.*

de•vel•op•ment /dĭ vĕl′ əp mənt/ n. **a.** the act of developing; growth. *The children enjoyed watching the kittens' development.* **b.** results; news. *What are the latest developments in the plans for a picnic?*

di•am•e•ter /dī ăm′ ĭ tər/ *n.* a straight line that passes through the center of a circle or other figure, dividing it into two equal parts. *The radius of a circle is half its diameter.* [Greek *dia*, through + *metron*, measure.]

diameter

di•e•ti•tian /dī′ ĭ tĭsh′ ən/ *n.* a person who specializes in creating healthful diets. *Our school dietitian plans nutritious meals.*

dif•fer /dĭf′ ər/ *v.* **a.** to be unlike. *The two nations differ in their languages and customs.* **b.** to disagree; to have unlike ideas or opinions. *We couldn't resolve our argument, so we agreed to differ.*

dif•fer•ence /dĭf′ ər əns/ *n.* **a.** a way in which people or things are not alike. *There is a big difference in size between a mouse and an elephant.* **b.** the amount by which one number is greater than another. *The difference between 10 and 12 is 2.*

dif•fer•ent /dĭf′ ər ənt/ or /dĭf′ rənt/ *adj.* **a.** not alike. *Summer is different from winter.* **b.** not the same; separate. *My cousin and I go to different schools.*

dif•fi•cult /dĭf′ ĭ kŭlt′/ or /-kəlt/ *adj.* **a.** hard; not easy to do or understand. *Learning to play chess is difficult.* **b.** hard to get along with. *He has a reputation for being difficult.*

di•ges•tive /dī jĕs′ tĭv/ or /dĭ-/ *adj.* relating to or serving the process by which food is changed so the body can absorb it. *The digestive system breaks down the food we eat into nutrients.*

di•men•sion /dī mĕn′ shən/ or /dĭ-/ *n.* a measurement of the length, width, or height of something. *The dimensions of the package are three feet in length, two feet in width, and one foot in height.*

dip•lo•mat /dĭp′ lə măt′/ *n.* a person skilled in dealing with other persons or governments. *The diplomats tried to lessen the tension between their countries.*

di•rect¹ /dĭ rĕkt′/ or /dī-/ *v.* **a.** to point out the way. *The road map directed us to the town.* **b.** to be in charge of; to manage. *A police officer directed traffic.* **c.** to order; to command. *The doctor directed Will to eat more fresh fruit.* [Latin *dīrect-*, perfect stem of *dīregere*, to give direction to, from *dis-*, apart + *regere*, to guide.]

Pronunciation Key

ă	pat	ŏ	pot	th	**th**in
ā	pay	ō	toe	*th*	**th**is
âr	care	ô	paw, for	hw	**wh**ich
ä	father	oi	noise	zh	vision
ĕ	pet	ou	out	ə	about,
ē	be	ŏŏ	took		item,
ĭ	pit	ōō	boot		pencil,
ī	pie	ŭ	cut		gallop,
îr	pier	ûr	urge		circus

di•rect² /dĭ rĕkt′/ or /dī-/ *adj.* **a.** straight; not roundabout: *a direct route.* **b.** honest; frank: *a direct answer.*

di•rec•tion /dĭ rĕk′ shən/ or /dī-/ *n.* **a.** managing; control. *The orchestra was under the direction of a famous conductor.* **b.** a point toward which one can face. *We walked in the direction of the bank.* **c.** **directions** an explanation of how to do something. *The directions were hard to follow.*

di•rect•ly /dĭ rĕkt′ lē/ *adv.* **a.** in a direct line; straight. *The city is directly north of us.* **b.** right away. *I'll be there directly.*

dir•ty /dûr′ tē/ *adj.* not clean; containing dirt. *Put all the dirty clothes into the washing machine.*

dis•a•gree•ment /dĭs ə grē′ mənt/ *n.* a dispute; a difference of opinion. *We had a disagreement over whose turn it was.*

dis•count /dĭs′ kount/ *n.* a reduction; an amount taken off a price. *Mary got a discount on the hat because it was on sale.*

dis•cus•sion /dĭ skŭsh′ ən/ *n.* a serious or thorough conversation. *Sandy and I had a long discussion about how to clean up our neighborhood.* [Latin *discuss-*, perfect stem of *discutere*, to discuss, from *dis-*, apart + *quatere*, to shake.]

dis•guise¹ /dĭs gīz′/ *v.* (**dis•guis•es, dis•guised, dis•guis•ing**) **a.** to change one's real appearance so that one will not be recognized. *In the play, the thief was disguised as a detective.* **b.** to hide; to mask; to cover up. *He disguised his anger by smiling.*

dis•guise² /dĭs gīz′/ *n.* a costume used to hide one's real identity: *a clown disguise.*

disk•ette /dĭ skĕt′/ *n.* a floppy disk on which computer data can be stored. *Dave stored his program on a high-density diskette.*

dis•pute¹ /dĭ spyo͞ot′/ *v.* (dis•putes, dis•put•ed, dis•put•ing) to argue; to debate; to have a different opinion about. *Our class disputed over the best date for the picnic.*

dis•pute² /dĭ spyo͞ot′/ *n.* argument; debate; quarrel. *Diplomats try to settle disputes between countries.*

dis•tance /dĭs′ təns/ *n.* the space between two points or places. *I live a short distance away.*

dis•tant /dĭs′ tənt/ *adj.* **a.** far away or long ago. *The speaker had traveled in distant lands.* **b.** not easy to talk with; keeping to oneself. *Shy persons can seem distant until you get to know them.*

dis•trict /dĭs′ trĭkt/ *n.* a part of a country, state, or county that has certain duties or functions. *We have school districts and voting districts.*

di•vis•i•bil•i•ty /dĭ vĭz′ ə bĭl′ ĭ tē/ *n.* the state of being able to divide without a remainder. *Factoring can show the divisibility of a number.*

DOB an abbreviation for "date of birth." *Write the date you were born in the space marked "DOB."*

doc•u•ment /dŏk′ yə mənt/ *n.* an official paper; any written record used as evidence for some fact. *Your birth certificate is an important document.* [Latin *documentum*, lesson, from *docēre*, to teach.]

do•nate /dō′ nāt′/ *v.* (do•nates, do•nat•ed, do•nat•ing) to give or contribute to a fund or a cause. *The class decided to donate the money from their bake sale to the animal shelter.*

doubt•ful /dout′ fəl/ *adj.* not sure; uncertain. *I am doubtful that we can finish the game in this rain.*

down•ward¹ /doun′ wərd/ *adv.* toward a lower place. *The car at the top of the hill rolled downward.*

down•ward² /doun′ wərd/ *adj.* going toward a lower place. *This downward path leads to the house.*

drought /drout/ *n.* a long period of time during which there is no rain. *The crops were ruined last summer by a two-month drought.*

du•ti•ful /do͞o′ tĭ fəl/ or /dyo͞o′-/ *adj.* careful about performing one's duty; obedient; respectful. *Darrell is a dutiful son who helps care for his bedridden mother.*

east•ward¹ /ēst′ wərd/ *adv.* toward the east. *The river runs eastward.*

east•ward² /ēst′ wərd/ *adj.* in or toward the east. *The pilot set an eastward course.*

ed•i•ble /ĕd′ ə bəl/ *adj.* capable of being eaten. *Many wild berries are not edible.*

-eer a suffix that means "someone who works in or is involved with": *engineer.*

ef•fort /ĕf′ ərt/ *n.* **a.** the use of one's strength or power; exertion. *Riding a bicycle uphill requires effort.* **b.** an attempt; a try. *Make an effort to finish by three.* [Latin *ex-*, out + *fortis*, strong.]

e•lec•tri•cian /ĭ lĕk trĭsh′ ən/ or /ē lĕk-/ *n.* a person who installs and repairs electrical equipment. *The electrician rewired the old house.*

electrician

e•lec•tron /ĭ lĕk′ trŏn/ *n.* one of the tiny particles of negative matter that travel around the nucleus of an atom. *Electrons have a negative charge.*

e•mer•gen•cy /ĭ mûr′ jən sē/ *n.* (e•mer•gen•cies *pl.*) a serious situation that requires something to be done right away. *The police are trained to respond quickly in an emergency.*

e•mo•tion /ĭ mō′ shən/ *n.* a strong reaction or feeling. *Anger is a common emotion.*

em•pire /ĕm′ pīr/ *n.* a number of countries led by a single, powerful ruler or emperor. *Years ago, the Roman Empire included most of the world then known in the West.*

em•ploy•ee /ĕm ploi′ ē/ *n.* a person who works for another person or for a business. *The bank had a picnic for all its employees.*

-ence a suffix, used to form nouns, that means: **a.** an act or a result of acting: *dependence.* **b.** a state or a quality: *absence.*

en•cy•clo•pe•di•a /ĕn sī klə **pē′** dē ə/ *n.* a book or group of books that gives general information on many different subjects. *Topics in an encyclopedia are usually in alphabetical order.*

en•dan•ger /ĕn **dān′** jər/ *v.* to put in danger; to harm. *Pollution endangers wildlife.*

en•gi•neer /ĕn jə **nîr′**/ *n.* **a.** a person trained to use science and math for practical purposes such as designing and building systems or equipment. *My big sister is an electrical engineer.* **b.** a person who operates an engine: *a train engineer.*

en•grave /ĕn **grāv′**/ *v.* (**en•graves, en•graved, en•grav•ing**) to carve designs or letters into a surface. *The jeweler engraved my initials on my watch.*

en•list /ĕn **lĭst′**/ *v.* **a.** to join a branch of the armed forces voluntarily. *Lydia wants to enlist in the Navy when she finishes high school.* **b.** to gain the support of. *The principal enlisted us all to help clean up the school yard.*

-ent a suffix used: **a.** to form adjectives that means "causing" or "being": *absorbent.* **b.** to form nouns that means "one who": *president.*

en•vi•ron•ment /ĕn **vī′** rən mənt/ *n.* **a.** the total surroundings that allow a living organism to grow and develop. *Congress has passed bills to protect our environment from pollution.* **b.** surroundings. *The library is a quiet environment for study.*

en•zyme /**ĕn′** zīm/ *n.* a protein substance produced by living organisms. *Enzymes help our bodies break down food.*

ep•i•der•mis /ĕp ĭ **dûr′** mĭs/ *n.* the outer layer of the skin. *Humans and plants both have an epidermis.*

-er a suffix, used to form nouns, that means: **a.** one who: *teacher.* **b.** thing that: *toaster.*

e•quip•ment /ĭ **kwĭp′** mənt/ *n.* the things needed for a special purpose; supplies. *Paper, desks, and chairs are all office equipment.*

e•quiv•a•lent¹ /ĭ **kwĭv′** ə lənt/ *adj.* identical; equal. *Twelve inches are equivalent to one foot.*

Pronunciation Key

ă	pat	ŏ	pot	th	thin
ā	pay	ō	toe	th	this
âr	care	ô	paw, for	hw	which
ä	father	oi	noise	zh	vision
ĕ	pet	ou	out	ə	about,
ē	be	ŏŏ	took		item,
ĭ	pit	ōō	boot		pencil,
ī	pie	ŭ	cut		gallop,
îr	pier	ûr	urge		circus

e•quiv•a•lent² /ĭ **kwĭv′** ə lənt/ *n.* something equal or identical. *The equivalent of 12 x 12 is 144.*

e•ro•sion /ĭ **rō′** zhən/ *n.* the wearing or washing away of the earth's surface. *Soil conservation can help control erosion from wind or water.*

erosion

er•ror /**ĕr′** ər/ *n.* a mistake. *I was happy because my spelling test had no errors.*

es•pe•cial•ly /ĭ **spĕsh′** ə lē/ *adv.* mainly; in particular; unusually. *My brother likes all sports, but he especially enjoys soccer.*

es•ti•ma•tion /ĕs′ tə **mā′** shən/ *n.* **a.** a rough calculation. *The engineer gave an estimation of the costs for the building project.* **b.** judgment; opinion. *It was the engineer's estimation that the project could be finished on time.*

etch•ing /**ĕch′** ĭng/ *n.* a design cut into a plate by the action of acid or the print made from such a plate. *The artist printed the etching from a metal plate.*

e•vent•ful /ĭ **vĕnt′** fəl/ *adj.* filled with many events or an important happening. *Our most eventful month was May, when we moved.*

eve•ry•bod•y /**ĕv′** rē bŏd′ē/ or /-bŭd′ē/ *pron.* all people; each person. *Everybody in our class went to see the parade.*

ex- a prefix that means: **a.** out of; away from: *expose.* **b.** former: *ex-senator.*

283

ex•act•ly /ĭg zăkt′ lē/ *adv.* **a.** precisely; without any change. *Do exactly as the teacher says.* **b.** true; quite so. *"Exactly!" exclaimed George in agreement.*

ex•am•ine /ĭg zăm′ ĭn/ *v.* (ex•am•ines, ex•am•ined, ex•am•in•ing) to look at closely to find out the condition of; to inspect. *Examine the apples before you buy them.*

ex•cel /ĭk sĕl′/ *v.* (ex•cels, ex•celled, ex•cell•ing) to do better than others; to perform at a high level. *Colleen excels in mathematics.*

ex•cel•lence /ĕk′ sə ləns/ *n.* something in which a person surpasses others. *The school offered an award for excellence in spelling.*

ex•cel•lent /ĕk′ sə lənt/ *adj.* very good. *Their excellent singing received loud applause.*

ex•cite•ment /ĭk sīt′ mənt/ *n.* an excited condition; the state of being stirred up. *The entrance of the tigers created great excitement among the circus crowd.*

ex•clam•a•to•ry /ĭk sklăm′ ə tôr′ē/ or /-tōr′ē/ *adj.* expressing a forceful statement or sudden cry. *An exclamatory sentence ends with an exclamation point.*

ex•hale /ĕks hāl′/ *v.* (ex•hales, ex•haled, ex•hal•ing) to breathe out. *Swimmers exhale with their faces in the water.*

ex•hib•it¹ /ĭg zĭb′ ĭt/ *v.* to display; to reveal publicly. *His paintings were exhibited at the art fair.*

ex•hib•it² /ĭg zĭb′ ĭt/ *n.* a public show or display. *The school's trophies are on exhibit in the front lobby.*

exhibit

ex•per•i•ence /ĭk spîr′ ē əns/ *n.* **a.** a living through an event or series of events; a doing or feeling something. *Watching the baby birds hatch was a special experience.* **b.** what one learns from doing things. *I gained business experience from my paper route.*

ex•per•i•ment¹ /ĭk spĕr′ ə mənt/ *n.* a trial or test to learn, discover, or prove something. *An experiment with litmus paper will show whether a substance is an acid or a base.*

ex•per•i•ment² /ĭk spĕr′ ə mənt/ *v.* to test something to learn, discover, or prove something about it. *The artist experimented with several shades of paint.* [Latin *experīmentum*, from *experīrī*, to try.]

ex•pert¹ /ĕk′ spûrt/ *n.* a highly skilled or knowledgeable person. *Police detectives often consult a fingerprint expert.*

ex•pert² /ĕk′ spûrt/ *adj.* having a great deal of skill or knowledge: *an expert carpenter.*

ex•po•nent /ĭk spō′ nənt/ or /ĕk′ spō′nənt/ *n.* a mathematical term that shows how many times the base number is to be multiplied by itself. *In the expression y^3, the 3 is an exponent.*

ex•press¹ /ĭk sprĕs′/ *v.* to tell; to make known. *Think for a moment before you try to express your idea.*

ex•press² /ĭk sprĕs′/ *adj.* quick and direct: *express mail.*

ex•pres•sion /ĭk sprĕsh′ ən/ *n.* **a.** a particular word or phrase. *"Hit the sack" is a slang expression for "go to bed."* **b.** a means of expressing something; an indication. *A sigh can be an expression of contentment.*

ex•tract¹ /ĭk străkt′/ *v.* **a.** to draw out or pull out by force: *extract a tooth.* **b.** to obtain a substance by a chemical process: *extract aluminum from bauxite.*

ex•tract² /ĕk′ străkt′/ *n.* **a.** a concentrated substance prepared from natural food or flavoring: *vanilla extract.* **b.** a passage from a literary work. *Our drama club presented extracts from Shakespeare's plays.*

fa•ble /fā′ bəl/ *n.* a brief tale or story, often with animal characters that speak and act like human beings, that teaches a useful lesson about human nature. *Her favorite fable is "The Tortoise and the Hare."*

fab • u • lous /făb′ yə ləs/ *adj.* **a.** belonging to legend or myth. *Elves are fabulous creatures.* **b.** amazing; wonderful. *It was a fabulous party.* [Latin *fābula*, fable.]

fac • tor[1] /făk′ tər/ *n.* **a.** any of the things that cause a certain result. *Time is an important factor to consider in cooking.* **b.** any of the numbers multiplied to obtain a product. *Factors of 21 are 3 and 7.*

fac • tor[2] /făk′ tər/ *v.* to separate into factors. *If you factor 21, you get 3 and 7.*

Fahr • en • heit /făr′ ən hīt′/ *adj.* of or according to the Fahrenheit scale, where the freezing point of water is 32° and the boiling point is 212°: *the Fahrenheit scale.*

faint[1] /fānt/ *adj.* **a.** lacking strength; weak and dizzy. *If you feel faint, sit or lie down.* **b.** unclear; dim. *A faint light came from a window in the house.*

faint[2] /fānt/ *v.* to lose consciousness and lie as if asleep because of illness, weakness, etc. *He fainted because he was very tired and hungry.*

fam • ine /făm′ ĭn/ *n.* an extreme shortage of food, causing widespread hunger. *The Red Cross shipped food and medicine to the areas of Africa hit by the famine.*

fan • ci • ful /făn′ sĭ fəl/ *adj.* imaginative; unreal. *Science fiction writers create fanciful worlds.*

fash • ion[1] /făsh′ ən/ *n.* **a.** a style of dressing or behaving. *Fashions change yearly.* **b.** way or manner. *She smiled in an odd fashion.*

fash • ion[2] /făsh′ ən/ *v.* to shape; to form. *Birds fashion nests of grass and twigs.*

fa • vor • a • ble /fā′ vər ə bəl/ or /fāv′ rə-/ *adj.* (**fa•vor•a•bly,** *adv.*) **a.** encouraging: *a favorable answer.* **b.** helpful: *favorable winds.*

fa • vor • ite[1] /fā′ vər ĭt/ or /fāv′ rĭt/ *adj.* most liked; preferred. *Broccoli is my favorite vegetable.*

fa • vor • ite[2] /fā′ vər ĭt/ or /fāv′ rĭt/ *n.* the one most liked or preferred. *Which is your favorite team in the World Series?*

fear • less /fîr′ lĭs/ *adj.* not afraid; brave. *The fearless kitten confronted the big dog.*

Pronunciation Key

ă	pat	ŏ	pot	th	thin
ā	pay	ō	toe	*th*	this
âr	care	ô	paw, for	hw	which
ä	father	oi	noise	zh	vision
ĕ	pet	ou	out	ə	about,
ē	be	ŏŏ	took		item,
ĭ	pit	ōō	boot		pencil,
ī	pie	ŭ	cut		gallop,
îr	pier	ûr	urge		circus

fee • ble /fē′ bəl/ *adj.* without much strength; weak. *Newborn animals are often feeble.*

fer • ti • liz • er /fûr′ tl ī′ zər/ *n.* something added to soil to make it more productive. *Compost makes a good garden fertilizer.*

fierce /fîrs/ *adj.* **a.** savage; wild. *The fierce lion growled and paced inside the cage.* **b.** violent. *The fierce wind blew down trees.*

film /fĭlm/ *n.* **a.** a thin, flat material coated with a chemical and used for taking photographs. *I put a new roll of film in my camera.* **b.** a motion picture. *Many old films are shown.* **c.** a thin coating: *a film of ice.*

fi • nal • ly /fī′ nə lē/ *adv.* at last. *I finally got the job done.*

fi • nance /fə năns′/ or /fī′ năns′/ *n.* the management of large amounts of money. *Bankers must be skilled in finance.*

fis • cal /fĭs′ kəl/ *adj.* relating to money matters. *A government's fiscal policy determines how much money it spends.*

flex • i • ble /flĕk′ sə bəl/ *adj.* **a.** capable of being bent. *The clay figures were still flexible enough to shape.* **b.** adjustable, changeable: *a flexible schedule.*

flop • py disk /flŏp′ ē dĭsk′/ *n.* a flexible plastic disk used to store computer data. *The information is stored on a floppy disk.*

floppy disk

flow • chart /flō′ chärt′/ *n.* a diagram showing the sequence of operations. *A flow chart is helpful in writing computer programs.*

flu • id /floo′ ĭd/ *n.* any substance, such as water or air, that flows easily. *"Drink plenty of fluids," the doctor advised.*

flut • ist /floo′ tĭst/ *n.* a person who plays a woodwind instrument called the flute. *The flutist and the oboist played a haunting duet.*

forc • i • ble /fôr′ sə bəl/ or /fōr′-/ *adj.* using or applying physical force: *a forcible entry.*

fore • man /fôr′ mən/ or /fōr′-/ *n.* a person in charge of a group of workers: *the construction foreman.*

for • get • ful /fər gĕt′ fəl/ or /fôr′-/ *adj.* tending to forget; unable to recall. *Because Sandra is often forgetful, she writes notes to remind herself to do things.*

for • mer¹ /fôr′ mər/ *adj.* coming earlier in time or before in position. *The former owner of this house painted the walls blue.*

for • mer² /fôr′ mər/ *n.* the first of two things talked about. *When Tom was given the choice of visiting Los Angeles or New York, he chose the former because he had never been to California.*

for • tu • nate /fôr′ chə nĭt/ *adj.* lucky. *You were fortunate to find the lost bracelet.*

frag • ment /frăg′ mənt/ *n.* **a.** a piece broken off. *The vase broke into fragments when it fell to the floor.* **b.** something incomplete. *An incomplete sentence is called a sentence fragment.*

freeze /frēz/ *v.* (**freez•es, froze, fro•zen, freez•ing**) **a.** to become ice; to turn to ice. *The lake froze during the night.* **b.** to chill something until it becomes cold and hard as ice. *We freeze the vegetables from our garden so they will last through the winter.*

fruit • less /froot′ lĭs/ *adj.* **a.** not producing any fruit. *The fig tree was fruitless.* **b.** unsuccessful; unproductive. *They conducted a fruitless search for the missing papers.*

-ful a suffix that means "full of" or "having," used to form adjectives: *joyful.*

ful • fill /fool fĭl′/ *v.* **a.** to bring into effect; to make real. *The team fulfilled their goal of having a winning season.* **b.** to finish; to complete. *Scouts must fulfill requirements to earn badges.*

fu • ri • ous /fyoor′ ē əs/ *adj.* **a.** very angry. *I was furious with myself for forgetting my homework.* **b.** strong; violent. *The furious storm raged for hours.*

fur • nace /fûr′ nĭs/ *n.* an enclosed structure in which to make a fire. *Furnaces are used to heat buildings, melt metal, and fire pottery.*

gal • ax • y /găl′ ək sē/ *n.* (**gal•ax•ies** *pl.*) a large group of stars. *Our solar system is part of the Milky Way galaxy.*

ga • rage /gə räzh′/ or /-räj′/ *n.* **a.** a building in which cars are kept. *She backed the car out of the garage.* **b.** a place where vehicles are repaired or stored. *The workers at the garage will install new brakes.* [French *garer*, to shelter.]

garage

gar • bage /gär′ bĭj/ *n.* spoiled food or waste matter that is thrown away. *We put our garbage in cans in the alley.*

ge • og • ra • pher /jē ŏg′ rə fər/ *n.* a person who specializes in the study of geography. *The geographer studied the terrain using maps.*

ge • og • ra • phy /jē ŏg′ rə fē/ *n.* **a.** the study of Earth and its features and inhabitants. *In geography we learn that trade and commerce depend upon rivers, mountains, and other natural features.* **b.** the landscape of a place. *The geography of Colorado is rugged.* [Greek *geō-*, from *gē*, earth + *graphein*, to write.]

ge • ol • o • gist /jē ŏl′ ə jĭst/ *n.* a person who specializes in the study of geology. *The geologist explained volcanic action.*

ge•ol•o•gy /jē ŏl′ ə jē/ *n.* the scientific study of the composition and history of the earth's structure. *Scientists use geology when they try to locate water or minerals underground.*

ge•om•e•try /jē ŏm′ ĭ trē/ *n.* the mathematical study of the measurements and relationships of solid and plane figures. *In geometry we learned that a circle has 360 degrees.* [Greek *geō-*, from *gē*, earth + *metron*, measure.]

glaze /glāz/ *n.* a coating applied to ceramics before firing. *After the pot was fired the glaze gave it a smooth, shiny surface.*

glo•ri•ous /glôr′ ē əs/ or /glōr′-/ *adj.* **a.** producing honor and glory; deserving praise. *The discovery of a way to prevent polio was a glorious triumph of medicine.* **b.** beautiful; brilliant. *This is a glorious day.* [Latin *glōria*, glory.]

golf /gŏlf/ or /gôlf/ *n.* a game played with a small hard ball and a set of clubs. *The object of golf is to hit the ball into certain holes using the fewest possible strokes.*

golf

good•ness /gŏŏd′ nĭs/ *n.* the condition of being good. *He determines the goodness of an apple by its taste.*

gor•geous /gôr′ jəs/ *adj.* very beautiful; stunning; magnificent. *From an airplane the view of the Grand Canyon is gorgeous.* [Old French *gorgias*, elegant.]

gram•mar /grăm′ ər/ *n.* the study of how words are arranged in sentences. *A knowledge of grammar helps us write effectively.*

graph•ic /grăf′ ĭk/ *adj.* **a.** vivid; strong; clear. *Your graphic description of the painting made it easier to find in the museum.* **b.** relating to art, printing, or engraving: *graphic arts.* [Greek *graphein*, to write.]

grav•i•ty /grăv′ ĭ tē/ *n.* the force that draws all objects toward the center of Earth. *A ball that is thrown into the air returns to the ground because of gravity.*

graze /grāz/ *v.* (**graz•es, grazed, graz•ing**) to eat grass in a field or pasture. *The cattle grazed by the river.*

Pronunciation Key

ă	pat	ŏ	pot	th	thin
ā	pay	ō	toe	*th*	this
âr	care	ô	paw, for	hw	which
ä	father	oi	noise	zh	vision
ě	pet	ou	out	ə	about,
ē	be	ŏŏ	took		item,
ĭ	pit	ōō	boot		pencil,
ī	pie	ŭ	cut		gallop,
îr	pier	ûr	urge		circus

grief /grēf/ *n.* great sorrow or sadness. *Everyone felt grief when the great leader became ill.*

grown-up /grōn′ ŭp′/ *adj.* not childish; mature; adult. *Jason asked for a grown-up bike for his birthday.*

guard•i•an /gär′ dē ən/ *n.* **a.** a person or thing that takes care of or protects. *Every citizen must act as a guardian of democracy.* **b.** a person appointed by a court to care for another person. *The form has a blank for the name of your parent or guardian.* [Old French *garder*, to guard.]

guide•book /gīd′ bŏŏk′/ *n.* a handbook of information for tourists. *The city guidebook lists museums, restaurants, and parks.*

hand•ker•chief /hăng′ kər chĭf/ *n.* a small square of cloth used for wiping the nose or worn as decoration. *Mr. Weiss wore a maroon handerkerchief that matched his tie.*

hard•ware /härd′ wâr′/ *n.* **a.** articles made from metal. *Nails, bolts, and wire are hardware.* **b.** machines or other physical equipment needed to perform a particular task:* computer hardware.*

her•i•tage /hěr′ ĭ tĭj/ *n.* that which is passed down from preceding generations; tradition. *The book* Roots *deals with the heritage of African Americans.*

Spelling Dictionary

home • ward[1] /hōm′ wərd/ *adv.* at or toward home. *The ship sailed homeward.*

home • ward[2] /hōm′ wərd/ *adj.* toward home: *the homeward journey.*

hon • or • ar • y /ŏn′ ə rĕr′ ē/ *adj.* given as a token of honor: *an honorary key to the city.*

hor • ri • ble /hôr′ ə bəl/ or /hŏr′-/ *adj.* **a.** causing horror; shocking; dreadful: *a horrible disease.* **b.** very unpleasant: *a horrible grating noise.*

horse • pow • er /hôrs′ pou′ ər/ *n.* a unit of power equal to the amount needed to raise a weight of 550 pounds one inch in one second. *An engine's strength is measured in horsepower.*

hue /hyo͞o/ *n.* a color or a shade or tint of a color. *The bright fabric contained some lovely red and purple hues.*

hus • band /hŭz′ bənd/ *n.* the man a woman is married to. *When they were married, her husband gave her a ring.*

hy • drau • lic /hī drô′ lĭk/ *adj.* powered by a liquid under pressure: *a hydraulic drill.*

hy • giene /hī′ jēn/ *n.* the science of keeping well; the study of rules of health. *We learn about hygiene in our health class.*

hymn /hĭm/ *n.* a song of praise. *The poet wrote a hymn in praise of nature.*

-ian a suffix, used to form nouns, that means "one who": *custodian.*

-ible a suffix, used to form adjectives, that means: **a.** capable of: *flexible.* **b.** tending toward: *sensible.*

i • de • al[1] /ī dē′ əl/ or /ī dēl′/ *n.* a perfect type; an idea of something that is perfect. *Our nation was founded on the ideal that citizens can govern themselves.*

i • de • al[2] /ī dē′ əl/ or /ī dēl′/ *adj.* perfect; exactly as one would wish. *A warm day and a clear sky are ideal conditions for a picnic.*

ig • no • rant /ĭg′ nər ənt/ *adj.* not having education or knowledge. *A person ignorant of history might think Brazilians speak Spanish.*

ig • nore /ĭg nôr′/ or /-nōr′/ *v.* (**ig•nores, ig•nored, ig•nor•ing**) to pay no attention to; to refuse to notice. *Anita ignored their silly remarks.*

il- a prefix that means "not": *illicit.* **Il-** replaces **in-** before words that begin with **l**.

il • le • gal /ĭ lē′ gəl/ *adj.* not legal; against the law. *In many states it is illegal to litter.*

il • leg • i • ble /ĭ lĕj′ ə bəl/ *adj.* (**il•leg•i•bly,** *adv.*) not able to be read; blurred or poorly written. *The handwriting on the old letter was nearly illegible.*

il • lit • er • ate /ĭ lĭt′ ər ĭt/ *adj.* unable to read or write. *Teaching illiterate persons to read will help them vote wisely and find new jobs.*

il • log • i • cal /ĭ lŏj′ ĭ kəl/ *adj.* senseless; not according to the principles of logic. *In Alice's Adventures in Wonderland, Alice finds herself in an illogical world.*

i • mag • i • nar • y /ĭ măj′ ə nĕr′ ē/ *adj.* not real; happening only in the mind. *Unicorns are imaginary animals.*

im • me • di • ate /ĭ mē′ dē ĭt/ *adj.* happening right away; without delay. *The immediate effect of the medicine was to stop his coughing.*

im • per • a • tive /ĭm pĕr′ ə tĭv/ *adj.* **a.** expressing a command. *An imperative sentence gives an order.* **b.** urgent; necessary. *It is imperative that you come at once.*

im • por • tance /ĭm pôr′ tns/ *n.* significance; value. *Never underestimate the importance of correct spelling.*

im • press /ĭm prĕs′/ *v.* **a.** to affect strongly or favorably. *Her fluent French impressed all of us.* **b.** to fix firmly in the mind. *He impressed upon us the need to remain quiet.*

in- a prefix that means "not": *inattentive.*

in • deed /ĭn dēd′/ *adv.* in fact; really. *This meal is indeed delicious.*

in • dict /ĭn dīt′/ *v.* to formally charge with a crime. *The grand jury indicted a suspect in the murder case.*

in•dus•tri•ous /ĭn dŭs′ trē əs/ *adj.* hard-working; diligent. *Industrious students usually enjoy school.*

in•for•ma•tion /ĭn′ fər mā′ shən/ *n.* knowledge; facts; something that is told. *They searched in the library for information about the history of Alaska.* [Latin *īnfōrmāre*, to inform, from *in-*, in + *fōrma*, form.]

in•hale /ĭn hāl′/ *v.* (**in•hales, in•haled, in•hal•ing**) to breathe in; to take air into the lungs. *The doctor told me to inhale deeply.*

in•her•it /ĭn hĕr′ ĭt/ *v.* **a.** to receive something from a person who has died. *Lisa inherited her aunt's ring.* **b.** to receive from a parent as a genetic trait. *Stuart inherited his father's blue eyes.*

in•her•i•tance /ĭn hĕr′ ĭ təns/ *n.* heritage; something inherited. *Our instinct for survival is an inheritance from many previous generations.*

in•no•cence /ĭn′ ə səns/ *n.* the state of being innocent; the absence of guilt or wrongdoing. *The suspect's alibi proved his innocence.*

in•no•cent /ĭn′ ə sənt/ *adj.* **a.** not guilty. *She claimed she was innocent of the crime.* **b.** harmless; having no bad effect: *an innocent trick.* **c.** unaware of evil. *An innocent child trusts everyone.*

in•put /ĭn′ po͝ot′/ *n.* anything put into a system to produce a result, or output. *For the computer program to work, your input must contain all the necessary data.*

in•sert /ĭn sûrt′/ *v.* **a.** to put into. *Insert a coin into the slot.* **b.** to add. *Insert an example in this paragraph to strengthen it.*

in•stance /ĭn′ stəns/ *n.* an example; a case. *In most instances students adjust quickly to new schools.*

in•stant¹ /ĭn′ stənt/ *n.* a short time; a moment. *The runner paused for an instant to catch his breath.*

in•stant² /ĭn′ stənt/ *adj.* immediate; taking place quickly. *She demanded an instant reply.*

in•stru•ment /ĭn′ strə mənt/ *n.* **a.** a tool. *A pen is a writing instrument.* **b.** a device for making music. *A piano is a musical instrument.* [Latin *īnstrūmentum*, tool, from *īnstruere*, to prepare.]

Pronunciation Key

ă	pat	ŏ	pot	th	thin
ā	pay	ō	toe	*th*	this
âr	care	ô	paw, for	hw	which
ä	father	oi	noise	zh	vision
ĕ	pet	ou	out	ə	about,
ē	be	o͝o	took		item,
ĭ	pit	o͞o	boot		pencil,
ī	pie	ŭ	cut		gallop,
îr	pier	ûr	urge		circus

in•sult¹ /ĭn sŭlt′/ *v.* to treat with rudeness; to hurt feelings on purpose. *It is not polite to insult someone.*

in•sult² /ĭn′ sŭlt′/ *n.* a rude or hurtful remark or act. *I meant that as a compliment, not an insult.*

in•sur•ance /ĭn sho͝or′ əns/ *n.* the business of guaranteeing to cover specified losses in the future, as in the case of accident, illness, theft, or death, in return for the continuing payment of regular sums of money. *Drivers in many states must maintain accident insurance.*

in•sure /ĭn sho͝or′/ *v.* (**in•sures, in•sured, in•sur•ing**) to arrange for a payment of money in case of loss or illness by paying regularly to an insurance company. *My parents insured our house against fire.*

inter- a prefix that means "between" or "among": *interlocking.*

in•ter•act /ĭn′ tər ăkt′/ *v.* to act on or influence each other. *After-school activities allow students to interact with each other.*

in•ter•change¹ /ĭn′ tər chānj′/ *v.* (**in•ter•chang•es, in•ter•changed, in•ter•chang•ing**) to switch the places of. *The parts of a jigsaw puzzle cannot be interchanged.*

in•ter•change² /ĭn′ tər chānj′/ *n.* **a.** a mutual exchange: *an interchange of ideas.* **b.** an intersection: *a highway interchange.*

interchange

in•ter•est rate /ĭn′ trĭst rāt′/ *n.* the rate charged for borrowing money. *Low interest rates encourage people to borrow money.*

in•ter•face /ĭn′ tər fās′/ *v.* (**in•ter•fac•es, in•ter•faced, in•ter•fac•ing**) to join or connect at a common point or surface. *The parts of an electrical system must interface smoothly.* [Latin *inter,* between + *faciēs,* face.]

in•ter•rog•a•tive /ĭn′ tə rŏg′ ə tĭv/ *adj.* asking a question. *An interrogative sentence ends with a question mark.*

in•ter•sect /ĭn′ tər sĕkt′/ *v.* to cross; to meet at a common point. *I'll meet you where Eighth Street intersects Main.* [Latin *inter,* between + *sect-,* perfect stem of *sēcare,* to cut.]

in•ter•state /ĭn′ tər stāt′/ *adj.* connecting two or more states: *an interstate highway.*

in•ter•view¹ /ĭn′ tər vyoo′/ *n.* a meeting of two people to discuss something. *The graduate had a job interview with an employer.*

in•ter•view² /ĭn′ tər vyoo′/ *v.* to meet and talk with in the hope of getting information. *The reporter interviewed the committee members.*

intra- a prefix that means "within": *intravenous.*

in•tra•mu•ral /ĭn′ trə myoor′ əl/ *adj.* consisting of participants from the same school: *intramural sports.* [Latin *intrā,* within + *mūrus,* wall.]

in•tra•state /ĭn′ trə stāt′/ *adj.* existing within the boundaries of a state. *Intrastate telephone rates may be higher than those for out-of-state calls.*

in•tro•duce /ĭn′ trə doos′/ or /-dyoos′/ *v.* (**in•tro•duc•es, in•tro•duced, in•tro•duc•ing**) **a.** to present; to bring into contact with. *Mrs. Rogers, may I introduce my mother?* **b.** to bring in. *New inventions introduce different ways of doing things.* [Latin *intrōdūcere,* from *intro,* within + *dūcere,* to lead.]

in•tro•duc•tion /ĭn trə dŭk′ shən/ *n.* **a.** being brought in or acquainted with. *Visiting the school board meeting was an introduction to politics.* **b.** the first part, as of a book. *Read the chapter introduction carefully.* **c.** a basic explanation: *an introduction to first aid.* [Latin *intrōduct-,* perfect stem of *intrōdūcere,* to bring in, to introduce.]

in•trude /ĭn trood′/ *v.* (**in•trudes, in•trud•ed, in•trud•ing**) to interrupt; to break in without being asked. *It's not polite to intrude on a private conversation.*

in•va•lid¹ /ĭn′ və lĭd/ *n.* an ill or injured person who needs care. *After he recovered from his injury, he was no longer an invalid.*

in•val•id² /ĭn văl′ ĭd/ *adj.* not authentic; questionable. *If your pass isn't signed by the teacher or the principal, it is invalid.*

in•ven•tion /ĭn vĕn′ shən/ *n.* a device, method, or process that is developed or created. *The electric light bulb and the phonograph are two inventions of Thomas A. Edison.*

invention

in•vert /ĭn vûrt′/ *v.* to turn upside down or inside out. *If you invert a bucket of sand, the sand falls out.*

in•vest /ĭn vĕst′/ *v.* to put money into something to make a profit. *Many Americans invest in savings bonds.*

in•vis•i•ble /ĭn vĭz′ ə bəl/ *adj.* not capable of being seen. *Her hearing aid is so tiny it is almost invisible.*

in•ward¹ /ĭn′ wərd/ *adv.* toward the inside or center. *The door opened inward.*

in•ward² /ĭn′ wərd/ *adj.* inside a thing or a person; inner: *inward doubts.*

-ion a suffix, used to form nouns, that means "the result of an action or process": *introduction.*

ir- a prefix that means "not": *irreversible.* **Ir-** replaces **in-** before words that begin with **r.**

IRA an abbreviation for "Individual Retirement Account." *I put the money from my summer job into an IRA.*

ir•ra•tion•al /ĭ răsh′ ə nəl/ *adj.* without reason or clear thought. *Many fears are irrational.*

ir•reg•u•lar /ĭ rĕg′ yə lər/ *adj.* not conforming to the usual rule or practice; different. *The coin is valuable because of its irregular markings.*

ir•re•sis•ti•ble /ĭr′ ĭ zĭs′ tə bəl/ *adj.* too strong to be resisted; compelling. *Although he was on a diet, his desire for the food was irresistible.*

ir•ri•gate /ĭr′ i gāt′/ *v.* (ir•ri•gates, ir•ri•gat•ed, ir•ri•gat•ing) to supply water to by a system of ditches or pipes. *Farmers irrigate land that does not get enough rain.*

IRS an abbreviation for "Internal Revenue Service." *Most adults file income tax reports with the IRS each year.*

isle /īl/ *n.* an island, especially a small one. *The Isle of Wight is located off the coast of England.*

▶ Isle sounds like **aisle.**

is•sue /ĭsh′ o͞o/ *v.* (is•sues, is•sued, is•su•ing) to circulate or distribute in an official capacity; to send out. *The principal issued a memo explaining the new fire drill procedure.*

i•tem /ī′ təm/ *n.* **a.** a separate article. *Which item shall we buy first?* **b.** a piece of news: *an item in a newspaper.*

jeal•ous /jĕl′ əs/ *adj.* worried about losing someone's affection to another person; resentful of another person's good fortune. *The toddler is jealous of the attention his new brother is getting.*

jew•el•ry /jo͞o′ əl rē/ *n.* jewels; ornaments of gold, silver, gems, etc. *The children enjoy dressing up in their grandmother's costume jewelry.*

jour•nal /jûr′ nəl/ *n.* a personal record of activities and feelings, kept on a regular basis. *Ramon kept a journal of his summer experiences.*

jour•nal•ist /jûr′ nə lĭst/ *n.* a person whose career is in writing, editing, or publishing news stories. *My mother is a journalist who covers courthouse news for the local paper.*

Pronunciation Key

ă	pat	ŏ	pot	th	thin
ā	pay	ō	toe	*th*	this
âr	care	ô	paw, for	hw	which
ä	father	oi	noise	zh	vision
ĕ	pet	ou	out	ə	about,
ē	be	o͝o	took		item,
ĭ	pit	o͞o	boot		pencil,
ī	pie	ŭ	cut		gallop,
îr	pier	ûr	urge		circus

kiln /kĭln/ or /kĭl/ *n.* an oven used to bake or fire ceramics. *The kiln must be very hot for the pottery to harden.*

kins•man /kĭnz′ mən/ *n.* a male relative. *A kinsman is a male relative, and a kinswoman is a female relative.*

kiln

knack /năk/ *n.* a special talent for doing something. *Philip has a knack for writing short stories.*

kneel /nēl/ *v.* (kneels, knelt or kneeled, kneel•ing) to rest on bent knees. *Be careful not to kneel in the dirt.*

knob /nŏb/ *n.* a rounded handle on a door, TV set, drawer, etc. *The knob on the right of the radio controls the sound.*

knowl•edge /nŏl′ ĭj/ *n.* everything that one knows or understands about something. *Her knowledge of baseball statistics is impressive.*

la•bel /lā′ bəl/ *n.* a small piece of paper used for identification or instructions. *When you buy canned or packaged food, you can read the label to find out the contents.*

la•bor /lā′ bər/ *n.* physical work. *Moving these stones is hard labor.*

Spelling Dictionary

la • goon /lə gōōn′/ *n.* a shallow body of water near or connected with a larger body of water. *A lagoon may be separated from the sea by sandbars.*

la • ser /lā′ zər/ *n.* an acronym for a device that strengthens light to produce a thin, powerful beam. *Lasers are used in industry, medicine, and communications.* [**L**ight **a**mplification by **s**timulated **e**mission of **r**adiation.]

leath • er /lĕ*th*′ ər/ *n.* the dressed or tanned hide of an animal. *Gloves and jackets made of leather are soft, warm, and durable.*

le • gal /lē′ gəl/ *adj.* permitted by law. *A left turn at this corner is not legal.*

leg • end /lĕj′ ənd/ *n.* a popular story handed down from earlier times. *The story of King Arthur and his knights is an English legend.*

leg • i • ble /lĕj′ ə bəl/ *adj.* (**leg•i•bly,** *adv.*) able to be read. *Check to be sure that your handwriting is legible.*

lei • sure /lē′ zhər/ *adj.* free; not busy. *Our leisure time was spent reading and listening to music.* [Latin *licēre,* to be permitted.]

lens /lĕnz/ *n.* (**lens•es** *pl.*) a piece of clear, curved glass or plastic used to bend light rays. *Lenses are used in eyeglasses, cameras, telescopes, and microscopes.*

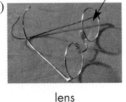
lens

-less a suffix, used to form adjectives, that means "without": *endless.*

li • brar • i • an /lī′ brâr′ ē ən/ *n.* a person who specializes in library work. *The librarian can help you find the materials you need for your report.*

li • cense /lī′ səns/ *n.* a document giving official permission; a permit. *Ms. Soto obtained a pilot's license after she learned how to fly a plane.*

lieu • ten • ant /lōō tĕn′ ənt/ *n.* an officer usually ranking next below a captain. *The army officer was promoted from second to first lieutenant.* [Old French *lieu,* in place of + *tenant,* past participle of *tenir,* to hold.]

lim • it /lĭm′ ĭt/ *n.* the greatest amount permitted. *The speed limit on this street is thirty miles an hour.*

lin • e • ar /lĭn′ ē ər/ *adj.* of or relating to a straight line. *A foot is a linear measurement.*

lin • guis • tics /lĭng gwĭs′ tĭks/ *n.* the science of language that deals with the nature and structure of speech. *Phonetics is a branch of linguistics that is especially useful in spelling.*

link • ing verb /lĭngk′ ĭng vûrb′/ *n.* a verb, such as a form of "be," that links the predicate of a sentence to the subject. *In the sentence "They seemed happy," "seemed" is a linking verb.*

lit • er • ate /lĭt′ ər ĭt/ *adj.* able to read and write. *In school we are taught to be literate.*

liv • er /lĭv′ ər/ *n.* a large organ of the body located near the stomach that produces digestive juices. *The work of the liver includes helping change food into fuel for the body.*

lo • cal /lō′ kəl/ *adj.* having to do with a certain place or a nearby area. *Our local news programs inform us about our own area.*

lo • ca • tion /lō kā′ shən/ *n.* a place; a position. *This quiet field is a good location for our campsite.* [Latin *locātiō,* a placing, from *locāre,* to place, from *locus,* place.]

log • i • cal /lŏj′ ĭ kəl/ *adj.* using logic; sensible. *When asked to make a decision, he made the logical choice.*

lone • some /lōn′ səm/ *adj.* lonely; sad from being alone. *My little sister kept my puppy from getting lonesome while I was at school.*

loose /lōōs/ *adj.* (**loos•er, loos•est; loose•ly,** *adv.*) not fastened tightly; slack. *I have a loose button on my coat.*

loud • ness /loud′ nĭs/ *n.* the state of being loud. *The loudness of a sound is measured in units called decibels.*

lu • nar /lōō′ nər/ *adj.* of or relating to the moon: *a lunar eclipse.*

-ly a suffix, used to form adverbs, that means "in a way that is" or "in the manner of": *quietly.*

ma·chin·er·y /mə shē′ nə rē/ *n.*
machines or machine parts. *Farm machinery has made it possible for farmers to grow larger crops.*

mag·a·zine /măg′ ə zēn′/ or /măg′ə zēn′/ *n.* a periodical publication that may contain articles, stories, or poems. *We receive two monthly magazines.*

man·ner /măn′ ər/ *n.* way; fashion. *The students left the bus in an orderly manner.*

mar·ble /mär′ bəl/ *n.* a kind of rock that can be polished to a smooth, shiny finish. *Many statues are carved from marble.*

ma·rim·ba
/mə rĭm′ bə/ *n.* an instrument played by striking wooden bars arranged in a musical scale; a large xylophone. *The marimba is of African origin.*

marimba

mar·riage /măr′ ĭj/ *n.* the state of being married; life as husband and wife. *The couple celebrated fifty years of marriage.*

mass /măs/ *n.* the volume or bulk of a body or object. *The mass of an object does not change when it is broken, melted, or frozen.*

ma·te·ri·al /mə tîr′ ē əl/ *n.* the parts or substances from which a thing is made. *The material for the roof was delivered before the workers arrived.*

mead·ow /mĕd′ ō/ *n.* a field in which grass or hay grows naturally. *The cows grazed in the meadow.*

meas·ure·ment /mĕzh′ ər mənt/ *n.*
a. the act of measuring or the process of being measured. *A gallon is a unit of liquid measurement.* **b.** the length, size, or amount of something. *Her waist measurement is twenty-five inches.*

mech·a·nize /mĕk′ ə nīz′/ *v.*
(**mech•a•niz•es, mech•a•nized, mech•a•niz•ing**) to equip with machinery: *mechanize a factory.*

Pronunciation Key

ă	pat	ŏ	pot	th	**th**in
ā	pay	ō	toe	*th*	**th**is
âr	care	ô	paw, for	hw	**wh**ich
ä	father	oi	n**oi**se	zh	vi**si**on
ĕ	pet	ou	**ou**t	ə	**a**bout,
ē	be	ŏŏ	t**oo**k		it**e**m,
ĭ	pit	ōō	b**oo**t		penc**i**l,
ī	pie	ŭ	c**u**t		gall**o**p,
îr	pier	ûr	**ur**ge		circ**u**s

me·di·um /mē′ dē əm/ *adj.* having, being, or occupying a middle position; moderate. *Warm the soup over medium heat.*

mel·o·dy /mĕl′ ə dē/ *n.* (**mel•o•dies** *pl.*) a series of musical tones making up a tune. *He whistled the melody of a popular song.*

-ment a suffix, used to form nouns, that means "the result of an action or process": *advancement.*

mer·chant /mûr′ chənt/ *n.* a person who buys and sells goods. *The three fabric stores in this area are owned by the same merchant.* [Latin *mercari,* to trade.]

me·tab·o·lism /mə tăb′ ə lĭz′ əm/ *n.* the physical and chemical processes that maintain life. *Doctors can check the rate of your metabolism.*

me·te·or·ite /mē′ tē ə rīt′/ *n.* a piece of a meteor that does not burn up completely in Earth's atmosphere and lands on the surface of Earth. *This rock may have been part of a meteorite.*

meth·od /mĕth′ əd/ *n.* a system; a way of doing something. *Broiling is one method of preparing fish.*

mid- a prefix that means "a middle part, time or location": *midway.*

mid·sum·mer /mĭd′ sŭm′ ər/ *n.* the middle of the summer. *We had our family reunion at the beach in midsummer.*

mid·way¹ /mĭd′ wā′/ *adv.* in the middle of the way or distance; halfway. *The equator circles Earth midway between the poles.*

293

mid•way² /mĭd′ wā′/ *adj.* in the middle of a way, distance, period of time, or succession of events: *at the midway point in the baseball season.*

mile•age /mīl′ ĭj/ *n.* the number of miles covered. *What was the total mileage of the trip?*

mil•i•tar•y¹ /mĭl′ ĭ tĕr ē/ *n.* the armed forces. *Soldiers and sailors serve in the military.*

mil•i•tar•y² /mĭl′ ĭ tĕr ē/ *adj.* having to do with the armed forces: *a military parade.*

min•ute¹ /mĭn′ ĭt/ *n.* **a.** one of the sixty equal parts into which an hour is divided; sixty seconds. *We were given ten minutes to do each part of the test.* **b.** the exact moment. *I recognized him the minute I saw him.*

mi•nute² /mī nōōt′/ or /-nyōōt′/ *adj.* tiny; very small. *Minute bits of dust floated through the ray of sunlight.*

mir•ror¹ /mĭr′ ər/ *n.* **a.** a glass or other reflective surface. *We saw the reflection in the mirror.* **b.** anything that gives a true account or picture. *The book is a mirror of modern society.*

mirror

mir•ror² /mĭr′ ər/ *v.* to reflect. *The setting sun was mirrored on the surface of the lake.*

mis- a prefix that means: **a.** bad; badly; wrong; wrongly: *misconduct.* **b.** failure; lack: *misfire.*

mis•be•have /mĭs′ bĭ hāv′/ *v.* (mis•be•haves, mis•be•haved, mis•be•hav•ing) to act badly or improperly. *Puppies sometimes misbehave by chewing on shoes.*

mis•chief /mĭs′ chĭf/ *n.* **a.** conduct or actions that cause or could cause harm, injury, or damage. *Mother asked me to stay out of mischief.* **b.** harmless and merry teasing or pranks. *My kitten is full of mischief.* [Old French *meschief*, misfortune.]

mis•for•tune /mĭs fôr′ chən/ *n.* bad luck. *It was his misfortune to lose his wallet.*

mis•in•form /mĭs′ ĭn fôrm′/ *v.* to give wrong or false information. *We were misinformed about the day of the party; it was Thursday, not Tuesday.*

mis•lead /mĭs lēd′/ *v.* (mis•leads, mis•led, mis•lead•ing) to guide in the wrong direction; to confuse. *A misspelled word may mislead the reader.*

mis•place /mĭs plās′/ *v.* (mis•plac•es, mis•placed, mis•plac•ing) to put in a wrong place; to mislay. *Megan searched for the notebook she had misplaced.*

mis•read /mĭs rēd′/ *v.* (mis•reads, mis•read, mis•read•ing) to read or understand incorrectly. *Because he misread the instructions, he couldn't assemble the kite.*

mis•trust¹ /mĭs trŭst′/ *n.* lack of trust. *Her mistrust showed in her frowning expression.*

mis•trust² /mĭs trŭst′/ *v.* to view without confidence. *Don't mistrust your ability; I think you'll do a great job.*

mis•use¹ /mĭs yōōs′/ *n.* incorrect or improper use. *The misuse of a word can cause confusion.*

mis•use² /mĭs yōōz′/ *v.* (mis•us•es, mis•used, mis•us•ing) to use wrongly or incorrectly. *Don't misuse the piano by banging on the keys.*

mod•er•ate /mŏd′ ər ĭt/ *adj.* within reasonable limits; not extreme: *a moderate price.*

mod•i•fi•er /mŏd′ ə fī′ ər/ *n.* a word, phrase, or clause that limits or qualifies the meaning of another word or group of words. *Adjectives and adverbs are modifiers.*

mod•ule /mŏj′ ōōl/ *n.* a self-contained unit of a spacecraft; a unit with a specific function. *The engineers at NASA designed a new space module.*

mo•men•tar•y /mō′ mən tĕr′ ē/ *adj.* (mo•men•tar•i•ly, *adv.*) brief; lasting a short time. *There was a momentary lull in the storm.*

mo•res /môr′ āz/ or /mōr′-/ *n. pl.* the customs accepted by a particular social group. *We should respect the mores of other societies.*

Spelling Dictionary

mor • tar /môr′ tər/ *n.*
a. a mixture of cement or lime with sand and water. *The construction worker laid bricks with mortar.*
b. a bowl in which substances are crushed or ground. *The pharmacist uses a mortar and pestle to grind the medicines.*

mortar and pestle

moun • tain • ous /moun′ tə nəs/ *adj.* having mountains; filled with or covered by mountains. *The western part of the United States contains many mountainous areas.*

mph or **m.p.h.** an abbreviation for "miles per hour." *The speed limit in our town is 30 mph.*

mul • ti • ple¹ /mŭl′ tə pəl/ *adj.* having many parts. *His multiple interests include sports, music, and movies.*

mul • ti • ple² /mŭl′ tə pəl/ *n.* a quantity that can be evenly divided by another quantitiy. *Four is a multiple of two.*

mul • ti • pli • cand /mŭl′ tə plĭ kănd′/ *n.* a number multiplied by another. *In 2 x 7, 7 is the multiplicand.*

mul • ti • pli • er /mŭl′ tə plī′ ər/ *n.* a number by which another number is multiplied. *In 2 x 7, 2 is the multiplier.*

mu • ral /myŏŏr′ əl/ *n.* a picture painted directly on a wall. *The artist designed a mural for the lobby of the auditorium.*

mus • cle /mŭs′ əl/ *n.* body tissue composed of fibers that tighten or loosen to move parts of the body. *The athlete was careful to stretch his muscles before the race.*

mu • si • cian /myŏŏ zĭsh′ ən/ *n.* a person who composes or performs music. *The players in an orchestra are expert musicians.*

mut • ton /mŭt′ ən/ *n.* the meat of a full-grown sheep. *In England, roast mutton is a popular dish.*

myth /mĭth/ *n.* a story or legend that attempts to account for something in nature. *Some myths deal with the early history of a nation.*

Pronunciation Key

ă	pat	ŏ	pot	th	thin
ā	pay	ō	toe	*th*	this
âr	care	ô	paw, for	hw	which
ä	father	oi	noise	zh	vision
ĕ	pet	ou	out	ə	about,
ē	be	ŏŏ	took		item,
ĭ	pit	ōō	boot		pencil,
ī	pie	ŭ	cut		gallop,
îr	pier	ûr	urge		circus

na • tion • al /năsh′ ə nəl/ *adj.* belonging to a nation. *The national flag of the United States has stars and stripes.*

nat • u • ral /năch′ ər əl/ *adj.* **a.** produced by nature; not artificial. *Wood is a natural substance.* **b.** having a particular character by nature. *Eileen has a natural love for art.* **c.** normal; usual; to be expected. *It is natural for winters in Florida to be warm.*

neb • u • la /nĕb′ yə lə/ *n.* (**neb•u•las** or **neb•u•lae** *pl.*) a cloudy mass seen among the stars at night. *On a clear night, you may see a nebula in the sky.*

nec • es • sar • y /nĕs′ ĭ sĕr′ ē/ *adj.* (**nec•es•sar•i•ly**, *adv.*) needed; required. *A balanced diet is necessary for proper nutrition.*

neigh • bor • hood¹ /nā′ bər hŏŏd′/ *n.* a distinctive part of a town or city in which people live. *In a big city, some neighborhoods have apartment buildings and others have houses.*

neigh • bor • hood² /nā′ bər hŏŏd′/ *adj.* relating to the neighborhood: *a neighborhood park.*

ner • vous /nûr′ vəs/ *adj.* **a.** of the nerves. *All the nerves in the body make up the nervous system.* **b.** excited; not calm. *The kitten became nervous when everyone crowded around.*

neu•tral /nōo′ trəl/ or /nyōo′-/ *adj.* **a.** not favoring either side. *During two world wars, Switzerland remained a neutral country.* **b.** neither acidic nor alkaline: *a neutral solution.*

neu•tron /nōo′ trŏn′/ or /nyōo′-/ *n.* a part of an atomic nucleus that has no electrical charge. *Both neutrons and protons are subatomic particles.*

niece /nēs/ *n.* the daughter of one's brother or sister or of one's spouse's brother or sister. *Your parents' nieces are your cousins.*

nim•bo•stra•tus /nĭm′ bō strā′ təs/ or /-străt′ əs/ *n.* a low gray cloud that brings rain, snow, or sleet. *A nimbostratus sometimes indicates the arrival of snow.*

ni•tro•gen /nī′ trə jən/ *n.* a gas that forms about four-fifths of the air we breathe. *Nitrogen has no color, taste, or odor.*

nom•i•nate /nŏm′ ə nāt′/ *v.* (**nom•i•nates, nom•i•nat•ed, nom•i•nat•ing**) to choose a candidate for an office; to name. *Mary was nominated for president of her class.*

non- a prefix that means "not": *nonmetal.*

non•fat /nŏn′ făt′/ *adj.* lacking fat solids or having the fat content removed: *nonfat milk.*

non•prof•it /nŏn prŏf′ ĭt/ *adj.* not set up for the purpose of making a profit. *A charity is a nonprofit organization.*

non•re•new•al /nŏn′ rĭ nōo′ əl/ or /-nyōo′-/ *n.* a not granting of an extension. *The barber was upset by the nonrenewal of his lease.*

non•re•turn•a•ble /nŏn′ rĭ tûr′ nə bəl/ *adj.* not able to be returned: *nonreturnable bottles.*

no•ta•ble /nō′ tə bəl/ *adj.* **a.** worthy of notice; remarkable. *Writing a book is a notable accomplishment.* **b.** prominent; distinguished. *He is a notable physicist.*

no•tice[1] /nō′ tĭs/ *n.* an announcement. *The notice on the bulletin board gives the dates of the field hockey games.*

no•tice[2] /nō′ tĭs/ *v.* (**no•tic•es, no•ticed, no•tic•ing**) to pay attention to; to take notice of; to see. *Joan noticed Barbara's new dress right away.*

nour•ish /nûr′ ĭsh/ or /nŭr′-/ *v.* (**nour•ish•es, nour•ished, nour•ish•ing**) to feed; to cause to grow by giving enough of the right food. *Water and sunlight nourish the flowers.*

nov•el[1] /nŏv′ əl/ *n.* a book-length fictional story. *Mark Twain wrote several novels.*

nov•el[2] /nŏv′ əl/ *adj.* new or unusual: *a novel idea.*

nu•cle•us /nōo′ klē əs/ or /nyōo′-/ *n.* (**nu•cle•i** or **nu•cle•us•es** *pl.*) the central, positively charged core of an atom, composed of neutrons and protons. *A nucleus contains almost all the mass of an atom.*

numb /nŭm/ *adj.* without sensation or movement. *If you don't wear warm gloves, your fingers may become numb with cold.*

nu•tri•tion /nōo trĭsh′ ən/ or /nyōo-/ *n.* eating; nourishment. *Proper nutrition helps maintain good health.*

nu•tri•tious /nōo trĭsh′ əs/ or /nyōo-/ *adj.* providing nourishment. *Apples are a nutritious snack.* [Latin *nūtrīre*, to nourish.]

o•a•sis /ō ā′ sĭs/ *n.* (**o•a•ses** *pl.*) a place in the desert where there is water. *Trees, shrubs, or grass might grow in an oasis.*

oasis

ob- a prefix that means "toward" or "against": *objection, obstacle.*

o•be•di•ence /ō bē′ dē əns/ *n.* the act of obeying rules or laws. *Crossing the street safely requires obedience to traffic laws.*

ob•ject[1] /əb jĕkt′/ *v.* to make objection; to protest. *They objected that the weather was too cold to play outside.*

ob•ject[2] /ŏb′ jĭkt/ *n.* **a.** a thing that can be seen or touched. *The little shop had many objects made of china.* **b.** a purpose; a goal: *the object of the game.*

ob•tain /əb tān′/ *v.* to get. *He obtained a ticket to the play.*

ob•vi•ous /ŏb′ vē əs/ *adj.* easy to see or figure out; clear; plain. *It is obvious that the movie is popular, since the theater is so crowded.*

oc•ca•sion /ə kā′ zhən/ *n.* **a.** a particular happening or event. *Holidays are special occasions.* **b.** an opportunity; a good chance. *I hope you find an occasion to call us while you are traveling.*

o•cean•og•ra•pher /ō′ shə nŏg′ rə fər/ *n.* a scientist whose specialty is the study and exploration of the ocean. *The oceanographer told us about the Gulf Stream.* [Greek *Ōkeanos,* a great river encircling the earth + *graphein,* to write.]

of•fer /ô′ fər/ or /ŏf′ ər/ *v.* **a.** to say that one is willing. *We offered to help Mr. Patel start his car.* **b.** to present as a suggestion. *The President offered a plan for peace.*

of•fi•cer /ô′ fĭ sər/ *n.* **a.** a person in a position of authority: *a bank officer; an army officer.* **b.** a policeman or policewoman. *Officer, which way is Oak Street?*

officer

OPEC an acronym for "Organization of Petroleum Exporting Countries." *OPEC's decisions affect the price we pay for oil.*

op•er•a•tion /ŏp′ ə rā′ shən/ *n.* **a.** the way in which something works. *Finally I understand the operation of an airplane.* **b.** a surgical treatment. *The patient recovered quickly after the operation.* [Latin *operātiōnem,* from *operāri,* to work.]

o•pin•ion /ə pĭn′ yən/ *n.* **a.** a belief or impression that cannot be proved. *Leon holds the opinion that soccer is more fun than football.* **b.** a judgment or verdict. *The judge handed down an opinion in favor of the plaintiff.*

op•po•nent /ə pō′ nənt/ *n.* a person or group that competes against another. *Our school's opponent for the game is Deerfield School.* [Latin *oppōnere,* to oppose.]

op•por•tu•ni•ty /ŏp′ ər tōō′ nĭ tē/ or /-tyōō′-/ *n.* (**op•por•tu•ni•ties** *pl.*) a time or chance that is right for doing something. *Let's find an opportunity to talk to Amy about the picnic.*

op•pose /ə pōz′/ *v.* (**op•pos•es, op•posed, op•pos•ing**) to be against; to act against. *The mayor opposed the building of a new highway.* [Latin *ob-,* against + *pos-,* perfect stem of *pōnere,* to put.]

op•po•site[1] /ŏp′ ə zĭt/ *adj.* contrary; completely different; exactly reverse: *opposite opinions.*

op•po•site[2] /ŏp′ ə zĭt/ *n.* the reverse of something else. *"Up" is the opposite of "down."*

op•po•site[3] /ŏp′ ə zĭt/ *prep.* across from. *The library is opposite the school.* [Latin *ob-,* against + *pos-,* perfect stem of *pōnere,* to put.]

op•ti•mism /ŏp′ tə mĭz′ əm/ *n.* a hopeful disposition; the belief that our world is the best of all possible worlds. *Juanita's optimism and sunny outlook on life make her fun to be around.*

or•di•nar•y /ôr′ dn ĕr′ ē/ *adj.* **a.** usual; normal. *The ordinary time it takes to drive downtown is twenty minutes.* **b.** not special; average: *an ordinary meal.*

-ous a suffix, used to form adjectives, that means "possessing" or "characterized by": *joyous.*

or•phan /ôr′ fən/ *n.* a child whose parents are absent or dead. *Oliver Twist is a story about an orphan.* [Greek *orphanos,* without parents.]

out•back /out′ băk′/ *n.* a rural, undeveloped part of a country, especially Australia and New Zealand. *Great distances separate the sheep stations of the Australian outback.*

Spelling Dictionary

phrase¹ /frāz/ *n.* **a.** a group of words that gives a single idea. *In "He swam during the summer," "during the summer" is a phrase.* **b.** a short expression: *a scientific phrase.*

phrase² /frāz/ *v.* (**phras•es, phrased, phras•ing**) to express in words. *Phrase your thoughts carefully.*

phy•si•cian /fĭ zĭsh' ən/ *n.* a medical doctor. *When you are ill, you should see a physician.* [Old French *fisique,* medical science, from Greek *physis,* nature.]

pi /pī/ *n.* a Greek letter (π) used as a mathematical symbol to represent a specific number (about 3.14). *Pi is the ratio of a circle's circumference to its diameter.*

pi•an•ist /pē ăn' ĭst/ or /pē' ə nĭst/ *n.* one who plays the piano. *It takes years of training to become a concert pianist.*

pi•geon /pĭj' ən/ *n.* a bird with a small head, stout body, and short legs. *Some pigeons are trained to carry messages.*

pigeon

pig•ment /pĭg' mənt/ *n.* **a.** a substance used to give color to something. *There are yellow pigments in the green paint.* **b.** a substance that gives color to plant or animal tissue. *Chlorophyll is the pigment that makes plants green.*

pipe•line /pīp' līn'/ *n.* a channel or pipe used to carry water, petroleum, or natural gas. *The Trans-Alaska Pipeline carries oil hundreds of miles.*

pit•i•ful /pĭt' ĭ fəl/ *adj.* causing emotions of sorrow and compassion. *The injured dog was a pitiful sight.*

plat•form /plăt' fôrm'/ *n.* any flat floor or surface raised above the area around it. *The train will be at the platform in five minutes.*

plumb•er /plŭm' ər/ *n.* a person whose job is putting in and fixing sinks, pipes, and other plumbing fixtures. *We called a plumber when the basement pipes started leaking.*

plu•ral¹ /ploŏr' əl/ *n.* the form of a word that means more than one of something. *The plural of "leaf" is "leaves."*

plu•ral² /ploŏr' əl/ *adj.* showing that more than one is meant. *The plural form of most words is made by adding -s or -es.*

P.M. or **p.m.** an abbreviation that means "in the afternoon or evening." *She is usually asleep by 10 P.M.* [Latin *post meridiem,* after noon.]

pol•i•cy¹ /pŏl' ĭ sē/ *n.* (**po•li•cies** *pl.*) a way of doing things. *The store's policy is to treat customers politely.*

pol•i•cy² /pŏl' ĭ sē/ *n.* (**po•li•cies** *pl.*) a contract between an insurance company and those who are insured. *The school has a fire insurance policy.*

pol•lu•tion /pə loō' shən/ *n.* a harmful impurity. *Water pollution causes many fish to die.*

pop•u•la•tion /pŏp' yə lā' shən/ *n.* the number of people living in a country, state, town, or other area. *The town's population has greatly increased in the past five years.* [Latin *populus,* the people.]

por•tion /pôr' shən/ or /pōr'-/ *n.* a part; a share. *A portion of the school day is spent in study hall.*

pose /pōz/ *v.* (**pos•es, posed, pos•ing**) **a.** to hold an expression or a position. *The parents posed with their children for a family portrait.* **b.** to present; to put forward: *pose a question.* [Latin *pausāre,* to rest, influenced by *pos-,* perfect stem of *pōnere,* to put, to place.]

po•si•tion /pə zĭsh' ən/ *n.* **a.** place; location. *The navigator marked the ship's position on a chart.* **b.** a job; employment. *My brother has a new position with another company.*

pos•i•tive /pŏz' ĭ tĭv/ *adj.* **a.** confident; certain; without doubt. *Gus is positive that his team will win.* **b.** approving; showing agreement: *a positive answer.* **c.** not negative: *a positive number.* [Latin *pos-* perfect stem of *pōnere,* to put, to place.]

pos•sess /pə zĕs'/ *v.* (**pos•sess•es, pos•sessed, pos•sess•ing**) to have; to own. *Heather's family possesses a sailboat.*

pos•ses•sive¹ /pə zĕs' ĭv/ *adj.* showing ownership. *A possessive pronoun indicates to whom something belongs.*

pos•ses•sive[2] /pə zĕs′ ĭv/ *n.* a word that shows possession. *Possessives such as "teacher's" and "its" are formed from nouns and pronouns.*

pos•si•bly /pŏs′ ə blē/ *adv.* perhaps; maybe. *Possibly we'll finish before noon.*

post•age /pō′ stĭj/ *n.* the cost of stamps needed to send a letter or package by mail. *The postage was forty cents.* [French *poste*, mail.]

post of•fice /pōst′ ô′ fĭs/ or /-ŏf′ ĭs/ *n.* **a.** an office or a building where people can buy stamps and mail letters or packages. *Mail these cards at the post office.* **b.** the public department in charge of mail. *The post office employs thousands of workers.*

pot•ter•y /pŏt′ ə rē/ *n.* pots, dishes, or ornaments made of clay that has been hardened by baking. *This shop sells beautiful pottery.*

pottery

POW or **P.O.W.** an abbreviation for "prisoner of war." *A great celebration awaited the POWs upon their return home.*

prac•ti•cal /prăk′ tĭ kəl/ *adj.* **a.** able to be done, used, or carried out. *Her practical solution took care of the problem.* **b.** dealing with facts rather than theory; concrete. *Her practical approach to children is a great help.*

pre•cious /prĕsh′ əs/ *adj.* **a.** having a high price; costing a great deal. *Diamonds are precious jewels.* **b.** much loved; dear. *Their precious child brought happiness to the parents.* [Latin *pretium*, price.]

pre•mi•er[1] /prĭ mîr′/ or /-myîr′/ or /prē′ mîr/ *adj.* first in importance; chief. *The economy was the premier concern of the voters.*

pre•mier[2] /prĭ mîr′/ *n.* the chief executive of a Canadian province. *Canadian premiers are leaders of their legislatures.*

pres•ent[1] /prĕz′ ənt/ *adj.* **a.** of the time between past and future; current: *the present moment.* **b.** at hand; not absent. *All the committee members were present for the final vote.*

Pronunciation Key

ă	pat	ŏ	pot	th	thin
ā	pay	ō	toe	*th*	this
âr	care	ô	paw, for	hw	which
ä	father	oi	noise	zh	vision
ĕ	pet	ou	out	ə	about,
ē	be	ŏŏ	took		item,
ĭ	pit	ōō	boot		pencil,
ī	pie	ŭ	cut		gallop,
îr	pier	ûr	urge		circus

pre•sent[2] /prĭ zĕnt′/ *v.* **a.** to give. *The prize was presented to the winner.* **b.** to offer; to bring up for consideration. *May I present a suggestion?*

pres•ent[3] /prĕz′ ənt/ *n.* a gift. *The present was colorfully wrapped.*

pres•sure /prĕsh′ ər/ *n.* the act of pressing; use of force. *We applied pressure to the orange to squeeze out the juice.*

price•less /prīs′ lĭs/ *adj.* very worthy; invaluable. *The art collection is priceless.*

prim•er[1] /prĭm′ ər/ *n.* a textbook for early grades. *The children took out their primers and began the lesson.*

prim•er[2] /prī′ mər/ *n.* an undercoat of paint to prepare a surface for further painting. *The painter applied a primer first.*

print•er /prĭn′ tər/ *n.* the part of the computer that produces printed matter. *The printer was not working; it needed new toner.*

prob•a•ble /prŏb′ ə bəl/ *adj.* (**prob•a•bly,** *adv.*) likely to happen. *The dark clouds and lightning mean that rain is probable.*

proc•ess /prŏs′ ĕs′/ or /prō′ sĕs′/ *n.* (**proc•ess•es** *pl.*) **a.** a system of operations in the production of something: *the process of canning fresh fruit.* **b.** a series of actions with an expected end: *the growth process.*

prof•it[1] /prŏf′ ĭt/ *n.* **a.** the amount of money made after all expenses have been subtracted. *The profits in some businesses are small.* **b.** a benefit; an advantage. *Woo found both profit and enjoyment in his music lessons.*

prof•it[2] /prŏf′ ĭt/ *v.* to benefit. *I can profit from your experience.*

prof•it•a•ble /prŏf′ ĭ tə bəl/ *adj.* (*prof•it•a•bly,* *adv.*) bringing profit or benefit. *The store had a profitable year.*

pro•gram•ming /prō′ grăm′ ĭng/ or /-grəm-/ *n.* the designing or planning of a computer program. *Students interested in computer science should study programming.*

prog•ress[1] /prŏg′ rĕs′/ or /prō′ grĕs′/ *n.* **a.** a movement forward. *The train made steady progress.* **b.** development; improvement: *the progress of science.*

pro•gress[2] /prə grĕs′/ *v.* to advance; to improve. *Sarah will progress in her ability to spell.*

proj•ect[1] /prŏj′ ĕkt′/ *n.* a plan; a scheme. *The girls' next project is to build a radio.*

pro•ject[2] /prə jĕkt′/ *v.* **a.** to throw or shoot forward. *An arrow is projected from a bow.* **b.** to cause to fall on a surface. *Movies are projected on a white screen.*

proof /pro͞of/ *n.* anything that shows that something is correct or true. *Do you have proof of your theory?*

prop•er /prŏp′ ər/ *adj.* **a.** correct; suitable. *A proper tool for smoothing wood is a plane.* **b.** indicating a particular person, place, or thing; belonging to one or to only a few. *Proper nouns, such as "Joan" and "Ohio," are always capitalized.*

pro•por•tion /prə pôr′ shən/ or /-pōr′-/ *n.* **a.** a part. *A large proportion of Earth is covered by water.* **b.** a proper relation. *This painting is in proportion to the size of the wall it hangs on.* **c.** a relation of equality between two ratios. *How do you find the missing element in a proportion?*

pro•tect /prə tĕkt′/ *v.* to guard; to defend; to keep from danger. *The police protect citizens from criminals.*

pro•tec•tion /prə tĕk′ shən/ *n.* watchful care; a keeping from danger. *The job of a gamekeeper is the protection of wildlife.*

pro•ton /prō′ tŏn′/ *n.* a positively charged subatomic particle. *Protons are found in the nucleus of an atom.*

prov•ince /prŏv′ ĭns/ *n.* **a.** a division of a country. *Canada is divided into ten provinces and two territories.* **b.** range of knowledge, activity, or authority. *The study of volcanoes falls within the province of geology.*

pro•vi•sion /prə vĭzh′ ən/ *n.* a condition. *One of the provisions for ordering tickets is that you must be a student.*

pub•li•ca•tion /pŭb′ lĭ kā′ shən/ *n.* **a.** the act or process of publishing printed matter. *The author was excited about the publication of her novel.* **b.** a book, magazine, or newspaper. *The library has more than twenty-five thousand publications.*

punc•tu•a•tion /pŭngk′ cho͞o ā′ shən/ *n.* the use of commas, periods, and other marks to make writing clearer. *In writing, correct punctuation is as important as correct usage.*

pun•ish /pŭn′ ĭsh/ *v.* to administer a penalty for a crime or misbehavior. *I will not punish you if you tell the truth.*

pur•chase[1] /pûr′ chĭs/ *v.* (**pur•chas•es, pur•chased, pur•chas•ing**) to buy. *We purchased folding chairs for the porch.*

pur•chase[2] /pûr′ chĭs/ *n.* a thing that is bought. *Mother's purchases will be delivered by the store.*

quad•ri•lat•er•al /kwŏd′ rə lăt′ ər əl/ *n.* a geometric figure with four sides and four angles. *The quadrilateral has four sides.*

quadrilateral

quo•ta /kwō′ tə/ *n.* **a.** due share; an allotment. *Not all the students used up their quota of free tickets.* **b.** a maximum number that may be admitted. *The club has a quota of ten new members each year.*

Spelling Dictionary

quo•ta•tion /kwō tā′ shən/ *n.* **a.** a passage that is quoted. *The speaker used quotations to illustrate his point.* **b.** a passage repeated from a well-known literary work. *"All the world's a stage" is a popular quotation from a play by Shakespeare.*

Pronunciation Key

ă	pat	ŏ	pot	th	thin
ā	pay	ō	toe	th	this
âr	care	ô	paw, for	hw	which
ä	father	oi	noise	zh	vision
ĕ	pet	ou	out	ə	about,
ē	be	o͝o	took		item,
ĭ	pit	o͞o	boot		pencil,
ī	pie	ŭ	cut		gallop,
îr	pier	ûr	urge		circus

ra•di•us /rā′ dē əs/ *n.* (**ra•di•i** or **ra•di•us•es** *pl.*) a straight line from the center of a circle to its edge. *The radius of a circle is half its diameter.*

rap•id /răp′ ĭd/ *adj.* fast; quick. *The rapid current carried the canoe down the river.*

ra•tio /rā′ shō/ or /rā′ shē ō′/ *n.* **a.** the quotient that shows the comparison of two numbers. *The ratio of 1 to 4 is 1/4.* **b.** comparison in size or quantity between two things. *The recipe mixes flour and sugar in the ratio of two to one.*

ra•tion•al /răsh′ ən əl/ *adj.* based on reason; logical. *After thinking it over calmly, Jeff made a rational decision to sell his car.*

re- a prefix that means: **a.** again: *rebuild.* **b.** backwards; back: *react.*

re•al es•tate /rē′ əl ĭ stāt′/ or /rēl′-/ *n.* land and all buildings and properties on it. - *Matt's mother sells real estate.*

real estate

re•bel[1] /rĭ bĕl′/ *v.* (**re•bels, re•belled, re•bel•ling**) to resist or oppose authority. *The workers rebelled against the unfair demands of their employer.*

reb•el[2] /rĕb′ əl/ *n.* a person who reacts against authority. *Rebels challenge tradition.*

re•ceipt /rĭ sēt′/ *n.* **a.** a written statement showing that money or goods have been received. *I signed the receipt when the package was delivered.* **b.** the act of receiving. *On receipt of the good news, we felt happy.*

re•ceive /rĭ sēv′/ *v.* (**re•ceives, re•ceived, re•ceiv•ing**) to get. *You should receive the letter in two days.*

re•ceiv•er /rĭ sē′ vər/ *n.* **a.** a person or a thing that receives something. *The sender of a letter puts the address of the receiver on the envelope.* **b.** the part in a radio, telephone, or TV that picks up the signals. *I held the receiver to my ear.*

re•cess /rē′ sĕs′/ *n.* (**re•cess•es** *pl.*) a brief rest from work. *During the morning we have a fifteen-minute recess.*

re•cip•ro•cal[1] /rĭ sĭp′ rə kəl/ *n.* either of a pair of numbers whose product is 1. *The reciprocal of 3/4 is 4/3, since 3/4 x 4/3 = 1.*

re•cip•ro•cal[2] /rĭ sĭp′ rə kəl/ *adj.* mutual; felt by both sides: *reciprocal interest.*

re•flect /rĭ flĕkt′/ *v.* **a.** to throw back from a surface, as light or heat. *A mirror reflects light.* **b.** to give back an image of. *The trees were reflected in the clear lake.* **c.** to show; to make apparent. *His work reflects great effort.*

re•fract /rĭ frăkt′/ *v.* to cause the path of light to bend. *The lens of the human eye refracts light.*

re•fuse[1] /rĭ fyo͞oz′/ *v.* (**re•fus•es, re•fused, re•fus•ing**) **a.** to turn down; to reject. *She refused my offer of help.* **b.** to be unwilling; to decline. *I refuse to let them bother me.*

ref•use[2] /rĕf′ yo͞os/ *n.* useless matter; rubbish; garbage. *Please put your refuse in the wastebasket.*

re•gion•al /rē′ jə nəl/ *adj.* **a.** characteristic of a large geographic area. *In the sunbelt states, the growth of cities has been a regional asset.* **b.** characteristic of a particular area: *a regional accent.*

reg•u•lar /rĕg′ yə lər/ *adj.* **a.** usual; normal; ordinary. *Our regular practice on Sunday is to have dinner in the afternoon.* **b.** frequent: *regular customers.* **c.** occurring at fixed intervals. *We make regular visits to the dentist.*

reign[1] /rān/ *n.* the time during which a leader rules. *During the queen's reign, the people enjoyed many improvements.*

reign[2] /rān/ *v.* to rule. *The king reigned for thirty years.*

re•lease[1] /rĭ lēs′/ *v.* to let loose; to set free. *If you release the door, it will close by itself.*

re•lease[2] /rĭ lēs′/ *n.* **a.** the act of letting go or setting free. *The rangers planned the release of the bear cubs they had raised.* **b.** freedom; relief. *After the test was over, I felt a sense of release.*

re•lief /rĭ lēf′/ *n.* the removal or ease of worry, pain, etc. *Imagine my relief when I remembered the right answer.*

re•main /rĭ mān′/ *v.* **a.** to stay. *We remained at home because of the rain.* **b.** to continue; to last without changing. *The weather remained warm until the last week of October.* **c.** to be left. *All that remains of the old house is the foundation.*

re•quire /rĭ kwīr′/ *v.* (**re•quires, re•quired, re•quir•ing**) **a.** to need. *Humans require food and water to live.* **b.** to demand; to command. *Good manners require that you use a knife and a fork when you eat.*

res•i•dence /rĕz′ ĭ dəns/ *n.* **a.** the place where one lives; home. *His residence is on Spruce Street.* **b.** the act or fact of living in a place. *His family took up residence in Spain while he was working there.*

res•i•dent /rĕz′ ĭ dənt/ *n.* **a.** a person who lives in a particular area. *When our family moved to Idaho we became residents of that state.* **b.** a doctor who is doing clinical training. *Ms. Barin is a third-year resident at the hospital.* [Latin *residēre*, to reside, from *re-*, back + *sedēre*, to sit.]

res•pi•ra•to•ry /rĕs′ pər ə tôr′ ē/ or /-tōr′ ē/ *adj.* pertaining to the process of breathing. *Smoking is hazardous to the respiratory system.*

re•spond /rĭ spŏnd′/ *v.* **a.** to answer; to reply. *Susan did not respond when I asked her a question.* **b.** to react. *The patient responded well to the medicine.*

re•spon•si•ble /rĭ spŏn′ sə bəl/ *adj.* (**re•spon•si•bly,** *adv.*) **a.** trustworthy; reliable. *A responsible student was chosen to collect the money for the field trip.* **b.** required to answer for something. *Who is responsible for turning off the lights when we leave the room?* **c.** deserving credit or blame for something. *The cold weather was responsible for the small crowd at the picnic.*

res•tau•rant /rĕs′ tər ənt/ or /-tə ränt′/ *n.* a place where meals are sold and served. *We ate dinner in a restaurant downtown.*

re•sult[1] /rĭ zŭlt′/ *n.* outcome; effect. *He was late to work as a result of a delay in traffic.*

re•sult[2] /rĭ zŭlt′/ *v.* to happen as an effect. *The cold, damp weather resulted in icy roads.*

re•ver•ber•ate /rĭ vûr′ bə rāt′/ *v.* (**re•ver•ber•ates, re•ver•ber•at•ed, re•ver•ber•at•ing**) to sound again; to echo. *The thunder reverberated through the mountains.*

re•vers•i•ble /rĭ vûr′ sə bəl/ *adj.* capable of being turned backward or inside out; able to be reversed. *Jo wore her reversible coat.*

rhom•bus /rŏm′ bəs/ *n.* (**rhom•bus•es** or **rhom•bi** *pl.*) a parallelogram with equal sides. *Is every square a rhombus?*

rhombus

rhythm /rĭth′ əm/ *n.* a regular, repeated movement in which a beat or accent rises and falls or occurs steadily. *The rhythm in music is often provided by the drums.*

ri•val[1] /rī′ vəl/ *n.* one who is trying to do better than another; one who competes. *The two friends were rivals for the same part in the school play.*

ri•val[2] /rī′ vəl/ *adj.* competing; being rivals. *The rival stores lowered their prices to attract more customers.*

round /round/ *v.* to express as a whole number. *In math class we are learning to round off numbers to the nearest five or ten.*

rou • tine¹ /rōō tēn′/ *n.* a standard set of activities performed regularly. *Each morning Ann goes through her exercise routine.*

rou • tine² /rōō tēn′/ *adj.* ordinary; not special: *a routine day.*

rpm or **r.p.m.** an abbreviation for "revolutions per minute." *A long-playing record turns at $33\frac{1}{3}$ rpm.*

ru • mor /rōō′ mər/ *n.* uncertain information spread by word of mouth; hearsay. *We heard a rumor that our math quiz was cancelled.*

sa • li • va /sə lī′ və/ *n.* the liquid that is secreted by glands in the mouth. *Saliva helps in the digestion of food.*

salm • on /săm′ ən/ *n.* (**salm•on** or **salm•ons** *pl.*) a large fish with silver scales and pink flesh. *Salmon swim upstream from salt water to fresh water to lay their eggs.*

SALT an acronym for "Strategic Arms Limitation Talks." *The United States and the former Soviet Union originated the SALT treaty.*

sanc • tion /săngk′ shən/ *n.* **a.** approval; support; encouragement. *The governor received public sanction for his views.* **b. sanc•tions** *n. pl.* a course of action several nations agree to take against a nation considered to have violated international law. *Governments may impose economic sanctions on another country for violations of human rights.*

sat • is • fac • tion /săt′ ĭs făk′ shən/ *n.* a feeling of being satisfied or contented. *Dan gets satisfaction from doing his job well.*

sat • is • fy /săt′ ĭs fī′/ *v.* (**sat•is•fies, sat•is•fied, sat•is•fy•ing**) **a.** to please; to fill a need or desire. *You can satisfy the baby by giving her a toy.* **b.** to put an end to. *Water will satisfy my thirst.*

Pronunciation Key

ă	pat	ŏ	pot	th	thin
ā	pay	ō	toe	*th*	*th*is
âr	care	ô	paw, for	hw	which
ä	father	oi	noise	zh	vision
ĕ	pet	ou	out	ə	about,
ē	be	ŏŏ	took		item,
ĭ	pit	ōō	boot		pencil,
ī	pie	ŭ	cut		gallop,
îr	pier	ûr	urge		circus

sauce /sôs/ *n.* a liquid that is served with food. *The chicken dish had a delicious ginger sauce.*

scarce • ly /skârs′ lē/ *adv.* hardly; barely. *There are scarcely any people awake at five o'clock in the morning.*

scar • ci • ty /skâr′ sĭ tē/ *n.* (**scar•ci•ties** *pl.*) a shortage in supply. *During a drought there is a scarcity of water.*

scheme /skēm/ *n.* **a.** a plan of action; a project. *We thought of a scheme for preventing graffiti.* **b.** a secret plot. *The scheme to give Mother a surprise party failed when she discovered the birthday cake.*

sci • en • tif • ic no • ta • tion /sī′ ən tĭf′ ĭk nō tā′ shən/ *n.* a method of writing numbers in terms of powers of ten. *In scientific notation the number 10,492 would be represented as 1.0492×10^4.*

scis • sors /sĭz′ ərz/ *n. pl.* a cutting tool consisting of two handles and two sharp blades fastened together. *Scissors can cut through paper or fabric.*

scu • ba /skōō′ bə/ or /skyōō′-/ *adj.* an acronym for a device with a mask, hose, and air tank used while swimming underwater.

scuba

Scuba divers often see schools of brightly colored tropical fish. [**S**elf-**c**ontained **u**nder**w**ater **b**reathing **a**pparatus.]

sculp • tor /skŭlp′ tər/ *n.* an artist who produces figures or designs that have depth. *Sculptors may choose to work in wood, stone, clay, or metal.*

ter•rain /tə rān′/ or /tĕ-/ *n.* a tract of land, especially with respect to its physical features. *From the airplane, we could see that the terrain below us was rugged.*

ter•ri•ble /tĕr′ ə bəl/ *adj.* (**ter•ri•bly,** *adv.*) **a.** causing terror or awe; alarming. *The monster in the movie was a terrible sight.* **b.** severe; intense; extreme. *The cold at the North Pole is terrible.*

ter•ri•to•ry /tĕr′ ĭ tôr′ ē/ or /-tōr′ ē/ *n.* (**ter•ri•to•ries** *pl.*) an area of land; a region. *Much of the territory in the central United States is used for farming.*

text /tĕkst/ *n.* **a.** written or printed words. *See the text under the map on page 73.* **b.** the words written by an author. *The novelist revised the text of the first chapter.*

theme /thēm/ *n.* **a.** a subject; a topic. *We selected school spirit as the theme of our discussion.* **b.** a short essay. *We write one theme a week in school.*

there•fore /*thâr*′ fôr′/ or /-fōr′/ *adv.* for that reason; consequently. *It turned the litmus paper blue; therefore, it must be a base.*

ther•mal /thûr′ məl/ *adj.* producing or caused by heat. *Skiers wear thermal clothing to protect themselves from the cold.* [Greek *thermē*, heat.]

ther•mom•e•ter /thər mŏm′ ĭ tər/ *n.* an instrument that measures and indicates temperatures. *The liquid in a thermometer expands and rises in the tube as the temperature rises.* [Greek *thermē*, heat + *metron*, measure.]

ther•mo•stat /thûr′ mə stăt′/ *n.* a device that automatically controls heating or cooling equipment. *The thermostat in our house keeps the temperature at 68 degrees.* [Greek *thermē*, heat + *-statēs*, one that causes to stand.]

the•sau•rus /thĭ sôr′ əs/ *n.* a book of synonyms and antonyms. *A thesaurus is a good place to find a more exact word.*

thief /thēf/ *n.* (**thieves** *pl.*) one who steals. *Our neighbor's dog was the thief that took our newspaper from the porch.*

thought•less /thôt′ lĭs/ *adj.* careless; inconsiderate. *It was thoughtless of you to invite only some of your friends.*

through /thrōō/ *prep.* **a.** in one side and out the opposite side. *Aleesha walked through the park to the library.* **b.** from the beginning to the end: *through the night.*

through•out /thrōō out′/ *prep.* **a.** during the entire time of. *Some states have warm weather throughout the year.* **b.** in every part of. *We looked for you throughout the building.*

thun•der•storm /thŭn′ dər stôrm′/ *n.* a heavy rainstorm with lightning and thunder. *That tree was struck by lightning during the thunderstorm.*

tim•pa•ni /tĭm′ pə nē/ *n. pl.* a set of kettledrums. *The timpani boomed out from the back of the orchestra.*

timpani

-tion a suffix, used to form nouns, that means "an action or process": *absorption.*

tire•less /tīr′ lĭs/ *adj.* not easily tired or fatigued. *Mother was tireless with her sewing project, spending hours on it until she finished.*

tire•some /tīr′ səm/ *adj.* tedious; boring. *Filing was the most tiresome part of the library job.*

tis•sue /tĭsh′ ōō/ *n.* **a.** a group of cells in a plant or animal that carry out a certain function: *skin tissue.* **b.** light, soft, thin paper or cloth. *I wiped my nose with a tissue.*

tomb /tōōm/ *n.* a burial place for the dead. *Egyptian pyramids are tombs.*

top•soil /tŏp′ soil′/ *n.* the surface layer of soil. *Flowers and shrubs grow best in rich topsoil.*

tour•ni•quet /tōōr′ nĭ kĭt/ or /tûr′-/ *n.* a cloth band used to temporarily stop the flow of blood through an artery. *A tourniquet should be applied only by someone well trained in first aid.*

tra•che•a /trā′ kē ə/ *n.* the passage that leads from the back of the mouth to the lungs. *The trachea carries air to the lungs.*

traf•fic /trăf′ ĭk/ *n.* the movement of people and vehicles. *There was very little traffic on the turnpike.*

trait /trāt/ *n.* a feature or characteristic. *We all inherit physical traits from our parents.*

trans•ver•sal /trăns vûr′ səl/ or /trănz-/ *n.* a line that intersects other lines. *When a transversal crosses parallel lines it forms sets of matching angles.*

trap•e•zoid /trăp′ ĭ zoid′/ *n.* a quadrilateral that has only one pair of parallel sides. *A trapezoid may have no equal sides.*

trav•el•er /trăv′ əl ər/ or /trăv′ lər/ *n.* a person who travels. *Many travelers visit the United States every year.*

tre•men•dous /trĭ mĕn′ dəs/ *adj*
a. marvelous; wonderful. *She made a tremendous catch.* **b.** terrible; dreadful. *The new dam saved the town from tremendous flood damage.* **c.** extremely large; enormous. *A tremendous wave rocked the boat.*

tribe /trīb/ *n.* a group of people who share a common ancestry, common customs, and a common leader. *The tribe moved west in their search for food.*

tril•lion /trĭl′ yən/ *n.* the number equal to one thousand billions. *The numeral for a trillion has twelve zeros.*

tril•o•gy /trĭl′ ə jē/ *n.* a group of three literary works or dramas related by theme. *The Lord of the Rings is a trilogy whose three volumes tell the story of a ring with mystical powers.* [Greek *trilogiā,* from *tri-,* three + *logos,* word, speech.]

tri•pod /trī′ pŏd′/ *n.* a three-legged stand for supporting a camera or other equipment. *A tripod can be adjusted to different heights.*

tripod

tri•umph¹ /trī′ əmf/ *n.* a great victory. *Eliminating smallpox was a triumph of medicine.*

tri•umph² /trī′ əmf/ *v.* to win; to achieve a victory; to succeed. *With practice, the boy was able to triumph over his fear of the water.*

trop•ics /trŏp′ ĭks/ *n. pl.* the region of Earth on both sides of the equator. *The weather in the tropics is usually hot and humid.*

Pronunciation Key

ă	pat	ŏ	pot	th	**th**in
ā	pay	ō	toe	*th*	**th**is
âr	care	ô	paw, for	hw	**wh**ich
ä	father	oi	noise	zh	vi**si**on
ĕ	pet	ou	out	ə	**a**bout,
ē	be	ŏŏ	took		it**e**m,
ĭ	pit	ōō	boot		penc**i**l,
ī	pie	ŭ	cut		gall**o**p,
îr	pier	ûr	urge		circ**u**s

tun•nel /tŭn′ əl/ *n.* a passage beneath the ground. *The mole dug a tunnel under the lawn.*

tur•ban /tûr′ bən/ *n.* a hat made of a scarf wound around the head. *The first turbans were worn as protection from the sun.*

tur•bu•lent /tûr′ byə lənt/ *adj.* disturbed or violently agitated. *The ocean became turbulent as the hurricane approached.*

typ•i•cal /tĭp′ ĭ kəl/ *adj.* being a certain type; like others in its category. *Saturday was a typical rainy day.*

ty•rant /tī′ rənt/ *n.* a person who rules very harshly or unjustly. *The citizens rebelled against the tyrant.*

ul•ti•mate /ŭl′ tə mĭt/ *adj.* **a.** farthest; last; final. *Being an outstanding teacher is my ultimate goal.* **b.** best; greatest. *Chess is the ultimate game of logic.*

un- a prefix that means "not" or "the opposite of": *unable; untie.*

under- a prefix that means "beneath" or "below in position": *underground.*

un•der•cov•er /ŭn′ dər kŭv′ ər/ *adj.* done in secret: *an undercover police investigation.*

un•der•ground /ŭn′ dər ground′/ *adv.* below the surface of the earth. *The tunnel led to an underground cavern.*

un•der•neath /ŭn′ dər nēth′/ *prep.* beneath; below; under. *Sean found the note that had been left underneath the doormat.*

un•der•pass /ŭn′ dər păs′/ *n.* a section of road that passes under another road or railroad. *The traffic noise echoed in the underpass.*

un•der•stand /ŭn′ dər stănd′/ *v.* (un•der•stands, un•der•stood, un•der•stand•ing) **a.** to know; to comprehend. *Do you understand how a vacuum cleaner works?* **b.** to learn; to hear. *I understand they are planning a trip.*

un•der•stood¹ /ŭn′ dər stŏŏd′/ *v.* past tense of **understand**.

un•der•stood² /ŭn′ dər stŏŏd′/ *adj.* assumed; implied. *It is understood that all sales are final.*

un•for•tu•nate /ŭn fôr′ chə nĭt/ *adj.* not fortunate; not lucky. *It is unfortunate that we missed the bus this morning.*

u•ni•form /yōō′ nə fôrm′/ *n.* the special clothes worn by persons of a particular order or service when they are on duty. *Police and firefighters wear uniforms so they will be recognized.* [Latin *ūnus*, one + *forma*, shape.]

uniform

un•ion /yōōn′ yən/ *n.* **a.** a joining to make a single thing. *The nation called the United States was formed by the union of the original thirteen states.* **b.** a group of workers formed to protect their interests with respect to wages and working conditions. *The union of postal employees accepted the new contract.* [Latin *ūnus*, one.]

un•pleas•ant /ŭn plĕz′ ənt/ *adj.* not pleasant; disagreeable. *That medicine has an unpleasant taste.*

un•voiced /ŭn voist′/ *adj.* produced without vibration of the vocal cords. *The consonant s is unvoiced, but z is voiced.*

up•ward /ŭp′ wərd/ *adv.* toward a higher place, level, or position. *The balloons floated upward when they were let go.*

u•su•al /yōō′ zhōō əl/ *adj.* common; ordinary. *The usual tool for driving a nail is a hammer.*

va•ca•tion /vā kā′ shən/ *n.* a period of time during which one is free from work or school. *My father gets a two-week vacation every year.*

val•u•a•ble /văl′ yōō ə bəl/ or /văl′ yə bəl/ *adj.* **a.** having great value or worth; important. *He is a valuable player on the team.* **b.** worth a great deal of money. *She keeps her valuable china on a high shelf.*

var•i•ous /vâr′ ē əs/ or /văr′-/ *adj.* of several different kinds; different. *I found shells of various sizes and shapes on the beach.*

VCR an abbreviation for "video cassette recorder." *We rented a VCR so we could tape the TV special.*

ve•loc•i•ty /və lŏs′ ĭ tē/ *n.* the rate at which an object moves in a specific direction; speed. *The coaches measured the velocity of the pitcher's fast ball.*

ver•dict /vûr′ dĭkt/ *n.* a decision reached by a jury or a judge at the end of a trial. *The jury handed down a verdict of "not guilty."*

vi•brate /vī′ brāt′/ *v.* (vi•brates, vi•brat•ed, vi•brat•ing) to move back and forth quickly. *The strings on a guitar vibrate when they are strummed.*

vic•to•ry /vĭk′ tə rē/ *n.* (vic•to•ries *pl.*) the act of winning; the defeat of the opposite side; triumph in a battle or contest. *The home team scored its first victory last night.*

vid•e•o¹ /vĭd′ ē ō/ *adj.* of or used in the transmitting and receiving of television images. *Our local record store will soon carry a line of video equipment.*

vid•e•o² /vĭd′ ē ō/ *n.* a videocassette tape; a recording on videotape. *Singers often create videos of their songs.* [Latin *vidēre*, to see.]

vil•lain /vĭl′ ən/ *n.* a wicked or evil character. *When the villain appeared onstage, the audience booed.*

vi•o•lin•ist
/vī′ ə lĭn′ ĭst/ *n.* a person who plays the violin. *John hopes to become a great violinist.*

violinist

vis•i•ble /vĭz′ ə bəl/ *adj.* able to be seen. *Because of the fog, the lights were no longer visible.*

vi•sion /vĭzh′ ən/ *n.* **a.** something that is or has been seen. *Jan was a vision of beauty in her costume.* **b.** the sense of sight. *He has perfect vision in both eyes.* [Latin *vis-*, perfect stem of *vidēre*, to see.]

vis•i•tor /vĭz′ ĭ tər/ *n.* a person who visits. *The visitor brought flowers.*

vis•u•al /vĭzh′ yoo əl/ *adj.* capable of being seen; visible. *The laser light show was a visual treat for the audience.*

voiced /voist/ *adj.* sounded with the vibration of the vocal cords. *The th sound in "this" is a voiced consonant sound.*

vol•ume /vŏl′ yoom/ or /-yəm/ *n.* **a.** the amount of space within an enclosed area. *Can you find the volume of this cube?* **b.** loudness. *Please turn down the volume of the radio.* **c.** one of a set of books: *a volume of the encyclopedia.*

vol•un•tar•y /vŏl′ ən tĕr′ē/ *adj.* (**vol•un•tar•i•ly,** *adv.*) done by choice or on purpose. *He made a voluntary decision to stay home and study.*

vol•un•teer /vŏl′ən tîr′/ *n.* one who offers to perform a service of his or her free will, usually without pay. *We need a volunteer to sell tickets to the school play.*

-ward a suffix, used to form adverbs or adjectives, that means "in a specified direction": *downward.*

wa•ter va•por /wô′ tər vā′ pər/ or /wŏt′ ər-/ *n.* water below the boiling point that is diffused as vapor in the atmosphere. *Water vapor forms in a steamy bathroom.*

wave•length /wāv′ lĕngth′/ *n.* the distance between any point on a wave and the same point on the next wave. *Light has a shorter wavelength than sound.*

weath•er•proof /wĕth′ ər proof′/ *adj.* able to be exposed to weather without damage. *Most houses are painted with weatherproof paint.*

weird /wîrd/ *adj.* strange; odd. *The group of people going to the costume party was a weird sight.*

whole•some /hōl′ səm/ *adj.* healthful. *The doctor gave us advice on the importance of exercise and wholesome meals.*

wind /wīnd/ *v.* (**winds, wound, wind•ing**) **a.** to wrap or coil around. *Wind the thread around the spool.* **b.** to turn or crank. *Who will wind the clock?*

won•der•ful /wŭn′ dər fəl/ *adj.* excellent; remarkable; marvelous. *What a wonderful sight the sunset is today!*

won•drous /wŭn′ drəs/ *adj.* wonderful. *The Perseid meteor shower is a wondrous August event.*

wood•cut /wŏod′ kŭt′/ *n.* a block of wood with a picture or design carved into it. *The artist carved the design into the block to form a woodcut.*

wor•ri•some /wûr′ē səm/ or /wŭr′-/ *adj.* causing concern or worry. *His jammed locker was a worrisome problem all day.*

worth•less /wûrth′ lĭs/ *adj.* without worth or value. *The photographs were worthless to everyone but the family members.*

would • 've would have.

wound¹ /wo͞ond/ *n.* an injury to the body. *The doctor put a bandage on the wound on my arm.*

wound² /wound/ *v.* past tense and past participle of **wind**.

wrist • watch /rĭst' wŏch'/ *n.* a watch worn on a band that fastens around the wrist. *The child was excited to get her first wristwatch.*

wristwatch

yield /yēld/ *v.* to surrender; to give up. *A traffic sign that says "yield" warns drivers to allow the other drivers to go first.*

USING THE Thesaurus

The **Writing Thesaurus** provides synonyms—words that mean the same or nearly the same—and antonyms—words that mean the opposite—for your spelling words. Use this sample to identify the various parts of each thesaurus entry.

- **Entry words** are listed in alphabetical order and are printed in boldface type.

- The abbreviation for the **part of speech** of each entry word follows the boldface entry word.

- The **definition** of the entry word matches the definition given of the word in your spelling dictionary. A **sample sentence** shows the correct use of the word in context.

- Each **synonym** for the entry word is listed under the entry word. Again, a sample sentence shows the correct use of the synonym in context.

- Where appropriate, **antonyms** for the entry word are listed at the end of the entry.

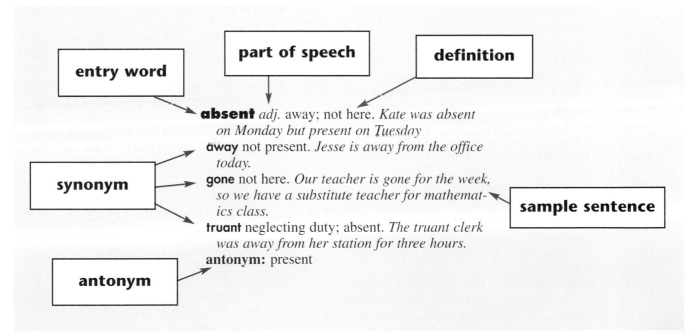

entry word | part of speech | definition

absent *adj.* away; not here. *Kate was absent on Monday but present on Tuesday*

away not present. *Jesse is away from the office today.*

gone not here. *Our teacher is gone for the week, so we have a substitute teacher for mathematics class.*

truant neglecting duty; absent. *The truant clerk was away from her station for three hours.*

antonym: present

synonym | sample sentence | antonym

absent *adj.* away; not here. *Kate was absent on Monday but present on Tuesday.*
away not present. *Jesse is away from the office today.*
gone not here. *Our teacher is gone for the week, so we have a substitute teacher for mathematics class.*
truant neglecting duty; absent. *The truant clerk was away from her station for three hours.*
antonym: present

accurate *adj.* correct; without mistakes. *The witness's testimony was accurate and consistent with the evidence.*
definite clear or exact. *The flight attendant gave a definite time for the flight's departure from the airport.*
exact precise; correct. *She noted the exact location of the accident.*
factual concerned with facts; truthful. *Horace gave a factual account of the game's ending.*
precise correct; exact. *Because the kit had precise directions, we could build the birdhouse easily.*
unerring without mistakes. *Because of her unerring performance, she was sure to win the gold medal.*
antonyms: incorrect, wrong

accuse *v.* to blame for wrongdoing. *The police did accuse him of speeding and reckless driving.*
blame to hold responsible for. *No one would blame you for mistaking one twin for the other.*
censure to criticize. *For not having the proper data in his research report, the decision was made to censure him.*
criticize to find fault with. *Do not criticize him until you know all the facts.*
reproach to blame. *Be a person of good character so no one can reproach you.*

achieve *v.* to reach; accomplish. *If you wish to achieve success, you must work hard.*
accomplish to succeed in completing. *We will accomplish the task in record time.*

attain to arrive at; gain. *She will attain her goal through hard work.*
antonym: fail

admit *v.* to acknowledge; confess. *The mayor did admit that she had not been aware of the problem.*
acknowledge to admit to be true. *The accountant must acknowledge that the mistake on the books was her fault.*
concede to admit as true. *The actor had to concede that he had not learned his lines on time.*
confess to own up; admit. *Sami confessed that the floor was flooded because he had left the water running in the sink.*
reveal to make known. *The investigation might reveal that the mistake was due to computer error.*

adorable *adj.* lovable; charming. *The stuffed animals were cuddly and adorable.*
attractive pleasing. *My brother and his wife are an attractive couple.*
captivating charming; fascinating. *The story is a captivating tale of two best friends.*
charming delightful; adorable. *The children in the play were totally charming.*
cute good-looking and lovable. *That baby is so cute and sweet!*
darling dear and attractive. *Your new puppy is just darling.*

advance *v.* to go forward. *Please advance to the front of the line.*
forge ahead to move forward. *She needed to forge ahead to win the race by just a few steps.*
proceed to move forward. *The cars continued to proceed slowly through the dangerous intersection.*
progress to go ahead. *The work on the new bridge continued to progress on schedule.*
promote to advance; move upward. *I was promoted to seventh grade.*

aged *adj.* old; having lived long. *The aged man was having difficulty walking.*
ancient very old; of great age. *The Colosseum is one of Rome's ancient ruins.*
elderly old. *In this program, elderly men and women spend time teaching the young children in the day-care center.*
antonym: young

amateur *n.* a person who participates in activities for fun, not money. *Even an amateur can become skillful with regular practice.*

hobbyist amateur. *The hobbyist compared his paintings to those displayed by the professionals.*

nonprofessional not professional; amateur. *In this tournament, a nonprofessional played with the golf pros.*

amaze *v.* to surprise or astonish. *The acrobat's ability to do high jumps really did amaze us.*

astound to surprise greatly; astonish. *The cost of the project continues to astound us.*

dazzle to astonish; overwhelm with beauty. *The splendor of the mansion will dazzle the tourists.*

fascinate to strongly attract or charm. *Tonight's featured news stories fascinate me.*

stun to overwhelm; shock; surprise. *The damage caused by the storm has to stun even the weather bureau.*

antisocial *adj.* avoiding the company of others. *It is a mistake to assume that a shy person is deliberately antisocial.*

hostile unfriendly; not sociable. *He gave me such a hostile look that I knew he did not want to be disturbed.*

unfriendly not friendly; hostile. *The unfriendly dog frightened me.*

unsociable not friendly; antisocial. *The child's parents scolded her for displaying unsociable behavior at the restaurant.*

appreciate *v.* 1. to see the value of something. *The recital made us appreciate my brother's hours of piano practice.* 2. to be thankful for. *I appreciate your help.*

be grateful to be thankful. *Sandra should be grateful for the opportunity to visit Paris.*

prize to highly value. *The actor seems to prize his privacy.*

value to think highly of. *I truly value my right to vote.*

approve *v.* 1. to give official consent to. *The board needs to approve the plans for the new gym.* 2. to have a good opinion of. *Do you approve of his choice of colors?*

accept to consent to. *The park manager must accept the bid for repairing the tennis courts.*

commend to praise; approve. *My instructor stopped to commend me for my performance in the play.*

endorse to support; approve. *The political party will endorse the President's reelection campaign.*

ratify to confirm; approve. *Both houses of Congress must ratify the law.*

aptitude *n.* a talent or ability for learning. *She has an aptitude for languages; she speaks French, German, and Italian.*

ability capability; power to do. *The runner had the ability to run the marathon in record time.*

capability ability to learn to do. *He has the capability to learn how to operate the new computer system.*

faculty ability; power to do something. *Her faculty to understand difficult ideas is admired by the entire staff.*

flair talent. *The artist had a flair for combining color and light in his paintings.*

sense power to perceive. *The reporter had the good sense not to pursue that line of questioning.*

talent natural ability. *Because of her talent, Donna was a soloist in the school's chorus.*

assign *v.* 1. to give out; distribute. *Our teacher does assign us homework every evening.* 2. to appoint to a position. *The teacher will assign him to be hall monitor this month.*

appoint to name for an office; select. *They decided to appoint Henry chairperson of the special events committee.*

commission to appoint; give authority to. *The committee voted to commission this artist to paint the President's portrait.*

consign to give out; deliver. *Which airfreight company did you consign the shipment to?*

delegate to appoint or send. *We decided to delegate Mitch to represent us at the meeting.*

name to appoint; choose. *The president of the company will name Carole vice president of marketing.*

associate *v.* to think of as related. *Most people associate tears with sadness, but many people cry when they are happy.*

connect to link; think of in relation to. *Many people connect seeing a robin for the first time with the beginning of spring.*

correlate to relate to another. *Did you correlate your choice of classes with your career goals?*

baffle *v.* to puzzle; bewilder. *The riddles will baffle the students.*

bewilder to puzzle; confuse completely. *All the aisles of shelves in the library bewilder Trisha and remind her of a maze.*

confound to puzzle; confuse. *The lack of detail in the instructions did confound me.*

confuse to bewilder. *Driving on diagonal streets can confuse my sense of direction.*

perplex to bewilder; confuse; puzzle. *The results of the student's experiment did perplex the professor.*

puzzle to perplex; baffle. *Tom's solution to that math problem did puzzle me.*

balance *v.* to make both sides equal; to weigh or measure in or as in a balance. *The clown tried to balance a chair on his head.*

equalize to make even; balance. *Tara attempted to equalize her study time and the time for swimming practice.*

offset to balance or set off. *The trip to Mexico offset the long hours of work needed to complete the project.*

barely *adv.* hardly; scarcely. *We could barely see the cars because of the fog.*

hardly only just; barely. *The teacher had hardly any time to prepare the students for the contest.*

only just barely; hardly. *He had only just begun to sing when the sound system broke down.*

scarcely barely; not quite. *Scarcely anyone was in the theater when I arrived for the second show.*

beyond *prep.* in a place farther away than; past. *The grocery store is just beyond the park.*

after behind. *Turn left after the second light.*

past farther on than. *If you go past the school, you have driven too far and you should turn around.*

browse *v.* 1. to look at in a leisurely way; skim through. *Sam began to browse through the magazines in the dentist's office.* 2. to feed on leaves. *Giraffes browse on tall trees.*

graze to feed on grass or trees. *After we milked the cows, we sent them out to the field to graze.*

scan to glance at; skim. *Looking for store coupons, Rosa needed to scan the ads in the newspaper.*

thumb through to browse; look casually. *Jackie will thumb through the mystery books in the library to find one that interests her.*

cancel *v.* to do away with; to call off. *The official had to cancel the game because of rain.*

neutralize to make neutral; to stop something from taking effect. *The antidote will neutralize the effect of the poison.*

repeal to take back; do away with. *Congress will repeal the unpopular tax law during the current session.*

revoke to withdraw; cancel. *The city can revoke a building permit if building codes are violated.*

capable *adj.* having the skill to; able to. *She is capable of fixing almost any machine.*

able having skill; capable. *Norm is able to swim thirty laps at a time.*

competent able; qualified. *Rose is a competent news reporter who always checks the facts of a story.*

proficient skilled; expert. *Kathryn is a proficient reader and speller.*

qualified competent. *Marietta was one of the qualified job applicants.*

carefully *adv.* with care; cautiously or thoroughly. *Peter dusted the tiny figurines carefully.*

cautiously very carefully; not taking any chances. *Victor cautiously approached the intersection where the accident had occurred.*

conscientiously careful to do the right thing. *Anita conscientiously attended each lecture in the series.*

gingerly very cautiously. *Anton gingerly picked up the pieces of broken glass.*

painstakingly very carefully; scrupulously. *Tina painstakingly fitted together all the pieces of the 1000-piece jigsaw puzzle.*

thoroughly very carefully, completing an entire task. *The vet thoroughly examined the injured bird.*

cautious *adj.* careful; keeping away from danger. *The bus driver was cautious in the storm.*
  careful showing care; watchful. *Carole was very careful while driving on the icy roads.*
  discreet very careful in what is said or done; wisely cautious. *She gave a discreet response to the impolite question.*
  unadventurous unwilling to take risks. *John is so unadventurous that he would not even think of going on the hiking trip through the park.*
  wary on guard; cautious. *You should be wary when walking on unlit streets alone at night.*
  antonym: careless

central *adj.* main; leading; chief. *What is the central idea that the author wants us to understand?*
  cardinal foremost; chief. *The cardinal rule for getting along with your friends is to respect them.*
  chief most important; main. *Corn is the chief crop raised by farmers in our state.*
  main foremost; most important. *Who was the main character in the story?*
  pivotal very important; central. *The President addressed the pivotal issues in his State of the Union Address.*
  principal most important; main. *Name the principal rivers in the United States.*

certainly *adv.* definitely; surely. *Certainly your grades will improve if you study hard.*
  absolutely certainly; without a doubt. *The star absolutely will attend the New York premiere of the movie.*
  definitely certainly; surely. *Without glasses, he definitely could not see the third line of the eye chart.*
  positively surely; absolutely. *This is positively the best restaurant in town.*
  undoubtedly without doubt; certainly. *Undoubtedly the game will be delayed because of rain.*

classify *v.* to sort; arrange according to category or class. *Librarians do not classify fairy tales with other fiction.*
  categorize to put into a category; classify. *For the lab test, we had to categorize items as PLANTS, ANIMALS, or MINERALS.*

grade to sort; place in classes. *We need to grade the peaches according to size.*
  sort to arrange by class; put in order. *Ray will sort the sales figures by product.*

cleanse *v.* to make clean; remove dirt from. *Always cleanse a cut or scrape before bandaging it.*
  clean to get rid of dirt; to make clean. *Be sure to clean behind your ears.*
  rinse to wash lightly. *The dentist told me to rinse my mouth out with salt water.*
  scour to make clean by rubbing; cleanse. *I will scour the tub until it shines.*
  scrub to rub hard; wash by rubbing. *We needed to scrub and wax the floors.*
  sponge to wipe clean. *Dad can sponge the dirt from Anna's scraped knee.*
  wash to clean with soap and water. *We will wash our hands and faces before we sit down to eat.*
  wipe to clean by rubbing. *Please wipe your feet before coming in the house.*

complain *v.* 1. to find fault. *Don't complain about a problem unless you're willing to help remedy it.* 2. to report something bad. *The neighbors called the police to complain about the noisy motorcycle.*
  accuse to place blame on. *The sales representative tried to accuse the mail service of delaying my order.*
  grumble to find fault; complain. *Jesse always seems to grumble about having too much homework to do.*
  protest to object to; complain strongly. *The coach decided to protest the referee's decision.*
  rail to complain bitterly. *The lawyer would rail against the injustice her client had experienced.*

conceit *n.* an exaggerated opinion of one's worth; vanity. *Conceit is an unattractive quality.*
  egotism too much concern with oneself; conceit. *His egotism led him to believe he could never be wrong.*
  self-esteem thinking well of oneself. *The success of her plan bolstered her self-esteem.*
  vainglory extreme pride; vanity. *The vainglory of the senator was one reason he was not reelected.*
  vanity too much pride; conceit. *The actor's vanity was greater than his talent.*

conclude *v.* to end; finish. *She concluded her speech and sat down.*

close to come together; to bring to an end. *The President closed his speech with a request for help from all the people.*

complete to make thorough; to get done. *Cheryl can complete her report before the deadline.*

end to stop; finish. *The story could end with the hero solving the mystery.*

finish to bring to an end; complete. *After I finish the book, I will lend it to my sister.*

terminate to put an end to. *When one partner left the company it was necessary to terminate the agreement.*

conduct *v.* to guide; lead. *The student will conduct the visitor through the new building.*

direct to manage; guide. *Matty tried to direct the actors in the movie.*

guide to show the way; lead. *The park ranger will guide us through the cave.*

lead to show the way; guide. *You can lead a horse to water, but you cannot make it drink.*

manage to guide; direct. *She continued to manage the account so well that its profits increased by fifty percent.*

usher to take to; escort. *The restaurant owner was pleased to usher us to our seats.*

confirm *v.* to make certain or sure. *The experiment will try to confirm her theory.*

authenticate to show to be valid; verify. *The scientific testing will authenticate the estimated age of the fossil.*

certify to confirm as true; guarantee. *This document does certify completion of the course.*

establish to prove; confirm. *The witness did establish the defendant's alibi.*

prove to show to be true or right. *The lawyer claimed she could prove her client's innocence.*

verify to confirm; prove the truth of. *Can scientific evidence be used to verify your conclusion?*

antonyms: contradict, disprove

connect *v.* 1. to join; link. *Before you turn on the water, connect the hose to the faucet.* 2. to join two ideas, events, etc., in the mind. *I connect clowns with the circus.*

bind to tie together; fasten. *We will bind the newspapers with twine before taking them to the recycling center.*

join to come together; connect. *Karen will join her friends at the theater.*

link to unite; connect. *The pieces of the puzzle link together perfectly.*

relate to connect ideas or events or things. *The increased attendance at home games is related to the team's long winning streak.*

unite to join together; combine. *The railroad does unite the two parts of the country.*

constant *adj.* never changing or stopping; happening again and again. *The constant beat of the rain put us to sleep.*

continual never stopping; over and over again. *The continual interruptions made it difficult for him to complete his work.*

persistent going on; continuing. *After most of my cold symptoms were gone, I still had a persistent cough.*

steady changing little; continuous. *The sun is finally shining after three days of steady rain.*

courage *n.* the quality of facing danger or a difficult task without giving in to fear. *It takes courage to admit your mistakes.*

bravery fearlessness. *The police officer won an award for bravery after saving the child from the fire.*

fortitude courage; firmness of convictions. *She has the fortitude to fight for what she believes is right.*

valor bravery; strength. *The valor of the colonists helped them win the American Revolution.*

cruel *adj.* wanting to make others suffer or causing them pain. *The cruel children threw stones at the birds.*

brutal extremely cruel. *The enemies waged a brutal battle against one another.*

insensitive slow to notice; uncaring. *The insensitive remark hurt her feelings.*

unkind harsh; cruel. *Children are sometimes unkind to one another.*

customary *adj.* based on custom; usual; routine. *A tuna sandwich and an apple are my customary lunch.*

everyday usual; not exciting. *This book details the everyday as well as the unusual events of the author's days living in the wilderness.*

habitual done by habit; regular. *We took our habitual evening walk along the beach.*

routine using routine; ordinary. *During one of our routine practices, the coach announced who would be the starting players in Saturday's game.*

traditional customary; handed down by tradition. *Turkey and cranberry sauce are two of the traditional foods for the Thanksgiving meal.*

usual common; ordinary; customary. *Although Lynne left for work at the usual time, she arrived fifteen minutes earlier than she expected.*

delicate *adj.* 1. light and pleasing to the senses. *This is a delicate perfume.* 2. carefully and expertly done; requiring careful workmanship. *Those are delicate repairs.* 3. fragile; easily broken or hurt. *Be careful with that delicate vase.*

dainty delicate in beauty; delicate in tastes. *The dainty spring flowers complemented the room's old-fashioned decor.*

exquisite very lovely; delicate. *This painting displayed by the museum is an exquisite example of impressionistic art.*

fine not coarse; delicate. *This fine cloth can be sewn into a beautiful summer suit.*

fragile easily broken; frail. *Because the package was marked fragile, I opened it very carefully.*

frail not very strong; easily broken. *My mother does not let anyone sit in the antique armchair because it is so frail.*

mild soft or lightly pleasing to the senses. *The mild aroma of the sauce made my mouth water.*

delightful *adj.* greatly pleasing; causing joy or delight. *We saw a delightful movie last night that made us remember our days as small children.*

charming delightful; very pleasing. *The child's retelling of "Goldilocks and the Three Bears" was charming.*

cheery pleasant; cheerful. *Sally sent me a cheery note when I was sick.*

enjoyable pleasant; able to be enjoyed. *We had an enjoyable time at the fair.*

lovely beautiful; pleasant. *It was a lovely evening at the concert.*

pleasurable agreeable; pleasant. *The cruise was a pleasurable way to spend a week.*

detain *v.* 1. to delay; hold back. *Heavy fog managed to detain their flight for two hours.* 2. to keep in custody. *They decided to detain the suspect for questioning.*

confine to restrict; limit. *At the meeting, we were asked to confine our comments to the topic being discussed.*

constrain to restrain; confine. *The restrictions placed on her project continued to constrain Natalie.*

delay to put off; hinder. *Because of switching problems, it was necessary to delay the train for an hour.*

hold up to stop; detain. *I knew the weather would hold up our departure.*

postpone to put off; delay. *It was decided to postpone the concert until a later date.*

retard to delay; hinder. *The lack of funds will retard the progress of the campaign.*

develop *v.* 1. to grow; come into being. *The bud will develop into a blossom.* 2. to build up; put to use. *Reading helps develop your mind.*

expand to enlarge; make or grow larger. *The class in geography will expand the student's knowledge of international relations.*

extend to stretch; increase. *Can you extend your answer to include the reasons for the American Revolution?*

grow to become bigger; develop. *Francesco is growing so quickly that he needs new shoes every three months.*

different *adj.* not alike. *Summer is different from winter.*

dissimilar unalike. *Our answers were so dissimilar that they could not be compared.*

diverse not alike; varied. *The candidates had diverse opinions on the issue.*

unlike not the same; different. *Although they are twins, they are very much unlike each other.*

varied having variety or choice. *The menu offered quite varied selections.*

antonyms: same, similar

difficult *adj.* hard; not easy to do or understand. *Learning to play chess is difficult.*

arduous hard to do; using much energy. *After her arduous workout, the gymnast wanted to do nothing but rest.*

hard difficult; troublesome. *At first, I had a hard time understanding what the toddler was trying to tell me.*

rigorous harsh; difficult. *Only after rigorous practice did I master the steps of the dance routine.*

tough hard. *Ed had a tough time trying to explain why he had not completed the project on time.*

antonym: easy

dirty *adj.* not clean; containing dirt. *Put all the dirty clothes into the washing machine.*

filthy very dirty; foul. *After playing in the mud, Johnny and Matthew were filthy from head to toe.*

foul very dirty; smelly. *The pollution released by the factory made the air foul.*

impure unclean; adulterated. *The addition of the incorrect chemical made the solution impure.*

antonym: clean

disguise *v.* 1. to change one's real appearance so that one will not be recognized. *In the play, the thief did disguise himself as a detective.* 2. to hide; mask; cover up. *He tried to disguise his anger by smiling.*

camouflage to conceal; disguise. *Chameleons camouflage themselves by changing their color.*

mask to cover or hide. *Al needed to mask his disappointment by cheerfully congratulating the winner.*

masquerade to disguise; falsely pretend. *To get the information he wanted, the private detective had to masquerade as a bartender.*

dispute *v.* to argue; debate; have a different opinion about. *Our class did dispute about the best date for the picnic.*

argue to discuss with someone who disagrees. *Abby would argue that her bedtime was much too early and that she should be allowed to stay up at least one hour longer.*

contend to argue. *Congress will contend that balancing the budget should be one of the country's highest priorities.*

contest to fight or dispute. *The defeated candidate did not contest the election returns, although the results were very close.*

debate to argue about; discuss pros and cons. *The city council will debate the need for additional taxes to pay for road repairs.*

disagree to quarrel; dispute. *If they disagree about who will be first, the friends will settle the argument by drawing lots.*

quarrel to argue; dispute. *I cannot quarrel with your account of the traffic accident.*

donate *v.* to give or contribute to a fund or cause. *The class decided to donate the money from the bake sale to the animal shelter.*

bestow to give as a gift. *France bestowed the Statue of Liberty on the United States for its centennial.*

confer to bestow. *The President will confer the Medal of Honor on three soldiers during the ceremony.*

contribute to give money or help. *Volunteers will contribute their time to the cleanup effort, since the storm left the city in a shambles.*

give to hand over. *We will give the clothes we collected for the poor to the local charity.*

grant to give what is asked. *The parent-teacher group voted to grant money to the school to build a new chemistry lab.*

effort *n.* 1. the use of one's strength or power; exertion. *Riding a bicycle uphill requires effort.* 2. an attempt; a try. *Make an effort to finish by three o'clock.*

attempt an effort or try. *The track star broke the record on his second attempt at the long jump.*

endeavor a strong attempt; effort. *The reporter's endeavor to gain an interview with the visiting official paid off when she agreed to speak with him.*

exertion effort. *The sheer exertion needed to complete the task on time was almost overwhelming.*

labor effort in doing. *The success of the summit made our labor to prepare for it worthwhile.*

error *n.* a mistake. *I was happy because my spelling test had no errors.*

blunder a foolish mistake. *Forgetting my mother's birthday was a real blunder.*

fault an error; a mistake. *A missing answer was the only fault I could find on my test paper.*

inaccuracy mistake. *It was an inaccuracy in the computer input that caused the program to fail.*

mistake error. *I corrected the mistake on my paper before I handed it in to the teacher.*

especially *adv.* mainly; in particular; unusually. *My brother likes all sports, but he especially enjoys soccer.*

notably in a notable manner; especially. *Karen is a good student in most subjects, but most notably in history and math.*

particularly especially; in particular. *The storm hit the eastern section of the city particularly hard.*

principally mainly. *Yvonne was the person principally responsible for the success of the school's fund-raising efforts.*

exactly *adv.* precisely; without any change. *Do exactly as the teacher says.*

accurately without errors. *The reporter accurately described the events leading to the tragedy.*

correctly without mistakes. *Andrew correctly named all the state capitals.*

definitely clearly; exactly. *It is definitely important to understand all the directions.*

literally precisely; actually. *Lynne followed the instructions for building the desk literally step by step.*

precisely exactly; in a precise manner. *What precisely is the total cost of the car when taxes are included?*

examine *v.* to look at closely to find out the condition of; inspect. *Examine the apples before you buy them.*

analyze to examine carefully. *The manager decided to analyze the reports to identify the trends in sales activity.*

audit to examine and check. *The state examiner will audit the bank's accounts once every two years.*

check to compare and examine. *The teacher will check the students' answers against the answer key.*

inspect to carefully examine. *Edna tried to examine the coat for flaws in the material.*

test to try out; examine. *The doctor used the chart to test my eyesight.*

excellence *n.* something in which a person surpasses others. *The school offered an award for excellence in spelling.*

merit something that deserves high praise; value. *The volunteer was honored for the merit of her work at our local children's hospital.*

quality excellence; merit. *The skill of the carpenter is reflected in the quality of the cabinet.*

superiority high in quality. *The superiority of this product makes it the best-selling stereo on the market.*

excitement *n.* an excited condition; the state of being stirred up. *The entrance of the tigers created great excitement among the circus crowd.*

ecstasy condition of great joy or delight. *The ecstasy of the occasion was evident on everyone's face.*

frenzy very great excitement. *The fans were in a frenzy when the home team won the World Series.*

thrill an exciting feeling. *I will always remember the thrill of my first summer vacation at the beach.*

exhibit *v.* to display; reveal publicly. *He decided to exhibit his paintings at the fair.*

display to put on view; show; exhibit. *The students will display their projects at the school's science fair.*

expose to show openly; make known; display. *The company's new product was first exposed to the public on national television.*

feature to draw special attention to. *The trade show will feature the latest technology.*

present to bring before the public. *The museum will present the works of the most noted realists.*

experience *n.* what one learns from doing things. *I gained business experience from my paper route.*

background past experience or knowledge. *My strong background in history helps me better understand today's political issues and events.*

knowledge what one knows and understands. *The new group had very limited knowledge of the music business.*

practice the condition of being skilled through repeated exercise. *The coach pointed out that sloppy practice doesn't make perfect.*

training practical education; experience. *Dan's training as a crime reporter helped him identify clues that could be used to solve the mystery.*

express *v.* to tell; make known. *Think for a moment before you try to express your idea.*

communicate to give information through writing or speaking, etc. *Her speech will communicate her viewpoint eloquently.*

convey to communicate. *Let me convey my best wishes for the success of your new business venture.*

delineate to describe in words. *Jeff will delineate the company's profit plan in his presentation to the board.*

phrase to express in a particular way. *Be sure to phrase your question so that only a "Yes" or "No" answer is needed.*

state to tell; say. *The mayor did clearly state his position on the property tax increase the council was proposing.*

verbalize to express in words. *I am going to verbalize my ideas to see if you think they will work.*

fabulous *adj.* amazing; wonderful. *It was a fabulous party.*

marvelous splendid; extraordinary. *We had a marvelous time at the annual charity ball sponsored by our organization.*

sensational outstanding; spectacular. *Both actors gave sensational performances on stage.*

spectacular marvelous; sensational. *The game ended with Sara's spectacular diving catch of the fly ball.*

splendid wonderful; excellent. *The restaurant offers a splendid choice of seafood as well as pasta dishes.*

striking very noticeable; fabulous. *Her striking rendition of the show's theme song brought the audience to its feet.*

wonderful causing wonder; remarkable. *We had a wonderful time vacationing in the Hawaiian Islands.*

fearless *adj.* not afraid; brave. *The fearless kitten confronted the big dog.*

bold without fear; daring. *Malcolm made a bold effort to outrun the older boys on the team.*

brave showing courage. *Jessie put on a brave smile as she entered the dentist's office for her appointment.*

courageous brave; fearless. *Saving the child was a courageous act by the firefighter, who received an award for his bravery.*

daring fearless; bold. *The daring high divers perform their spectacular acts every day.*

gallant brave; noble. *The gallant efforts of the volunteers helped protect the homes from being flooded.*

antonyms: afraid, frightened

feeble *adj.* without much strength; weak. *Newborn animals are often feeble.*

faint dizzy; weak. *Evelyn felt faint as she stood to give her speech in the school auditorium.*

flimsy slight; frail. *Anton gave a flimsy excuse for being late for his class.*

frail weak; feeble. *Although she appeared frail, Maxine was quite strong for her size.*

infirm lacking strength; feeble. *The patient was too infirm to walk without help.*

fierce *adj.* 1. savage; wild. *The fierce lion growled and paced inside the cage.* 2. violent. *The fierce wind blew down the trees.*

ferocious savage; very cruel. *The ferocious animal bared its teeth as it growled.*

furious violent; very fierce. *The furious storm tore roofs off houses and uprooted trees.*

raging violent. *The raging winds blew down power lines and tree branches.*

savage cruel; fierce. *The savage fight ended with both wild dogs bleeding and limping away.*

flexible *adj.* capable of being bent. *The clay figures were flexible and could be formed into any shape.*

pliable easily bent. *Because the vines were pliable, we could easily shape them into a wreath.*

pliant easily bent; flexible. *The sculptor heated the steel to make it pliant for forming the pieces of an enormous mobile.*

supple bending easily; flexible. *The supple dancer leaped and twirled throughout the ballet performance.*

former *adj.* coming earlier in time or before in position. *The former owner of this house painted the walls blue.*

earlier before; previous. *The author's earlier novel was better written that this one.*

previous earlier; coming before. *I did not see this exhibit on my previous visit to the museum.*

prior earlier than; before. *The coach gave a stirring speech prior to the start of the game.*

fortunate *adj.* lucky. *You were fortunate to find the lost bracelet.*

happy lucky; fortunate. *It was a happy co-incidence that my friend and I were in the same class.*

lucky having good luck. *We were lucky to get tickets for the playoff games from Pat's mother.*

furious *adj.* very angry. *I was furious with myself for forgetting my homework.*

angry feeling or showing anger. *Her angry tone of voice let me know she was not pleased.*

irate very angry. *The long delay made me irate because I knew I would miss my connecting flight.*

wrathful very angry. *With a wrathful roar, the tiger leaped to protect her cubs.*

garbage *n.* spoiled food or waste matter that is thrown away. *We put our garbage in cans in the alley.*

debris ruins; rubbish. *The stadium was filled with debris left by the fans.*

refuse waste; rubbish. *Keep the park clean by throwing your refuse in one of the trash containers.*

rubbish trash; waste. *It is illegal to burn rubbish in most communities.*

trash rubbish. *The students filled three bags with the trash picked up from the baseball field.*

waste refuse; unused materials. *It would be wrong to let so much food go to waste.*

glorious *adj.* beautiful; brilliant. *This is a glorious day.*

brilliant splendid; magnificent. *The actor's brilliant performance as Hamlet was given rave reviews in the newspaper.*

magnificent splendid; grand. *The magnificent work of the artist was displayed in the art museum.*

splendid glorious; brilliant. *We had a splendid time on the cruise through the canal.*

grief *n.* great sorrow or sadness. *Everyone felt grief when the great leader became ill.*

mourning expression of grief. *The flags were flown at half-mast in mourning for the victims of the disaster.*

sadness sorrow. *I was filled with sadness as I waved good-bye to my friend who was moving to a city on the west coast.*

sorrow sadness; grief. *She felt sorrow that her injury would cause her to give up the sport she loved so well.*

woe great grief; distress. *The young boy's woe over his lost puppy was replaced by his joy when the puppy was found.*

horrible *adj.* 1. causing horror; shocking; dreadful. *Jim let out a horrible scream.* 2. very unpleasant. *The old blender makes a horrible grating noise.*

awful terrible; very bad. *I went to the dentist so that he could look at the tooth that was causing the awful pain.*

frightful dreadful; terrible. *The monster rising out of the marsh was a frightful sight for the hunters.*

ghastly shocking; horrible. *The critic did not recommend the movie because it was filled with ghastly violence.*

grim frightful; horrible. *The storm was a grim reminder of our helplessness against nature's power.*

horrid terrible; very unpleasant. *The warm spring weather was a welcome relief from the horrid cold of last winter.*

shocking painfully surprising; horrible. *The damage caused by the forest fire was shocking even to firefighters who had battled other forest fires.*

ideal *adj.* perfect; exactly as one would wish. *A warm day and a clear sky are ideal conditions for a picnic.*

absolute free from imperfection; pure. *The quality of the diamond was absolute.*

perfect without defect; unspoiled. *The park's fall foliage made a perfect backdrop for the movie's opening and closing scenes.*

sublime grand; noble. *Her sublime contribution to American literature will long be remembered.*

superior best; high in quality. *The weather conditions were superior for the Mackinac sailing race.*

ignore *v.* to pay no attention to; to refuse to notice. *Anita tried to ignore their silly remarks.*

disdain to look down on; scorn. *The typist would disdain the use of a typewriter when a computer could be used.*

disregard to pay no attention to; neglect. *Fred was luckily not hurt when he decided to disregard the safety procedures.*

scorn look down upon; reject. *Traitors are scorned for betraying their countries.*

shrug off disregard. *Carrie tried to shrug off the pain and continued to run in the race.*

immediate *adj.* happening right away; without delay. *The immediate effect of the medicine was to stop his coughing.*

instantaneous coming at once; immediate. *The officer's response to the call for emergency assistance was instantaneous.*

quick sudden; swift. *When the bell rang, the students made a quick dash for the door.*

importance *n.* significance; value. *Never underestimate the importance of correct spelling.*

consequence importance. *Do you understand the consequence of this event to our history?*

gravity seriousness; importance. *The gravity of the situation was not lost on her.*

significance consequence; importance. *The significance of building the new factory is the creation of four hundred new jobs.*

value importance; worth. *The report had little value for the marketing department.*

impress *v.* to affect strongly or favorably. *Her fluent French did impress all of us.*

affect to stir the feelings. *The story of the young boy who saved his mother will affect you greatly.*

awe to fill with wonder. *The splendor of the painting always seems to awe the museum visitors.*

touch to affect with feeling. *Her quiet support always manages to touch me.*

insult *v.* to treat with rudeness; to hurt feelings on purpose. *It is not polite to insult someone.*

affront to offend; insult. *The dignitary was affronted by what he thought were inappropriate comments by the press.*

flout to treat with contempt. *Jim was suspended for three games for flouting team rules.*

offend to hurt the feelings of; unpleasantly affect. *The comedian's crude remarks managed to offend most of the audience.*

slur to insult; slight. *The rumors will slur the reputation of the governor.*

intrude *v.* to interrupt; to break in without being asked. *It's not polite to intrude on a private conversation.*

encroach to intrude; trespass. *The ranchers claimed that the farmers encroached on their grazing lands.*

interfere to get in the way of. *The unexpected meeting will interfere with my plans for the day.*

interrupt to break into. *Because constant phone calls interrupt my work, I will be late in submitting my report.*

irregular *adj.* not conforming to the usual rule or practice; different. *The coin was valuable because of its irregular markings.*

abnormal different from the ordinary; unusual. *Temperatures in the fifties are abnormal for this time of year.*

atypical not typical; irregular. *This is atypical behavior for a two-year-old.*

erratic irregular; uncertain. *The erratic schedule made it difficult for us to make plans ahead of time.*

fitful irregular; stopping and starting. *The class's attention during the lecture was fitful at best.*

uneven not uniform or regular. *The uneven performance of the leading tenor disappointed the theatergoers.*

antonyms: regular, normal, typical

jealous *adj.* worried about losing someone's affection to another person; resentful of another person's good fortune. *The toddler is jealous of the attention his new brother is getting.*

envious showing or feeling envy. *My sister is envious of my musical talent.*

grudging jealous. *He gave a grudging acknowledgment of my success in his field.*

knowledge *n.* everything that one knows or understands about something. *Her knowledge of baseball statistics is impressive.*

comprehension power or act of understanding. *The detective had total comprehension of the facts of the case.*

insight understanding and wisdom. *Her insight into the problem helped us immensely.*

understanding knowledge; comprehension. *Jake's understanding of math has helped him in science class.*

wisdom knowledge; judgment. *Wisdom was an important trait that contributed to his success as a ruler.*

labor *n.* physical work. *Moving these stones is hard labor.*

chore a difficult or disagreeable thing to do. *It is a real chore to clean out the barn.*

drudgery hard or disagreeable work. *The drudgery of working in the factory left the workers tired and bored.*

toil hard work. *The toil of years as a sales representative paid off when he was made a supervisor.*

work effort in doing something. *Some people say hard work is its own reward.*

legal *adj.* permitted by law. *A left turn at this corner is not legal.*

authorized granted permission; approved. *The biography was an authorized account of the President's days in the White House.*

lawful according to the law. *The lawful removal of the hazardous materials was monitored by state investigators.*

legitimate allowed by law. *She had a legitimate claim to the company's assets.*

limit *n.* the greatest amount permitted. *The speed limit on this street is thirty miles an hour.*

boundary limiting line; border; limit. *The Mississippi River forms the boundary between Illinois and Missouri.*

bounds boundaries; limits. *He kept his fears for her safety in bounds as he watched her perform the stunt.*

confines limits; boundaries. *He felt safe within the confines of his home.*

extent size, amount, or length. *What is the extent of your knowledge of the political process?*

location *n.* a place; position. *This quiet field is a good location for our campsite.*

place space or location. *We should set up our business in a place near the train station.*

position place; location. *The radio dispatcher asked the officer to describe her present position.*

site position or place. *This is the site of an ancient burial ground.*

spot a place. *What a lovely spot for a flower garden!*

lonesome *adj.* lonely; sad from being alone. *My little sister kept my puppy from being lonesome while I was at school.*

desolate forlorn. *The elderly woman felt desolate from the lack of company.*

forlorn miserable from being left alone. *The forlorn puppy brightened when the family returned from a day at the museum.*

lonely longing for company; lonesome. *You might be lonely when you first move to a new town.*

manner *n.* way; fashion. *The students left the bus in a quiet and orderly manner.*

fashion the way a thing is done; manner. *That conductor leads the orchestra in a fashion that inspires great performances.*

form way of doing something; method. *The judges rated the skater's form high but thought her routine was ordinary.*

mode manner; method. *His mode of operation was disliked by most employees.*

way manner of doing something. *She had a pleasant way of making everyone feel comfortable.*

material *n.* the parts or substances from which a thing is made. *The material for the roof was delivered before the workers arrived.*

element simple substance. *A question on the science test asked what elements are used to make steel.*

matter what things are made up of; material. *Water is a liquid matter that becomes solid when it freezes.*

substance material; matter. *Hydrogen and oxygen are the two substances that form water.*

meadow *n.* a field in which grass or hay grows naturally. *The cows grazed in the meadow.*

grassland land with grass often used as pasture. *The pampas are grasslands located in South America.*

lea grassy field; meadow. *The sheep graze on the lea during the day.*

pasture grassy field used for grazing. *In the evening, I help lead the cows home from the pasture.*

prairie large level or rolling grasslands. *The settlers left Pennsylvania to farm the Illinois prairie.*

melody *n.* a series of musical tones making up a tune. *He whistled the melody of a popular song.*

music arrangement of musical sounds. *I know the music for that song but I cannot remember the words.*

tune piece of music; melody. *What is the name of that lively tune the band just finished playing?*

merchant *n.* a person who buys and sells goods. *The three fabric stores in this area are owned by the same merchant.*

dealer a person who buys and sells for a living. *The car dealer was offering rebates on all new cars and selling all used cars at reduced prices.*

retailer a retail merchant or dealer. *The retailer promised to deliver the new appliances to my home before the end of the week.*

trader a person who buys and sells. *My older brother is a trader on the stock exchange.*

method *n.* a system; a way of doing something. *Broiling is one method of preparing fish.*

means the way something is done or brought about. *By what means do you plan to follow up on this account to ensure that we keep the customer happy?*

procedure way of doing something; method. *The doctor said that the ultrasound test is a simple procedure that would take very little time to complete.*

routine regular method. *She begins her morning routine by jogging two miles and then showering before she prepares breakfast.*

system way of getting things done; method. *Classifying plants by size is one system of rating them for pricing.*

tactics procedures; methods. *The parachutist changed her tactics when she realized that she could not open the chute by pulling the rip cord.*

minute *adj.* tiny; very small. *Minute bits of dust floated through the ray of sunlight.*

diminutive very small; minute. *She is so diminutive that she has trouble buying clothes.*

little small; not large. *I could not coax the baby into eating even a little bit of the vegetables.*

minuscule very small; minute. *You can see even the most minuscule cells through this microscope.*

tiny very small; wee. *The baby's fingers are so tiny!*

mischief *n.* harmless and merry teasing or pranks. *My kitten is full of mischief.*

antics odd acts; pranks. *The antics of the clowns amused the audience.*

caper prank; trick. *The teacher did not find our little caper in the classroom funny.*

prank playful mischief; trick. *I fell for their prank when I screamed at the sight of the plastic mouse.*

trick prank; mischief. *Every April Fool's Day Frank pulls the same trick on us and we always act as if we are fooled.*

misfortune *n.* bad luck. *It was his misfortune to lose his wallet.*

calamity great misfortune. *Many people were affected by the calamity caused by the flood.*

disaster great misfortune; events causing suffering. *The city set up temporary shelters for those who lost their homes in the hurricane disaster.*

ill fortune bad luck. *It was my ill fortune to be in the wrong place at the wrong time.*

misadventure unfortunate accident; bad luck. *Our trip started out with a misadventure when we had a flat tire just a mile from home.*

mishap unlucky accident. *Because of some mishap, we lost our electricity for three hours.*

tragedy great misfortune; terrible event. *The strain of reporting the tragedy was visible on the face of the news reporter.*

moderate *adj.* within reasonable limits; not extreme. *The price of the dress was moderate.*

gentle not harsh; moderate. *The beginners' slope has a gentle incline that new skiers can handle.*

mild not severe; temperate; moderate. *We were pleased that there was only a mild wind blowing across the lake.*

reasonable fair; inexpensive. *The rents for apartments in this city are reasonable.*

temperate moderate; using self-control. *She gave a temperate response to the rude question.*

momentary *adj.* brief; lasting a short time. *There was a momentary lull in the storm.*

brief lasting only a short time. *By a chance meeting, I had a brief visit with an old friend.*

instantaneous happening in an instant. *My reaction to the cold water in the pool was instantaneous.*

short not long. *She will be leaving for the airport in a short time.*

natural *adj.* 1. produced by nature; not artificial. *Wood is a natural substance.* 2. having a particular character by nature. *Eileen had a natural love of art.*

crude in a natural or raw state. *Thousands of barrels of crude oil are refined here every day.*

inbred instinctive; natural. *She has an inbred sense of humor that helps her handle almost any situation.*

instinctive not learned; natural. *Animals have an instinctive desire to take care of their young.*

native born into; natural. *Deer seem to have a native ability to sense danger.*

raw in a natural state. *Wood is one of the raw materials we use in our industry.*

unspoiled in a natural state. *The national forests have an unspoiled beauty that everyone can appreciate.*

necessary *adj.* needed; required. *A balanced diet is necessary for proper nutrition.*

basic fundamental. *Keyboarding is a basic skill for secretaries.*

essential needed; required. *Flour and spices are essential ingredients for this recipe.*

integral necessary; essential. *American history is an integral part of the school curriculum.*

key very important; essential. *This is a key concept for students to understand before completing their assignments.*

requisite necessary; required. *The student submitted the requisite records for enrolling in school.*

vital necessary; essential; very important. *The pollution of our environment is a vital concern for all the nations of the world.*

nervous *adj.* excited; not calm. *The kitten grew nervous when everyone crowded around.*

anxious uneasy; worried. *Eloise was anxious about trying out for the varsity volleyball team.*

excitable easily aroused; nervous. *The excitable dog has to be taught to obey commands under all circumstances.*

high-strung nervous; excitable. *The trainer led the high-strung horse back to its stall after the race.*

jumpy easily excited; uneasy. *Dave was jumpy as he waited to learn if his application was accepted.*

overwrought excited; nervous. *The young child was overwrought with fear when the thunder began.*

restless uneasy. *The restless reporters paced the floor as they waited for the news conference to begin.*

tense keyed up; strained. *The student driver was tense about taking the driving test.*

uneasy restless; nervous. *The five-year-old child was uneasy about spending the night away from home for the first time.*

neutral *adj.* not favoring either side. *During two wars, Switzerland remained a neutral nation.*

detached not influenced by others; impartial. *The detached decision of the umpire did not favor the home team.*

fair-minded unprejudiced; just. *The attorney asked the jury to be fair-minded and to consider only the facts when making their decision.*

impartial fair; showing no favor to one side or another. *Judges of Olympic events should remain impartial and rate the athletes on their performances alone.*

objective without bias; impersonal. *Reporters try to present an objective view of a story.*

unbiased not prejudiced; fair. *The committee gave an unbiased assessment of the effectiveness of the city services.*

notable *adj.* 1. worthy of notice. *Writing a book is a notable accomplishment.* 2. prominent; distinguished. *He is a notable physicist.*

distinguished famous; very important. *The distinguished stage actor had never appeared in a movie.*

eminent famous; distinguished. *The eminent poet won the Nobel Prize for literature.*

famous well-known; noted. *That famous athlete endorses only products she actually uses.*

great remarkable; famous. *Abraham Lincoln was a great United States President.*

outstanding well-known; remarkable. *Dr. Salk's polio vaccine was an outstanding contribution to medicine.*

prominent well-known; important; distinguished. *The prominent attorney had lost only one case during her career.*

remarkable worthy of notice. *The remarkable story of the little girl's rescue was featured in all the newspapers.*

renowned famous. *The chef is renowned for his exquisite dishes.*

striking very noticeable. *She bears a striking resemblance to her mother.*

notice *v.* to pay attention to; take notice of; see. *Will Joan notice Barbara's new dress right away?*

detect to find out; discover. *I did not detect any differences in the way the machine was operating.*

distinguish to see or hear clearly. *Were you able to distinguish the last few notes in that song?*

observe to see and note. *I observed the accident from my office window and called the police.*

perceive to observe; be aware of. *He did not perceive the car pulling up beside him.*

sight to see. *The bird-watcher tried to sight the eagle soaring through the sky as it circled its aerie.*

view to see; look at. *Through the kitchen window we could view the children playing.*

numb *adj.* without sensation or movement. *If you don't wear warm gloves, your fingers may become numb from the cold.*

dull not felt sharply; vague. *I had a dull ache in my shoulder from carrying the heavy grocery bags.*

insensitive not sensitive; numb. *My brother seems to be insensitive to both heat and cold.*

nutritious *adj.* providing nourishment. *Apples are a nutritious snack.*

healthful good for one's health. *For a healthful diet, eat foods from each of the major food groups.*

nourishing promoting growth. *What I need now is a nourishing meal and some rest.*

wholesome good for one's health. *Be sure to eat a wholesome breakfast to start your day out right.*

object *v.* to make objection; to protest. *They started to object that it was too cold to play outside.*

demur to show disapproval; object. *The idea of selling the club's building made the president demur.*

disapprove to show or express dislike. *My parents disapprove of violent movies.*

oppose to be against. *The mayor was opposed to the bill the city council passed.*

protest to make objections. *The students wanted to protest the cancellation of the field trip.*

take exception to to object. *The teacher takes exception to our chewing gum in class.*

object *n.* a thing that can be seen or touched. *The little shop had many objects made of china.*

article a particular thing; item. *She unfortunately left several articles of clothing in the locker room.*

item separate thing or article. *How many items did you buy at the supermarket?*

novelty small and unusual object. *My sister bought a novelty as a vacation souvenir.*

thing an object or substance. *Because I like my room to be neat, I always put my things away after using them.*

obtain *v.* to get. *How did he obtain a ticket to the play?*

acquire to get as one's own; obtain. *Kim studied to acquire the knowledge needed to be a competent mathematician.*

gain to come to have; get. *I gain on-the-job experience when I work in the governor's office.*

get to come to have; obtain. *Please get the encyclopedia from the shelf for me.*

procure to get by effort; obtain. *The organization was able to procure funds for their project from the state.*

secure to get; obtain. *Will it be possible to secure tickets for tonight's concert?*

obvious *adj.* easy to see or figure out; clear; plain. *It is obvious that the movie is popular, since the theater is so crowded.*

apparent plain to see or understand. *It is apparent to me that you do not want to go out to dinner.*

conspicuous easily seen. *What do people mean when they say that someone was conspicuous in his or her absence?*

evident easy to see or understand; clear. *That he was a talented musician was evident as soon as he started to play.*

manifest apparent to the mind or eye. *The perfection of the diamond was manifest to the curator.*

plain easy to understand; clear. *Her directions for finding her house were plain to me.*

occasion *n.* 1. a particular happening or event. *Her birthday was a special occasion.* 2. an opportunity; a good chance. *I hope you find an occasion to call us while you are traveling.*

affair any happening. *The governor's ball was a wonderful affair that I will long remember.*

chance favorable time; opportunity. *I didn't have a chance before now to thank you for your generous contribution to our organization.*

circumstance event; occasion. *It was an unfortunate circumstance that made me miss my flight.*

episode a single happening. *Winning the award was a memorable episode in the actress's life.*

event an important happening. *The wedding was the biggest event of the year for the family.*

occurrence event; happening. *The solar eclipse was such an unusual occurrence that I did not want to miss it.*

opportunity a good chance; occasion. *We have the opportunity to travel to Europe this summer.*

offer *v.* 1. to say that one is willing. *We did offer to help Mr. Elliot start his car.* 2. to present as a suggestion. *The President will offer a plan for peace.*

bid to offer to pay. *We expected to have to bid at least $1,000 to obtain the antique vase.*

extend to offer; grant. *The government can extend emergency aid to the flood victims.*

give to offer; present. *The professor gave a lecture titled "Earth's Tomorrow."*

grant to give; confer. *In that tale, a fish can grant three wishes.*

present to offer formally; give. *The Medal of Honor was presented to the courageous soldier in a special ceremony.*

propose to put forward; suggest. *I propose that we delay the meeting until all the information we need is available.*

suggest to propose; offer. *I suggest that the group meet at my house this week.*

tender to offer formally. *She can tender her resignation to be effective in two weeks time.*

opponent *n.* a person or group that competes against another. *Our school's opponent for the game is Deerfield School.*

competitor person or group who competes; rival. *That company is a business competitor of our company.*

enemy person or group that hates or tries to harm another; rival. *The soldier never really knew who the enemy was.*

foe enemy; rival. *I didn't know if Margaret was a friend or a foe.*

opposition any opponent. *The senator takes pride in being in "the loyal opposition."*

rival person who tries to get the same thing as another; competitor. *Angela and Ted are friends even though they are business rivals.*

ordinary *adj.* 1. usual; normal. *The ordinary time it takes to drive downtown is twenty minutes.* 2. not special; average. *Her outfit made her look quite ordinary.*

average usual; ordinary. *The book gave an account of an average day in a small coastal village.*

common ordinary; usual. *Her common response when we ask to stay up late is "No."*

customary according to custom; usual. *Ed did not take his customary route to work this morning.*

general common to many; not special. *The general store offers a variety of goods from fresh fruit to sewing needles.*

habitual done by habit; regular. *Jean is a habitual reader who especially enjoys mystery novels.*

normal usual; regular. *It is my normal practice to read in bed before I go to sleep.*

regular fixed by custom; normal; usual. *Because it was a holiday, we were allowed to stay up past our regular bedtime.*

usual common; ordinary. *Fruit and cheese are my usual afternoon snack.*

partial *adj.* 1. not complete. *We saw a partial eclipse of the moon.* 2. inclined to favor one side. *An umpire should never be partial when he makes a decision.*

abridged shortened; incomplete. *I read the abridged version of the novel.*

biased favoring one side; prejudiced. *Some players thought the referee made biased decisions that affected the game's outcome.*

disposed inclined; partial. *She is more disposed to like traditional furnishings than contemporary ones.*

incomplete lacking some part; unfinished. *The directions I was given were incomplete, so I had a difficult time finding the office.*

one-sided partial; biased. *That driver gave a one-sided account of the accident.*

unfinished not complete. *The road work was still unfinished after six months.*

partner *n.* a person who shares something or joins with another. *The boys were partners on the camping trip.*

associate companion; partner. *Lena is an associate in our firm.*

colleague coworker; associate. *Let me introduce my colleague who will work with you on your project.*

companion someone who goes along with. *Marta is my traveling companion.*

co-owner business partner; associate. *Jason is the co-owner of this restaurant.*

passage *n.* 1. a way used for passing. *The passage led to the back staircase.* 2. part of a writing or a speech. *The passage about whales includes much interesting information.*

aisle long, narrow passage. *Both parents walked the bride down the aisle.*

alley narrow back street; path. *She drove down the alley carefully to avoid the trash cans kept there.*

approach way of reaching a place. *The sidewalk was the only approach to the front of the house.*

entryway a passage for entering. *The building's entryway is a long narrow hall that leads to a set of elevators.*

excerpt passage from a book. *We read an excerpt from one of Scott O'Dell's award-winning books.*

hall passage; entryway. *That hall will lead you to the kitchen and dining room.*

path a passageway for walking or riding. *We rode our bikes on the bicycle path in the park.*

selection portion of a text. *We read a selection about growing up on a farm in Iowa.*

text a short passage; written words. *The speaker memorized the text of his speech before delivering it.*

vestibule passage or hall for entering; entry. *We left our coats on the coatrack in the vestibule.*

pause *v.* to stop for a short time. *He will pause to get a glass of water.*

break off to stop suddenly. *She had to break off the telephone conversation to check the oven.*

cease to put an end to; stop. *The interruptions made the speaker cease his presentation.*

discontinue to put an end to. *After the snow, they had to discontinue train service until the tracks could be cleared.*

halt to stop for a time. *A power outage will halt the use of all electrical equipment.*

rest to pause. *She had to rest for a moment before continuing to read to the class.*

stop to interrupt briefly. *Can you stop at the store on your way home from work to pick up a few items?*

performance *n.* the way in which someone or something functions. *Your performance on the test was very good.*

administration the managing of a business. *The administration of a law firm depends on the caseload.*

execution a carrying out or doing. *The execution of the day's work was her highest priority.*

implementation a carrying out. *The policy's implementation was easier than we thought it would be.*

permit *v.* to let; allow; give consent to. *Please permit me to read your magazine.*

allow to permit; let. *I am not allowed to eat corn on the cob because of my braces.*

authorize to give formal approval. *Were you authorized to sign company checks?*

license to permit by law. *I am licensed to sell real estate in this community.*

sanction to authorize; allow. *Congress can sanction the investigation of one of its members.*

tolerate to allow or permit. *The librarian does not tolerate any noise in the reading room.*

pitiful *adj.* causing emotions of sorrow and compassion. *The injured dog was a pitiful sight.*

miserable poor; pitiful. *The tenement was a miserable place to live.*

sad causing sorrow. *The devastation caused by the forest fire was a sad sight to see.*

sorry wretched; poor. *Due to the sorry condition of the flooded fields, the farmer had to delay planting indefinitely.*

wretched miserable. *For the poor to be living in such wretched housing is a disgrace.*

population *n.* the number of people living in a country, state, town, or other area. *The town's population has greatly increased in the past five years.*

inhabitants persons or animals that live in a place. *The town's inhabitants gathered for the annual spring festival.*

people body of citizens. *The people supported new taxes for education.*

populace the common people. *The tornado warnings were broadcast to the populace by the civil defense.*

public the people in general. *The news conference informed the public of the congressional ruling.*

pose *v.* 1. to hold an expression or position. *The parents and children need to pose for a family portrait.* 2. to present; put forward. *May I pose a question?*

model to pose for an artist or photographer *He was hired to model clothing for ads in local magazines.*

offer to suggest; propose. *The suggestions offered could help us meet our goals.*

propose to put forward an intention or plan. *One committee member will propose sponsoring a fund-raising event.*

stand to take or keep a certain position. *Early photography required people to stand motionless for a long time.*

position *n.* place; location. *The navigator marked the ship's position on a chart.*

locality a particular place and/or the area around it. *That restaurant is in the locality of City Center Plaza.*

location position or place. *That building is in a bad location because it is not near public transportation.*

site position or place. *Our city had hoped to be the site of the next world's fair.*

situation site; location. *The situation of the castle offered protection from rebel subjects.*

positive *adj.* confident; certain; without doubt. *Gus is positive that his team will win.*

assured sure; certain; bold. *Her assured manner led me to believe that she knew the best way to get there.*

confident having confidence; sure. *Ellen is confident that she answered all the test questions correctly.*

convinced believing; sure; positive. *Convinced that he was better than the competition, Dan felt he would win the race.*

secure sure; certain. *Because of her expertise, Janet knew a promotion to vice president was secure.*

sure free from doubt; certain. *We checked the stock to be sure all the materials we needed were available.*

possibly *adv.* perhaps; maybe. *Possibly we'll finish by noon.*

conceivably imaginably. *The flight could conceivably arrive on time despite the delay in its departure.*

maybe possibly. *Maybe we can meet for lunch sometime next week.*

perchance perhaps. *Call to see if we perchance can still buy concert tickets.*

perhaps maybe. *Since you must get up early, perhaps you should go to bed now.*

probably more likely than not. *We will probably have a history quiz tomorrow.*

practical *adj.* able to be done, used, or carried out. *Her practical solution solved the problem.*

applicable capable of being applied. *"Honesty is the best policy" is a rule that I have found to be applicable to most situations.*

down-to-earth practical; realistic. *Marty's down-to-earth advice helped me handle the situation easily.*

realistic practical. *Because the plan would have been expensive to carry out, it was not a realistic solution to the housing shortage in our community.*

useful helpful; practical. *Expanding the public transportation system would be a useful means of solving the rush-hour traffic problems.*

precious *adj.* having a high price; costing a great deal. *Diamonds are precious jewels.*

costly expensive; of great value. *That costly painting was the only addition the museum made to its collection this year.*

priceless extremely valuable. *The artifacts from the archaeological discovery are a priceless national treasure.*

valuable of worth; having value. *Alphonse's valuable coin collection is always kept in the bank's vault.*

present *adj.* of the time between past and future; current. *Are you busy at the present moment?*

contemporary of the present time; modern. *The class contrasted the works of contemporary poets with those of late nineteenth century poets.*

current of the present time. *Every morning in homeroom, we read the paper and discuss current events.*

modern of the present time. *We are remodeling our kitchen to give it a more modern look.*

up-to-date modern; extending to the present time. *Models in fashion magazines always wear the most up-to-date styles.*

present *n.* a gift. *The present was colorfully wrapped.*

alms money or gifts to help the poor. *Our club collects alms for the poor and distributes them to organizations throughout the county.*

donation gift; contribution. *The senator made a donation of his letters to the Library of Congress.*

gift a present or donation. *This is my Father's Day gift for my dad.*

legacy a gift by will of money or property. *The candlesticks are my grandmother's legacy to me.*

probable *adj.* likely to happen. *The dark clouds and lightning mean that rain is probable.*

impending likely to happen soon; about to happen. *The construction crew worked furiously to meet the impending deadline.*

liable likely. *Be sure to lock the gate, or the dog is liable to run away.*

likely probable. *The teacher asked what the likely results of the experiment would be.*

presumable probable; likely. *The presumable cause of the highway closings was the drifting snow.*

process *n.* 1. a system of operations in the production of something. *Describe the process of canning fresh fruit.* 2. a series of actions with an expected end. *Learning is a continual process.*

course line of action; way of doing. *What is your course of action for completing the project on time?*

mechanism means by which something is done. *The mechanism for winning the election was set into action after the primary.*

method system of getting things done. *The methods used for the cleanup effort proved to be effective.*

procedure way of doing things. *The use of parliamentary procedure ensures that our meetings run smoothly.*

profit *v.* to benefit. *I can profit from your experience.*

benefit to receive good; profit. *The increased taxes will be used to benefit the schools and libraries in the state.*

gain to profit; get as an advantage. *What do you hope to gain by extending the store hours?*

reap to get as a return or reward. *If you exceed your sales quota, you will reap an increase in the percentage of your bonus.*

progress *n.* 1. a movement forward. *The train made steady progress.* 2. development; improvement. *Scientific progress has changed the way we think about the world.*

advance movement forward; progress. *The advances in scientific knowledge help us solve today's problems.*

advancement improvement; promotion. *Technological advancements have changed the way people live, work, and play in our country.*

development growth; process of developing. *Good nutrition is important to a child's physical development.*

expansion process of expanding; growth. *The expansion of the railroads across the United States resulted in greater settlement of the West.*

growth process of growing; development. *The personal computer industry spurred the growth of many software-producing companies.*

headway motion forward; progress. *Our boat had been making headway in the race until the wind shifted.*

improvement better condition or situation. *His program of exercise and diet is responsible for the improvement in his health.*

promotion an advance in rank or importance. *Her promotion to office manager was a result of hard work and dedication.*

rise an advance in rank, power, etc. *He said that his rise to stardom did not happen overnight but resulted from many years of hard work.*

R

rapid *adj.* fast; quick. *The rapid current carried the canoe down the river.*

fast moving or acting quickly. *The runners kept up a fast pace throughout the race.*

fleet swiftly moving; rapid. *Being fleet of foot, the runner passed us easily.*

hasty in a hurry; quick. *Mom waved a hasty good-bye as she ran to catch the commuter train.*

quick fast and sudden. *The boss's quick reply to my request for vacation enabled me to make arrangements well in advance.*

speedy rapid; fast. *Our class sent a card to our teacher wishing her a speedy recovery from the flu.*

swift very fast. *The express train provides a swift commute into the city.*

antonym: slow

rational *adj.* based on reason; logical. *After thinking it over calmly, Jeff made a rational decision to quit the team.*

judicious wise; sensible. *Sherman made a judicious decision to remain in school and complete his degree.*

logical of logic; reasonable. *It is logical to think that studying hard will help you get good grades.*

reasonable according to reason; sensible. *She had a reasonable excuse for being late to school.*

sane having or showing good sense. *Slowing down is a sane reaction to driving in bad weather conditions.*

sensible having or showing good sense or judgment. *Her ideas for improving the customer service department seemed sensible.*

sound rational; reasonable. *My counselor gave me sound advice about which courses to take.*

rebel *v.* to resist or oppose authority. *The workers wanted to rebel against the unfair demands of their employer.*

defy to set oneself openly against authority. *My brother meant to defy my parents by staying out long after his curfew.*

mutiny to rebel. *The sailors tried to mutiny against the ship's captain.*

protest to object strongly. *We protested the referee's decision without success.*

resist to act against; oppose. *Helen Keller at first resisted all efforts to help her learn to communicate.*

revolt to fight against leadership. *The people revolted against their leaders and called for democracy.*

receive *v.* to get. *You should receive the letter in two days.*

acquire to get as one's own. *I will acquire the deed for the property from my parents.*

obtain to come to have. *If you are able to obtain the needed materials, please let me know as soon as possible.*

secure to get; obtain. *Because he lacked a credit record, he was unable to secure a car loan.*

take to get; receive. *Mom says I don't take criticism very well.*

recess *n.* a brief rest from work. *During the morning, we have a fifteen-minute recess.*

break a short interruption in work. *Michael reads the newspaper during his break.*

pause a brief stop or rest. *The noise of the passing train forced a pause in the debate.*

respite a time of relief and rest. *The cease fire gave the people a respite from fear.*

spell a brief period of time. *Before starting a new project, Lorenzo relaxed for a spell by chatting with a coworker.*

refuse *v.* 1. to turn down; reject. *She might refuse my offer of help.* 2. to be unwilling; decline. *I refuse to let them bother me.*

decline to turn away from; refuse. *I hope you will not decline my luncheon invitation.*

disdain to scorn. *Wanting to be independent, the toddler disdained all attempts to help him put on his boots.*

reject to refuse to take. *The managers voted to reject the proposal to expand the sales force.*

scorn to regard with contempt. *The officer scorned the driver's efforts to avoid a ticket.*

spurn to reject with scorn. *The teen spurned the requests for dates from younger schoolmates.*

regular *adj.* 1. usual; normal; ordinary. *Our regular practice on Sunday is to have dinner in the afternoon.* 2. frequent. *Joe is a regular customer.* 3. occurring at fixed intervals. *We make regular visits to the dentist.*

established set up on a firm or lasting basis. *We have an established Monday morning meeting to discuss the week's activities.*

habitual done by habit; steady. *She is a habitual customer of this restaurant.*

periodic occurring or appearing at regular intervals. *Make sure you take your car in for periodic oil changes.*

recurrent occurring again; repeated. *I have had a recurrent dream that I cannot explain.*

routine a fixed or regular method of doing things. *Brushing my teeth is part of my routine activity.*

unexceptional ordinary; commonplace. *The performance of the football team was unexceptional this year.*

uniform not varying; regular. *The uniform length of time between classes is five minutes.*

release *v.* to let loose; set free. *If you release the door, it will close by itself.*

discharge to release; let go; dismiss. *He was discharged from the army after serving his term of duty.*

excuse to free from duty; let off. *Because of parent-teacher conferences, we were excused from school an hour early.*

exempt to make free; release. *The IRS would not exempt the organization from income taxes.*

free to make free; set loose. *We tried to free the firefly we had caught.*

let go to release; free. *The hostages were let go by their captors.*

let loose to set free; release. *We let loose the injured bird once its wing had healed.*

relieve to take another's place. *I relieved the night-shift nurse from duty at 7 A.M.*

unleash to let go. *She liked to unleash the dog and let him run loose in the park.*

relief *n.* the removal or ease of worry, pain, etc. *Imagine my relief when I remembered the right answer!*

alleviation relief; lessened severity. *The program called for the alleviation of poverty in the United States.*

diversion a turning away; relief. *Tennis is a diversion that takes my mom's mind off her business worries.*

relaxation the relief from work or effort. *For relaxation after school, I take a short walk through the neighborhood.*

reprieve temporary relief. *The postponement of the test day gave us a welcome reprieve.*

respite a putting off; delay; reprieve; a time of relief. *The clearing gave us a respite from the week-long storms that had hit our area.*

rest freedom; relief. *After a period of rest, we were refreshed and ready to begin working on the project again.*

remain *v.* 1. to stay. *We want to remain at home because of the rain.* 2. to continue; to last without changing. *The weather remained warm until the last week of October.* 3. to be left. *All that remains of the old house is the foundation.*

be left to remain. *This chair will be left for the next tenant of the apartment.*

endure to keep up; last. *The pyramids have lasted for ages and are now being restored to make sure they will continue to endure.*

hover to stay in or near. *The small child began to hover near her mother as the guests arrived for the party.*

last to hold on; continue. *The flowers will last for at least a week if you water them.*

linger to stay on; remain. *My cough lingered for days after the other cold symptoms were gone.*

loiter to linger idly. *The students like to loiter in the hall before the bell rings for the start of class.*

reside to live in a place for a long time. *My parents have resided in the same home since my first birthday.*

responsible *adj.* 1. trustworthy; reliable. *A responsible student was chosen to collect the money for the field trip.* 2. required to answer for something. *Who is responsible for turning off the lights when we leave the room?*

accountable liable; responsible. *The clerk was held accountable for banking all receipts.*

dependable reliable; trustworthy. *Vanessa is a dependable baby-sitter.*

liable under obligation; responsible. *Customers are liable for any merchandise they break.*

reliable worthy of trust; dependable. *The reporter's information came from a reliable source in the government.*

unfailing never failing; always ready when needed. *The accountant paid unfailing attention to every detail of the account.*

result *n.* outcome; effect. *He was late to work as a result of a delay in traffic.*

aftermath a result or consequence. *We had a long cleanup effort in the aftermath of the storm.*

consequence a result; an effect. *Being in the play-offs was a consequence of winning our last three games.*

outgrowth a result; an effect. *Organizing the recycling club was a natural outgrowth of our interest in the environment.*

upshot conclusion; result. *The upshot of the meeting was that we would plan a new campaign strategy for the student elections.*

satisfaction *n.* a feeling of being satisfied or contented. *Dan gets satisfaction from doing his job well.*

contentment satisfaction; ease of mind. *Her contentment with the results of the flower show was obvious from her expression.*

fulfillment accomplishment or satisfaction. *I was able to find great fulfillment from my work in the Peace Corps.*

gratification something that satisfies or pleases. *The parents' gratification for all their hard work came in seeing their child graduate from college.*

pleasure something that pleases or gratifies. *It brought me great pleasure to see my photographs displayed in the school hall.*

scarcely *adv.* hardly; barely. *There are scarcely any people awake at five o'clock in the morning.*

faintly dim; not clear. *The deer on the side of the road was only faintly visible to those of us driving in the dusk.*

imperceptibly very slightly. *The flaws in the material were almost imperceptibly noticeable to us.*

slightly a little; scarcely. *I know that area of the city only slightly.*

scheme *n.* 1. a plan of action; a project. *We thought of a scheme for preventing graffiti.* 2. a secret plot. *The scheme to give my mother a surprise party failed when she discovered the birthday cake.*

conspiracy secret planning; plot. *The investigation proved the assassination attempt was not a conspiracy, but rather the action of one person.*

design scheme; plan. *The investor had designs on our company until we reorganized all our operations.*

intrigue crafty dealings; scheming. *The novel focused on the intrigue of international spying.*

maneuver skillful plan, movement, or scheme. *Through a series of financial maneuvers, the employees hoped to purchase the company.*

strategy skillful planning and management. *The coach reviewed the game strategy with us before the start of the second half.*

tactic procedure or method for gaining advantage. *Her game-winning tactic was to keep her opponent running from one end of the court to the other.*

secondary *adj.* not ranking first. *Her primary concern was content, and her secondary concern was style.*

inferior lower in rank, position, or importance. *On the police force, a rank of detective is inferior to the rank of captain.*

minor less important; of lower rank. *The amount of salary increase was a minor issue compared to the need for job security.*

subordinate having less importance; secondary. *My role in helping to prepare for the conference was only a subordinate one.*

subsidiary auxiliary; supplementary. *Workbooks are subsidiary components of the textbook program.*

seize *v.* to take hold of suddenly; grasp; grab. *He seized her hand and shook it eagerly.*

apprehend to seize; arrest. *The jewel thief was not apprehended until the end of the movie.*

capture to take by force; seize. *The English managed to capture Quebec during the French and Indian War.*

catch to grasp or seize. *Try to catch the ball on the fly for an automatic out.*

clasp to hold firmly; grasp. *The child must clasp his mother's hand as they cross the street.*

grab to seize suddenly; snatch. *I had to grab my coat and run quickly so that I would not miss the bus.*

snatch to seize suddenly; grasp. *The thief tried to snatch the purse and run away before the young woman was even aware of what had happened.*

take to seize; catch; capture. *After a short battle, the enemy managed to take the fort.*

senseless *adj.* without meaning; pointless. *Watching that television program was a senseless waste of time.*

foolish unwise; silly. *It was a foolish mistake to leave my bicycle unlocked while I was inside the store.*

inane foolish; senseless. *The inane comment by the celebrity was overlooked by the reporters.*

meaningless without meaning; not making sense. *All of the preparations became meaningless when the conference was canceled.*

pointless without meaning or purpose. *It is pointless to try to reason with a two-year-old who demands to get his own way.*

silly without sense or reason. *Danielle's response to the question was silly because she didn't understand what was being asked.*

unsound not valid; not supported by evidence. *She gave some unsound advice that did not help us achieve our goal.*

antonyms: sensible, meaningful

shield *v.* to protect; guard. *This umbrella will shield you from the rain.*

defend to keep safe; protect. *The Americans were unable to defend New York City against the British in 1776.*

protect to defend; guard. *The dikes help protect the city from flooding.*

safeguard to keep safe; protect. *Every child should be given the vaccine to safeguard against polio.*

screen to protect or hide from. *The protective glasses screen the welder's eyes from the sparks.*

shelter to protect; shield. *The Underground Railroad tried to shelter slaves as they escaped to the North.*

siege *n.* the surrounding of a place for a long time in order to capture it. *The city was under siege for three weeks.*

assault a violent attack. *Wolfe led the British in their successful assault on Quebec.*

attack a use of force or weapons against a person or group. *The Civil War began with the Confederate attack on Fort Sumter.*

blitz sudden, violent attack. *During World War II, Poland surrendered after the German blitz.*

bombardment a vigorous attack. *The troops could not maintain their position during the bombardment.*

incursion a sudden attack. *The Minutemen responded quickly to the news of the British incursion.*

invasion an entering by force of an enemy. *Napoleon's invasion of Russia was not successful.*

onslaught a vigorous attack. *The defenders could not check the onslaught of invading soldiers.*

raid a sudden attack. *The pirates led raids against ships that were returning to Europe filled with gold.*

silence *n.* the absence of noise or sound; stillness. *There was silence while the principal spoke.*

hush a stopping of noise. *A sudden hush fell over the room when the President entered.*

peace a condition of quiet and order. *The peace of the afternoon was broken when the baby woke from her nap.*

quietness state of stillness; silence. *The quietness in the classroom surprised me.*

reserve a silent manner. *His reserve at parties made people think he was unfriendly.*

reticence tendency to be silent. *Calvin Coolidge was a President known for his reticence as well as for his dry wit.*

stillness absence of noise or movement; silence. *The stillness of the night was broken by the ambulance sirens.*

sullenness ill-humored silence. *His sullenness made me uncomfortable, so I left the room.*

antonyms: noise, clamor

similar *adj.* almost but not quite the same; alike but not identical. *The two girls wore similar clothes.*

alike like one another; similar. *Everyone says that my sister and I look alike.*

corresponding similar; alike. *General Grant and General Lee had corresponding roles in their armies.*

matching alike; similar. *The matching patterns complemented the room's decor.*

solemn *adj.* serious; earnest; grave. *He made a solemn promise.*

critical very important; serious. *She had to make a decision that would be critical to her future.*

sedate serious; calm. *His sedate behavior contrasted to my excitement.*

serious earnest; sincere. *He paid serious attention to the report so that he could review the findings with his superior.*

stubborn *adj.* not easily persuaded; having one's own definite idea. *Lee was stubborn and refused to follow my suggestions.*

adamant not giving in readily; unyielding. *Our teacher is adamant about having us turn in all of our assignments on time.*

determined firm; resolute. *She is determined to become a professional skater.*

headstrong stubborn; obstinate; rashly determined. *The headstrong toddler refused to let anyone help her get dressed.*

obstinate not giving in; stubborn. *Theo gave obstinate support to the effort even after it was obvious it would fail.*

opinionated stubborn about one's opinions. *His opinionated comments left little doubt about where he stood on the issue.*

persistent not giving up even in a difficult situation. *Betty was persistent in her efforts even after she broke her ankle.*

tenacious stubborn; persistent. *The tenacious salesclerk did not want us to leave the store without making a purchase.*

willful wanting or taking one's own way; stubborn. *It seems the only word the willful two year old knows is "NO."*

success *n.* a favorable result or outcome; achievement. *Hard work often brings success.*

accomplishment something done with skill, knowledge, or ability; achievement. *Her athletic accomplishments are evident from her many trophies and other awards.*

achievement thing achieved; feat. *She would not rest on the past achievements but continued to strive for excellence in her field.*

fortune prosperity; success. *Obtaining the contract was an unexpected fortune that will help us gain recognition.*

mastery victory; success. *His mastery over his disability is a remarkable achievement that can inspire us all.*

victory success in a contest. *The principal congratulated the team for its victory.*

talent *n.* special ability; natural skill. *She had a great talent for writing short stories.*

aptitude natural tendency; talent; ability. *Grandma Moses did not display her aptitude for painting until late in her life.*

expertise expert skill. *The expertise of a whittler can be seen in the details of his or her carvings.*

flair natural talent. *Alexandra has a flair for giving successful parties.*

genius great natural ability. *Thomas Edison's genius was not evident when he was a boy.*

gift special talent. *Christina's voice was a gift that all opera fans could appreciate.*

knack special skill or talent. *She has a knack for making people feel comfortable.*

tease *v.* to bother or irritate by making jokes, asking questions, nudging, etc. *The sign at the zoo asked the visitors not to tease the animals.*

badger to keep on teasing. *My brother badgered me about my skating until I threatened to tickle him.*

bait to tease or harass. *She tried to bait me into falling for one of her practical jokes.*

banter to tease playfully. *They bantered entertainingly throughout the evening.*

harass to disturb or tease continually. *People get angry if you harass them, even if you do it in fun.*

pester to annoy; vex. *I don't like it when my younger sister pesters me to take her shopping with me.*

tedious *adj.* tiresome; boring. *The politician's speech became so tedious that a few listeners got up to leave.*

boring dull; uninteresting. *The new movie playing at the local theater is boring.*

drab monotonous; dull. *The drab surroundings of our neighborhood made me wish for just one day in a beautiful park.*

dull boring; uninteresting. *The dull plot did not hold our attention for long.*

insipid lacking interest or spirit. *The insipid comments of the reporter made me wonder why he was assigned to that story.*

monotonous wearying because of its sameness. *The story line of that program had become so monotonous that I stopped watching it.*

stale not fresh or interesting. *Every time I see him he tells me the same old stale jokes.*

uninspired dull; tiresome. *The performances were so uninspired that I fell asleep.*

wearisome tiresome; tedious. *The wearisome hours of practice make me wish for a vacation from ballet lessons.*

temporary *adj.* lasting for a brief time; not permanent. *While our teacher was ill, we had a temporary teacher.*

passing not lasting; fleeting. *He had had a passing interest in airplanes when he was young.*

short-lived lasting a short time. *The player was a short-lived substitute for the first-string quarterback.*

transitory passing soon or quickly. *Dizziness was a transitory feeling that I had after getting off the ride.*

tenant *n.* a person who pays rent for the use of a house, apartment, or other property. *In that tall apartment building there are several hundred tenants.*

boarder a person who pays for meals and rooms in another's house. *To help pay for their house, my parents always take in a boarder.*

lodger a person who lives in a rented room or house. *College students are lodgers in our house.*

occupant one who occupies or has possession of a place. *The occupant of the apartment is there only through December.*

renter one who rents a place to live. *The renter of this apartment pays extra for garage parking.*

roomer one who rents a room or rooms for lodging. *The college is always looking for homes for roomers.*

thoughtless *adj.* careless; inconsiderate. *It was thoughtless of you to invite only some of your friends.*

careless not thinking; done without thought. *A careless mistake lowered my final grade.*

heedless careless; thoughtless. *The driver of the car seemed to be heedless of the traffic laws.*

inattentive not attentive; negligent. *The inattentive student did not understand the lesson.*

tactless without tact or thought. *Her tactless comment hurt my feelings.*

unthinking thoughtless; careless. *I made an unthinking error on my spelling test that resulted in a lower grade than usual.*

trait *n.* a feature or characteristic. *We all inherit physical traits from our parents.*

attribute a quality or trait. *Blue eyes are an attribute of my family.*

property quality or power of something. *A property of copper is that it conducts electricity.*

quality nature, kind, or character. *The quality of this material is excellent.*

tremendous *adj.* extremely large; enormous. *A tremendous wave rocked the boat.*

colossal huge; gigantic. *The bridge was a colossal structure that spanned the river.*

enormous extremely large. *The package was not only enormous but also so heavy I could not carry it.*

gigantic giant; huge. *The circus featured gigantic elephants in the opening parade.*

huge very big; extremely large. *The earthquake left a huge crevice in the ground.*

immense very large; huge. *In the early 1800s an immense portion of our country was still unexplored.*

turbulent *adj.* disturbed or violently agitated. *The ocean became turbulent as the storm approached.*

boisterous violent; rough. *The boisterous crowd demanded free elections.*

chaotic extremely confused; disorganized. *The hurricane-damaged school was a chaotic mess.*

riotous boisterous; disorderly. *The riotous behavior of the citizens signaled the beginning of the revolution.*

stormy disturbed; violent. *The council meeting ended in a stormy argument over tax assessments.*

unruly hard to control; disorderly. *The unruly student was given two weeks in detention after school.*

violent acting or done with strong, rough force. *The violent storm raged for hours along the coast before it hit the mainland.*

wild violently excited; out of control. *The trapped animal lashed out in a wild frenzy as it tried to free itself from the hunter's net.*

ultimate *adj.* best; greatest. *Chess is the ultimate game of logic.*

extreme very great; very strong; the highest degree. *It was an extreme pleasure to meet the President of the United States.*

maximum largest; highest; greatest possible. *The maximum number of videos that will be distributed is 25,000.*

superior higher in quality; greater; better. *She has a superior command of the English language.*

supreme highest in rank or authority. *Eisenhower was the supreme commander of the allied forces in Europe during the latter half of World War II.*

undercover *adj.* done in secret. *They are conducting an undercover police investigation.*

clandestine secret; concealed. *Early labor unions held clandestine meetings to keep employers from finding out about them.*

covert kept secret; hidden. *The Senate investigated the covert actions of the CIA.*

secretive not frank or open. *She was secretive about the plans for the new company.*

stealthy done in a secret manner; sly. *The stealthy investigation revealed the officer's role in the bribery case.*

understand *v.* to know; comprehend. *Do you understand how a vacuum cleaner works?*

comprehend to understand. *It is difficult to comprehend the effects of the radiation.*

digest to think over for understanding. *I found it hard to digest his comments since I did not agree with them.*

discern to see clearly; perceive. *I found it difficult to discern the truth when so many viewpoints were presented.*

grasp to understand; comprehend. *He grasped the meaning of the event immediately.*

realize to understand completely. *I realized that success was dependent on hard work.*

unpleasant *adj.* not pleasant; disagreeable. *The medicine had an unpleasant taste.*

disagreeable not to one's liking; unpleasant. *I find yard work to be a disagreeable task.*

distasteful unpleasant; offensive. *Her distasteful comments offended everyone in the room.*

various *adj.* of several different kinds; different. *I found shells of various sizes and shapes on the beach.*

distinct different in quality or kind. *The students had distinct abilities and talents.*

miscellaneous not all of one kind or nature. *I filed the memo with other miscellaneous information.*

mixed formed of different kinds. *She gave her mother a gift of mixed nuts.*

sundry several; various. *I selected a pen from the sundry items offered as party favors.*

varied of different kinds. *From the varied selection of recordings, I chose one featuring a jazz pianist.*

visible *adj.* able to be seen. *Because of the fog, the lights were no longer visible.*

apparent plain to see. *The location of the tower was apparent as soon as we entered the forest preserve.*

discernible capable of being seen. *The lights of the city were discernible as we approached the shore.*

distinct easily seen. *The outline of the building was distinct even at night.*

in sight visible. *The ship was in sight of people on the shore long before it docked at the pier.*

perceptible able to be seen; perceived. *The lines on the highway were barely perceptible because of the snow.*

weird *adj.* strange; odd. *The group of people going to the costume party was a weird sight.*

  curious strange; unusual. *The two-story gabled house looked curious among all of the ranch homes.*

  eerie fearful; weird. *I got an eerie feeling while walking through the empty building after working hours.*

  peculiar strange; odd. *Just before the storm, the sky was a peculiar color of grayish orange.*

  strange unusual; weird. *She had a strange look on her face when I entered the room.*

wonderful *adj.* excellent; remarkable, marvelous. *What a wonderful sunset we are having tonight!*

  fabulous wonderful; exciting. *We had a fabulous vacation when we took the Concorde to Paris, where we boarded the Orient Express.*

  spectacular wonderful; grand. *The Fourth of July fireworks display was spectacular last year.*

  superb grand; excellent. *We had a superb view of the skiing trails from our chalet at the resort.*

yield *v.* to surrender; give up. *A traffic sign that says "Yield" warns drivers to surrender the right of way.*

  give in to admit defeat; yield. *It was not easy for my boss to give in to my demand for fewer working hours.*

  relinquish to give up; let go. *To avoid a family argument, I relinquished my claim to the property.*

  submit surrender; yield. *Did Antoine submit to his parents' wishes, or did he apply to Temple University instead?*

  surrender give up; yield. *The team refused to surrender their lead in the game.*